Hiking and Climbing
in the
Great Basin National Park

A Guide to Nevada's Wheeler Peak, Mt. Moriah and the Snake Range

Michael R. Kelsey

Kelsey Publishing
456 E. 100 N.
Provo, Utah, USA 84601
Tele. 801-373-3327

First Edition May 1988
Copyright 1988 Michael R. Kelsey All Rights Reserved
Library of Congress Catalog Card Number 87-083590
ISBN 0-9605824-8-7

Distributors for Kelsey Publishing
Please write to one of these companies when ordering any of Mike Kelsey's books. His other books and a price list are at the back of this book.

Primary Distributor
Wasatch Publishers, Inc., 4647 Idlewild Road, Salt Lake City, Utah, 84124, Tele. 801-278-3174

Alpenbooks, P.O. Box 27344, Seattle, Washington, 98125, Tele. 206-672-9316
Banana Republic, 175 Bluxome Street, San Francisco, California, 94107, Tele. 800-527-5200
Bookpeople, 2929 Fifth Street, Berkeley, California, 94710, Tele. 800-227-1516
Canyon Country Publications, P.O. Box 963, Moab, Utah, 84532, Tele. 801-259-6700
Gordon's Books, 2323 Delgany, Denver, Colorado, 80216, Tele. 303-296-1830
Many Feathers—Southwestern Books, 5738 North Central, Phoenix, Arizona, 85012, Tele. 602-266-1043
Mountain 'n Air Books, 3704 1/2 Foothill Blvd., La Crescenta, California, 91214, Tele. 818-957-5338
Quality Books(Library Distributor), 918 Sherwood Drive, Lake Bluff, Illinois, 60044, Tele. 312-295-2010
Recreational Equipment, Inc.(R.E.I.), P.O. Box 88126, Seattle, Washington, 98188, 800-426-4840
(Or check at any of their local stores).

In the **UK** and **Europe**, and the rest of the world contact:
CORDEE, 3a De Montfort Street, Leicester, England, UK, LE1 7HD, Tele. 0533 543579

Printed by Press Publishing, 1600 W. 800 N., Provo, Utah.

All fotos by the author, unless otherwise stated.
All maps, charts, and cross sections drawn by the author.

FRONT COVER

BACK COVER

Front Cover
1. Wheeler Peak, seen from Bald Mtn.
2. Bristlecone pine in the Wheeler Cirque Basin
3. Old log cabin at the St. Lawrence Mine
4. The North Face of Mt. Moriah

Back Cover
5. Bristlecone pine on the summit of Eagle Peak
6. Baker Lake, just south of Baker Peak
7. Miners cabins near Johnson Lake
8. Winter climbing and camping
9. Giant quaking aspens in Johns Wash
10. Winter Climbing, north ridge of Lincoln Peak

Table of Contents

Acknowledgments

There were many people who offered help and information for this book, but special thanks should go to the following people. The person who spent more time than anyone looking at this manuscript and who was willing to give advice, information, and lots of time, was Paul Demeule. He is the District Ranger of the Ely Ranger District on the Humboldt National Forest in Ely. He and his staff were very helpful in proof reading the manuscript as well.

The author also interviewed Wayne Gonder of Garrison, John Osborne of the Big Wash Ranch east of Garrison, Joe Eldridge of Baker, Richard Swallow of Spring Valley, Shirley George Robison, formerly of Baker and now of Ely, and Ferrel Hansen of the Ely Chamber of Commerce,

And as usual, my mother Venetta Kelsey, helped proof read the manuscript on more than one occasion. She also watches the business when the author is on the road.

The Author

The author experienced his earliest years of life in eastern Utah's Uinta Basin, namely around the town of Roosevelt. Then the family moved to Provo, Utah, where he attended Provo High School, and later BYU, where he earned a B.S. degree in Sociology. Shortly thereafter he discovered that was the wrong subject, so he attended the University of Utah, where he received his M.S. degree in Geography, finishing in June, 1970.

It was then real life began, for on June 9, 1970, he put a pack on his back and started traveling for the first time. Since then he has traveled to 130 countries and island groups. All this wandering has resulted in a number of books written and published by himself: *Climbers and Hikers Guide to the Worlds Mountains(2nd Ed.); Utah Mountaineering Guide, and the Best Canyon Hikes(2nd Ed.); China on Your Own, and the Hiking Guide to China's Nine Sacred Mountains(3rd Ed.); Canyon Hiking Guide to the Colorado Plateau(2nd Revised Printing); Hiking Utah's San Rafael Swell; Hiking and Exploring Utah's Henry Mountains and Robbers Roost;* and *Hiking and Exploring the Paria River.*

GBNP from the east. Left to right, Pyramid, Baker and Jeff Davis(Wheeler) Peak.

Part I--Introduction

When the idea first came to mind to do a book on America's newest national park, it was thought that a simple trail guide would be in order. Then it was found there weren't that many trails in the park, but a lot of good and easy routes to climb instead. It was also found there were some very steep(vertical for the most part) north faces on several mountains. Finally, it was decided to include the northern end of the Snake Range in this book, because it would give hikers and climbers a broader look at some real wilderness, away from the national park setting. So the book evolved, and into a hiking, climbing and travel guide to the Great Basin National Park and the South Snake Range, as well as Mt. Moriah(North Snake Range) of the Humboldt National Forest of extreme eastern Nevada.

The climbing and hiking part of this book grew into a guide for all of those who like to be in the mountains. There are easy trail hikes for people of all fitness levels, like the ones to Baker and Johnson Lakes, the ones up the South Fork of Baker and Timber Creeks, and the Icefield Trail to the foot of the Wheeler Peak Rock Glacier and the Ancient Bristlecone Pine Forest.

There are hikes to the peaks, for those who like altitude, but not a dangerous climb. Most hikes or climbs in this book are of this nature. But also included, are some rock and snow and ice routes up some of the north faces. These include: the Northeast Face of Wheeler Peak from the Wheeler Cirque Basin; the North Face of Baker Peak and Mt. Washington; and the North and Northeast Face of Lincoln Peak. These are difficult, and possibly at times dangerous climbs, and for experts only.

In doing research in the American Alpine Club Journal(from 1953 to 1987), the author found nothing written up on either the North or South Snake Range. There has been some good climbs made on Wheeler's Northeast Face, but until now hasn't been documented or publicized. So it appears that the Snake Range and Great Basin National Park has lots of virgin rock climbs for those who like the challenge of difficult routes.

Since there are several old ghost town sites and hundreds of mines pocking the mountain sides, it was decided to include some information on the history of the mines, the old and now totally abandoned town sites, and the geology of the region. These ghost towns include Osceola and Hogum, located on the north end of the South Snake Range; and Black Horse, found on the southwestern side of the North Snake Range. Minerva and Shoshone are also mining camps or ghost towns, but these two places aren't nearly so old or interesting.

While several of these old mining camps occupy valley locations, others are high in the cirque basins of the Snake Range. The two best examples of these mining camps are the old Johnson Tungsten Mine at Johnson Lake, at the head of Snake Creek; and the St. Lawrence Mine, high on the south face of Mt. Washington. These sites are like outdoor museums, and should now be protected with the new national park status.

At the heart of the Great Basin National Park are the Lehman Caves. These have been part of America's national monument system since 1922. Today, the headquarters of the new national park is found in the old national monument facilities. A history of the discovery and development of Lehman Caves has also been included in this book.

One of the best and most interesting attractions in the park are the ancient bristlecone pines. Most of these trees are in the southern half of the South Snake Range and in areas made up of limestone rock. But the more picturesque and fotogenic stands of bristlecones are at the higher elevations of Mt. Washington, on the summit area of Eagle Peak, on the southwest part of The Table-- just north of the high peaks of Mt. Moriah, and in one big grove of very old specimens at the bottom end of the Wheeler Peak Rock Glacier. One tree there was found to be 4900 years old, and is(rather was) to date the oldest living thing ever found on earth.

For those who might be more interested in a wilderness setting as opposed to more popular areas in a national park, there's Mt. Moriah. It is one of the largest wild and scenic mountain areas in Nevada. As of 1988, the Mt. Moriah Massif, or the North Snake Range, had been placed on a list of potential wilderness areas. It's still under study as a Wilderness Study Area(WSA), and Forest Service people in Ely say it has the best chance of any region in Nevada of eventually becoming an official Wilderness. Very few people know about this mountain.

So this book has evolved into something for almost everybody; from the hard-rock climbers, to the scramblers, the backpackers, the mountaineers, and hopefully even for some who wouldn't normally call themselves hikers at all.

History of Great Basin National Park

Before discussing America's newest national park, an historical background of National Forests in the region and Nevada needs to be addressed. On March 3, 1891, an act of Congress vested to the President of the United States the power to create our National Forests. Later, President Theodore Roosevelt established the Nevada National Forest on February 10, 1909. This was the first step taken to preserve and regulate the mountain areas of the public lands in the state of Nevada.

Still later, there was a name change; Nevada National Forest became the Humboldt and the Toiyabe National Forests. Generalizing, the Humboldt Forest is in eastern Nevada, while the Toiyabe covers the higher mountains in the central part of the state. Recently, a small part of the Humboldt National Forest in the South Snake Range was set aside as the Great Basin National Park.

The founder and first chief of the Forest Service was Gifford Pinchot. His philosophy of *"the greatest good for the greatest number over the long time"* is the foundation of our country's conservation policy. Both Pinchot and T. Roosevelt have to be considered co-founders of the conservation movement in America.

Since 1909 the Snake Range has been administered by the U.S. Forest Service. In 1922, Lehman Caves was set aside as a National Monument, but still administered by the Forest Service. In 1933, administration of Lehman Caves was transferred to the National Park Service. In 1959, the Forest Service created the Wheeler Peak Scenic Area, a kind of intermediate step in the direction of national park status.

Finally, on October 27, 1986, the Great Basin National Park was formerly created by Congress, a date and event which will forever change the lives of local residents. On August 15, 1987, dedication ceremonies were conducted at Lehman Caves, and America's newest national park became reality.

For the people of White Pine County, this was the end of a long and sometimes tiresome battle over how the Snake Range, and especially the Wheeler Peak area should be managed. For those who wanted to make Wheeler Peak a national park, it took seven decades to get it through Congress. For those who opposed the national park concept, it was seven long decades of defense.

The first time it was suggested Wheeler Peak be made into a national park came in the early 1920's. It was at this time that C. C. Boak, a mining engineer from Tonopah, Nevada, helped to form national monument status for Lehman Caves. It was in about 1924, according to Robert S. Waite, that Boak proposed the boundaries of Lehman Caves be enlarged to include Lehman and Baker Creeks and Wheeler Peak, and that it should be classed as a national park, rather than just a monument. This happened about two years after the caves were made into a national monument.

Boak approached Senator Key Pittman about the proposal, and he also became interested. There was a campaign in the newspapers, and eventually the governer got into the fray, despite opposition from local ranchers and miners who refused to give up their range land and mining claims. Eventually Senator Pittman introduced a bill in Congress in June 1924, but it was soundly defeated by the grazing and mining interests. The idea was finally dropped because of lack of interest, and nothing more happened with the idea for the next 31 years.

According to Robert S. Waite's 1974 dissertation on Wheeler Peak and the Snake Range, there were two events in 1955, which led to the second attempt to create a Great Basin National Park. The first event was at a meeting of the Chamber of Commerce in Ely. At that time it was suggested that Wheeler Peak and Lehman Caves be combined into a new national park. Apparently there was no follow up proposals, and the idea died.

Later on, and in late summer of 1955, two men by the names of Weldon F. Heald and Albert Marshall, did some climbing and backpacking in the Wheeler Peak region, and were startled to find a piece of the northern Rockies inside the deserts of the Great Basin. The local ranchers and miners knew of the small "glacieret" or "rock glacier" high in the Wheeler Peak Cirque Basin all along, but to those two outsiders it was a new discovery.

Heald, after seeing the "glacier", got excited about the place and eventually wrote an article in *Pacific Discovery* magazine. He also contacted the Chamber of Commerce in Ely and started his own campaign for some kind of national recognition of Wheeler Peak. Later, Heald wrote numerous stories in magazines and newspapers to promote essentially the same ideas as had been proposed back in 1924.

During the period from about 1956 through 1961, a number of people got on the national park bandwagon, but the opposition began to organize too. In 1957, a half hour-long, 16mm film about the proposed park was produced, and copies of it were sent all over the country. In 1959, 10,000 copies of an attractive brochure were printed and distributed nation wide.

In 1956, the head of the National Park Service instructed some of his people to make a preliminary inspection of the area, and this was followed by a more detailed study in the fall of 1958. At the end of the first survey, which included several trips into the backcountry and around the range, the NPS recommended that the area should not be promoted as a national park. But after more pressure was brought to bear on the NPS, they ended up making a second survey, using different people. The people working on the second study, thought it a good idea to make it a park.

This is when the opposition began to be organized. The local ranchers, the people making a living in the timber industry, the mining interests, the fish and wildlife people, the hunters, and the Forest Service, were all opposed to the idea of creating a national park. They all felt it could be better managed under the multiple use concept.

Partly as a result of the second survey of the South Snake Range by the NPS, the Forest Service announced the creation of the Wheeler Peak Scenic Area, a much smaller version(1/5th the size) of what had been proposed as a national park. This scenic area would be run something like a small wilderness area, but would still be under partial multiple use. This was a compromise to having a real genuine national park. The Wheeler Peak Scenic Drive was begun in 1960 and completed in about 1962.

In September 1959, a bill was introduced into both houses of Congress, but when the hearings were set, one locally, the other in Washington, there was a lot more opposition to the park than there was in favor. One of the main reasons the bill never did pass, was the newly discovered beryllium deposit on the western side of Mt. Washington. Under the bill as it was then written, this ore body could not be mined. The bill failed to pass.

In 1961, Yet another bill was introduced into congress, but this time there were a number of compromises having to do with grazing rights, hunting and mining, and the area of the proposed park was much reduced. This time around, the Nevada Fish and Game Commission, a national sportsman group, plus the National Wildlife Federation opposed the park idea. Finally in January 1962, the bill did pass in the Senate, but failed in the House. In the months after the defeat, there were people on both sides attempting to make compromises, but the plan was stopped.

During the years 1976 through 1979, there was a third attempt to make Wheeler Peak a national park. This attempt never did get much steam, and the opposition pushed it away quickly.

Finally, the last time anyone tried to create a Great Basin National Park, was in the early 1980's. This last attempt was instigated by the Ely and White Pine County Chamber of Commerce and was inspired this time by the poor economic situation of White Pine County(Ely is the county seat).

Mining has always been the mainstay in the economy of this part of Nevada, but in 1979, one of the more important mines in the area, the one at Ruth, closed down. Later, in 1983, the big Kennecott Smelter closed, and Ely lost one quarter of it's population overnight. There were about 9500 people in Ely in 1979; about 7200 residents in 1983. During one period of time in the early 1980's, unemployment in Ely and the county was about 25%.

Unashamedly, the primary reason for the Chamber of Commerce backing the Great Basin National Park idea, was the need to create new jobs and employment. Whether or not having a new national park nearby will boost the economy as they have hoped, will remain to be seen. Certainly there are many more visitors to the region, but whether it will fill the vacuum left by the closing of some mines will also remain to be seen.

Other reasons put fourth by the Chamber of Commerce as being favorable for a new national park were as follows. Lehman Caves was already there, and drawing some attention, and their facilities could be used as the national park headquarters. There was Wheeler Peak and its small ice field and rock glacier which are very unique in the Great Basin. Because of the high altitude of the mountain range, 7 or 8 different life zones in North America are represented, and some felt a need for a park representing these various ecosystems of the Great Basin. Other people simply felt it was high time for a national park somewhere in the Great Basin and the state of Nevada.

Another important factor, one favoring national park status, was the discovery of the oldest trees in the world, the bristlecone pines. One tree named WPN-114, located at the bottom of the Wheeler Peak Rock Glacier, was found to be 4900 years old. This perhaps more than anything else, helped put Wheeler Peak on the map. But the most determining reason for the desire to create a national park, was as stated before, the economic situation of eastern Nevada.

With these themes in mind, the Chamber of Commerce got Representative Harry Reed involved(he is now Senator Reed). Reed first began the process of introducing legislation in October, 1985. After a long and hard fought battle, the bill finally passed on October 27, 1986. The dedication of Great Basin National Park took place on August 15, 1987.

While "Mainstreet" and the Ely Chamber of Commerce were pushing for the national park, there was another group of people who organized themselves in opposition to the creation of the park. This group was the Free Enterprise Associates. It included people like George Swallow, Tony Locke and Shirley Robison of Ely, and Joe Griggs and Dean Baker of Baker, the little town at the eastern foot of Wheeler Peak.

The opposition point of view included these points: First, there were the grazing interests. The cattlemen had been in this country at least since 1869, and their livelihood depended on cattle and

GREAT BASIN N. P. AND THE SNAKE RANGE

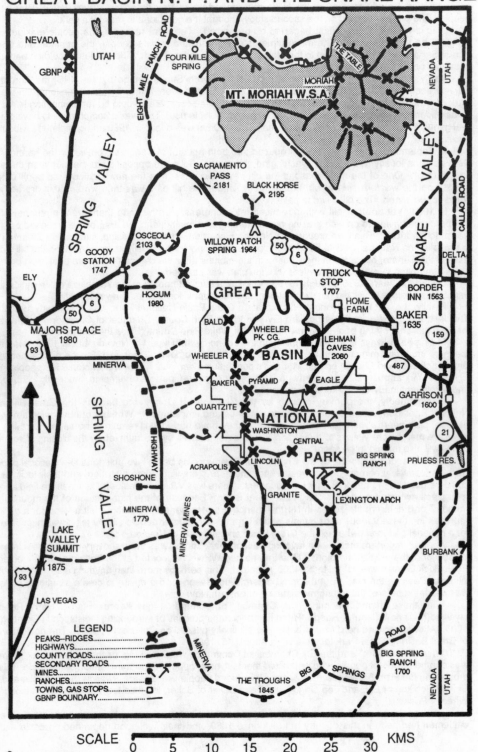

NEVADA
UTAH
GBNP

FOUR MILE SPRING

EIGHT MILE RANCH ROAD

THE TABLE

MORIAH

MT. MORIAH W.S.A.

NEVADA
UTAH

SNAKE VALLEY

CALLAO ROAD

SACRAMENTO PASS 2181

BLACK HORSE 2195

OSCEOLA 2103

WILLOW PATCH SPRING 1964

50
6

DELTA

GOODY STATION 1747

Y TRUCK STOP 1707

HOME FARM

BORDER INN 1563

ELY

HOGUM 1980

GREAT

BAKER 1635

50
6

MAJORS PLACE 1980

BALD

WHEELER PK. CG.

LEHMAN CAVES 2080

159

93

MINERVA

WHEELER

BASIN

BAKER PYRAMID

EAGLE

487

GARRISON 1600

QUARTZITE

NATIONAL

WASHINGTON

21

N

CENTRAL

PARK

SPRING

ACRAPOLIS

LINCOLN

BIG SPRING RANCH

PRUESS RES.

SHOSHONE

GRANITE

LEXINGTON ARCH

VALLEY

MINERVA 1779

MINERVA MINES

LAKE VALLEY SUMMIT

93

1875

BURBANK

LAS VEGAS

LEGEND

PEAKS–RIDGES............
HIGHWAYS.................
COUNTY ROADS...........
SECONDARY ROADS.......
MINES.....................
RANCHES..................
TOWNS, GAS STOPS.......
GBNP BOUNDARY.........

MINERVA

ROAD

BIG SPRING RANCH 1700

NEVADA
UTAH

THE TROUGHS 1845

BIG SPRINGS

SCALE 0   5   10   15   20   25   30 KMS

8

The trailhead sign at the Wheeler Peak Campground.

Jeff Davis to the left, Wheeler Peak to the right. From Bald Mountain.

summer grazing privileges in the mountains. The number of cattle they could raise, was very much dependent on their summer range. Since none of the ranchers had ever heard of a national park with grazing privileges preserved, they naturally were against national park status. In the end, Great Basin National Park is probably the first national park in America to retain all previous grazing privileges for all time.

Another powerful group was the mining lobby. Mining began in 1969 in White Pine County, and has always been the largest employer in the county. Although mining hasn't always been really big in the Snake Range, it still does have some important mineral deposits. At sometime in the future, depending on the price of various metals, mines could be reopened, putting many miners to work. In the end, the boundaries of the park were drawn to exclude some of the potentially better mining prospects. The still-valid mining claims on private property on the south face of Mt. Washington were removed from the park boundaries to preserve the right to mine, if and when economic conditions become favorable. The final bill passed by Congress, made the park about half the original size proposed.

The Forest Service and the Bureau of Land Management(BLM), are the agencies who care for Federal public lands in the west. One of their themes over the years has been the "Multiple Use" concept of land management. Many people in the Forest Service thought that by making a national park in the South Snake Range, it not only would lock up a parcel of land and take it out of the multiple use category, it would also bring more publicity, therefore much more use. In such cases, the end result is "multiple abuse", rather than the use it was intended for.

One forest ranger pointed out three factors which can add up to a good and successful national park. He believed GBNP fell short on all three points. First, in order for a park to attract and hold people for extended stays, a water based recreation experience is a critical component. Great Basin has only a handful of small streams, and the several lakes it does have, are accessible to hikers only.

Second, a park of this size with limited attractions, would do better if it were close to a large population center, so it would have a steady supply of visitors. Wheeler Peak and Great Basin National Park are a long way from nowhere! The closest large cities around are Salt Lake City to the northeast, and Las Vegas to the south. Each city is a long way from the park.

Third, close proximity to an established and well used US and Interstate Highway would help to bring in visitors. There are no Interstates in the area; and US Highway 50-6, the main east-west highway nearest the park, has the reputation as being the "Loneliest Highway in America".

Other factors presented by people against the creation of the park were the excessive costs of running a remote park of this type. Before the park was created, the Forest Service administered the range very well and at a much reduced cost to the tax payers.

The loss of hunting privileges was another key point. In recent years the deer herds have been expanding, and it was thought this trend would continue, making too many deer for the range. Also, a few years back, Rocky Mountain Bighorn Sheep were introduced to the Wheeler Peak area, and the first hunt took place about the time the park was created. Now this hunting recreation is gone, except for possibly late season hunts in the foothills of the park.

Another point brought out against the park idea, involved the possibility that the Wheeler Peak region, and canyons leading into the area, would be over developed by the Park Service, destroying many of the special attractions found in the wilderness. The Forest Service had suggested that Wheeler Peak be made into a wilderness area instead. It was thought that excessive development such as roads, more campgrounds, and new housing for park employees, would be expensive to the tax payer, and would negatively effect the real thing parks are intended to do--preserve the natural environment.

There was also the economic situation, which park opponents brought to everyones attention. In the year or two before the national park bill was passed, all of the Humboldt National Forest, which made up approximately 486,000 hectares(1.2 million acres) of land, had an annual budget of about $500,000. At the same time, the Lehman Caves National Monument budget was about $250,000.

Today, the National Forest budget and the amount of land supervised, is about the same; whereas the budget for the GBNP is $800,000. That's to take care of about 31,000 hectares(76,000 acres) of land. In the year or two before the park was created, the Forest Service had one full-time and three seasonal employees, to take care of what is today the GBNP(excluding the Lehman Caves N. M.). The budget at that time for the Wheeler Peak Scenic Division(South Snake Range) of the Humboldt National Forest was about $60,000 a year.

After all the wrangling and arguing there were concessions on both sides of the table, and the park created. Here are some of the key points of the bill which finally passed Congress on October 27, 1986. It is simply called, the *Great Basin National Park Act of 1986*.

The Lehman Caves National Monument, designated on January 24, 1922,........is hereby abolished and the lands incorporated within the Great Basin National Park.

After notice and opportunity for public hearing, the Secretary(of the Interior) shall prepare a management plan for the park.......within three years after the enactment of this act. Such plan may be amended from time to time.

The Secretary shall permit grazing on lands within the park to the same extent as was permitted on such lands as of July 1, 1985. Grazing within the park shall be administered by the National Park Service.

At request of the permittee, or at the initiative of the Secretary, negotiations may take place at any time with holders of valid existing grazing permits on land within the park, for an exchange of all or part of their grazing allotments for allotments outside the park.

Existing water-related range improvements(stock tanks) inside the park may be maintained by the Secretary or the persons benefiting from them, subject to reasonable regulation by the Secretary.

Now that the battle has either been won or lost, and the park created for better or for worse, the next step is to come up with a management plan for the future use of the park. In the three years following the inception of the park, a management plan will be created and begun. During this time period the public will be asked to write letters and make suggestions regarding the future use and regulations of the national park. This grace period will extend to October 27, 1989. Interested citizens are requested to send comments and suggestions to the Great Basin National Park, Baker, Nevada, 89311. If you'd like to obtain a copy of the entire 3 1/2 page Great Basin National Park bill, write to the GBNP.

Accommodations in the Region

Campgrounds

There are six campgrounds and one picnic site in the Great Basin National Park. Below is a table explaining what is available. These sites are very similar to other Forest Service campgrounds in the mountain west, because before the GBNP came to be, they were built and maintained by the Humboldt National Forest out of Ely, Nevada.

All campgrounds, except the two undeveloped sites on Snake Creek, have toilets, camp tables, campfire sites, places for tents, and parking. There is water at all developed sites, but as of 1987, some of the campgrounds had not yet had their water quality approved, so campers were requested to boil, filter or treat the water before drinking. But soon monies will be available, and approved drinking water systems will be installed. When this happens, the GBNP will charge a fee for camping. If, when you arrive, the camping is for free, then you can assume the water system has yet to be approved, even through there may be water in the taps. Inquire at the park visitor center.

The two sites on Snake Creek, the Shoshone and the Snake Creek Campgrounds, used to be a little better than they are today(1988). At one time there were more tables at each location, but some were taken away and used elsewhere. You can still camp there OK; there just aren't as many tables. In other words, they are now considered undeveloped or primitive campsites. There are many such sites along Snake Creek as you drive up canyon, most of which are for one family or a small group.

Name of Site	Elevation	Season of use?	Camping Units	Water?
Baker Ck. Campground	2317	Summer	17	Yes
Upper Lehman Ck. CG.	2400	Summer	24	Yes
Lower Lehman Ck. CG.	2350	All Year	11	Yes
Wheeler Peak CG.	3033	Summer	37	Yes
Snake Creek CG.	2350	Summer	2	Creek
Shoshone CG.	2500	Summer	2	Creek
Lehman Caves Picnic Site	2080	Summer	No	Yes

Besides these sites in the South Snake Range and in the Great Basin National Park, there are two other road side parking spots or primitive campsites nearby. One is on Highway 50-6 not far to the southeast of Sacramento Pass and very near mile post 88. This is called Willow Patch Spring, at 1964 meters. There's a sign stating, "radiator water only"; pointing to the south side of the road. This is an undeveloped spring, so don't drink the water. It has several picnic tables under some trees.

Another road side parking place with tables, is at Conners Pass, at 2354 meters. It's just west of Majors Place on Highway 50-6, and on the way to Ely. Have water in your vehicle before arriving at either of these places. There is no charge to stay at either campsite. These are not the greatest places to spend a night, because they're right on the highway.

Camping on BLM or Forest Service Lands

For those people coming from the eastern USA, Canada or elsewhere, please keep in mind that most of the land in the state of Nevada, and about 70% of land in Utah is owned and managed by the Federal Government. In the west, these Federal lands are managed by the Bureau of Land Management(BLM) and the Forest Service. All this land is public domain. Most of the land right along the highway, and in the dry desert areas is BLM land, but as you get into the mountains, it's likely managed by the Forest Service.

As you drive along the highways toward the GBNP, you will notice there are very few fences. Unfenced land is known as open range. In these areas, you can simply drive off the highway onto a side road, and camp anywhere. For a quiet and peaceful sleep, drive a km off the pavement somewhere and camp or park for the night. Since it's your land, why not leave a clean campsite as you would anywhere else?

If you come to areas with ranches or towns in sight, or any sign of civilization, you'll likely see some fences. Behind these fences, the land is likely privately owned. There are however, lots of places where there are fences along the highway, but which is still public domain. These fences are there to keep range cattle off the highway. You can also camp or park in most of these areas too; once you've passed over a cattle guard(Texas Gate), or through an unlocked gate. Obviously, if you see a sign stating, *No Trespassing,* then look someplace else.

By using these public lands to camp or park on, you will have a very quiet place to rest and at no charge. However, you must go prepared with all the food and water you'll need for the duration of your stay.

Towns and other Highway Outposts

Ely, Nevada Ely is located to the west of GBNP and is a town of about 10,000 people. It's a big enough place to have a number of motels, shops and a couple of supermarkets. It's the best place in the area to shop for anything and everything. There are also three bookstores, all in the older west end of town. They are Sportsworld, The Book Store, and Times Stationary. Ely is a regional center and the county seat, and has a Forest Service ranger station, a large BLM office, Fish and Game office, weather station, airport, etc. It's the biggest little town in eastern Nevada. Do your shopping there if you can; there isn't much else going on when you get close to the park. East of Ely and until you get to Delta or Milford in Utah, there are no other supermarkets or auto parts stores. It's about 100 kms from Ely to Baker, with only two gas station-restaurants in between.

Delta, Utah If you're approaching the GBNP from the northeast and along Highway 50-6, this is the last good place to do any serious shopping or to have major repairs done on your car. Delta is a farming community of maybe 3500 people. It has a couple of supermarkets and a pretty good main street. It's the center of a rather prosperous farming belt and in recent years, the very large coal-fired Intermountain Power Plant was built north of town. It's about 160 kms from Delta to Baker, Nevada, and not a gas station in between, except for one in Hinckley, 8 or 10 kms south of Delta, and the Border Inn at the Utah-Nevada state line.

Milford, Utah If you're heading for GBNP from the southeast and along Utah State Highway 21, Milford, Utah is the last of the "larger" little towns you'll pass. This town has some larger stores and a motel or two, and a population of perhaps 1000. From Milford to Garrison, which is right on the Utah-Nevada line, is about 125 kms with not one gas station in between.

Pioche, Nevada Pioche is located about 130 kms directly south of Majors Place, on Highway 93. There are no gas stations in between. Pioche is an old mining town of about 700 people, but today it's been built up and now depends on tourism for it's livelihood. It has many shops and stores along it's main street, and is the last(or first) place south of GBNP to do serious shopping.

Baker, Nevada This town is located on the east side of the range, just 10 kms downhill from park headquarters at Lehman Caves. Even through it's a very small town, it's the biggest community found on the area map. Population is near 60 in town, but maybe 150 if you count the Home Farm school and the national park employees. It's main street is a winner with the inception of the national park. This is the last place to fuel up if you're heading for Lehman Caves or Wheeler Peak via the east side routes.

Baker has but one gas station, which handles Diesel and propane, groceries in a new large room for the 1988 season, and a small garage which makes minor repairs. There's one motel, the Silver Jack. Also there's one snack bar, a couple of gift shops, and two restaurant-bars. Some of these

Main street in Baker, Nevada(most of it).

Garrison is even smaller than Baker.

services may be curtailed in winter, especially the snack bar. There's also a small part-time post office, at zip 89311.

Baker has a school to handle all children in the valley from the 3rd grade up through the 8th. Kindergarten and the 1st and 2nd grades are held in Garrison, Utah. High school students on the Nevada side of the line have a choice of being bused to Ely each day; or of finding a family to live with in Ely during the school year(a subsidy is paid to these students). While Garrison is at the Mormon end of the valley, Baker is the hangout for "Gentiles"(non-Mormons).

Garrison, Utah After Baker, this is the next largest community in the immediate area; in fact, it's the only other town. Garrison is just across the state line in Utah. With 50 to 55 residents, which includes some of the ranchers nearby, you'd better not blink or you'll miss this one.

Garrison has but one commercial facility, and that's the Wheeler Peak Service. It's a gas station-grocery store complex, which has perhaps the best selection of groceries in the valley. They also run a part time repair and garage service, as well as stocking Diesel and propane. To use this place, you first have to ring the door bell. Business is slow, but likely to pick up as a result of the new park.

Garrison has a small but new Mormon church, built out of a couple of double-wide mobile home trailers. It also has a small part-time post office with zip 84728. Garrison has a school for all children in the valley, and from both sides of the state line, from kindergarten through the 2nd grades, while Baker has school for grades 3 through 8.   All high school students from the Utah side of the state line, go to Delta, Utah, and find homes to live in while attending high school. The distance from Garrison to Delta is around 160 kms.

The Border Inn, Utah-Nevada This place is located east of GBNP and on Highway 50-6, right at the Utah-Nevada state line. It has a small restaurant and bar, a motel, and a gas station(with Diesel, and the pumps on the Utah side of the line). They also offer showers for hikers or travelers. Open year-round, and 24 hours a day.

The "Y" Truck Stop, Nevada This restaurant-bar and gasoline-Diesel station is located 8 kms northwest of Baker on Highway 50-6, between mile posts 94-95, and at the junction of US Highway 50-6 and Nevada State Highway 487--the turnoff to Baker. They also have trailer hookups, and in the spring of 1988, were building laundry and shower facilities. They remain open year-round.

Majors Place, Nevada This restaurant-bar and gas station is located 43 kms southeast of Ely and at the junction of Highways 50-6 and 93. This is about halfway between the park and Ely. They also have trailer hookups and are open year-round. They should have Diesel fuel as well?

Lehman Caves Giftshop, Nevada This small gift and curio shop, along with a small restaurant, is found in the same building as the GBNP headquarters and the visitor center at Lehman Caves. It will be open during the busier six months of the year. The national park visitor center in the same building, sells books related to the Great Basin and Nevada.

At one time there have been gas stations located at Goody Station and at a small facility near the top of Sacramento Pass, but they were out of business as of 1987. Shoshone and Minerva are now abandoned, and Osceola and Hogum have been ghost towns for many years.

Climate and Weather Information

The following climatic date will illustrate better than words, the weather patterns in the region surrounding Great Basin National Park. The weather stations covered are Delta and Garrison, Utah; and Lehman Caves, Ely and Pioche, Nevada. The altitude various from 1409 meters at Delta in the east, to 2080 meters at Lehman Caves.

Note that the valley locations have the hottest temperatures in the summer heat, but can also have slightly colder temps in the winter. This occurs because of a temperature inversion. During the winter months, and especially from about mid-November until the first part of February, there tends to be cold air trapped in the valleys of the Great Basin.

This situation begins to occur right after a frontal passage. There's always colder air coming in at the end of a storm or cold front. This cold air flows down hill(as does water) and into the lower basins. Then if a high pressure system builds up and becomes strong(normally a good weather pattern in winter), warmer Pacific air over-rides the cold air in the valleys. The cold air then stays trapped until the next storm comes through the region, to scoop out the fog with strong winds.

During these periods of warm, calm, and sunny days, the weather and hiking conditions are simply wonderful in the mountains. If you're hoping to do some winter climbing, pick a time when it's foggy in Salt Lake City. Foggy periods tend to settle in on Salt Lake mostly from mid-November through mid-February. The only drawback to climbing during this period of time(late November through mid-February), is that the snow tends to be more soft and powdery than it is in March.

Remember, the following charts are in **metric**. Centigrade(C) = F(Fahrenheit) - 32 x .555, and 1 inch = 2.54 cms. Precipitation stated in centimeters(cms). See the Metric Conversion Chart for help. It's at the beginning of the Hiking Section.

Delta, Utah 1409 meters(from 1938-1986)

Month	Daily Max. Temp (C)	Daily Min. Temp (C)	Record High Temp (C)	Record Low Temp (C)	Average Precip
January	3.4	-10.0	17.7	-31.6	1.37
February	7.4	-6.7	23.3	-30.0	1.45
March	11.9	-3.4	27.2	-22.2	2.13
April	17.2	3.3	31.1	-10.5	2.06
May	23.1	5.4	34.4	-6.1	2.41
June	29.5	9.9	41.1	-3.9	1.09
July	34.1	14.4	42.7	3.3	1.14
August	32.7	13.3	43.3	2.8	1.40
September	27.0	7.7	38.3	-4.4	1.91
October	19.8	2.5	31.6	-18.9	1.83
November	10.6	-4.6	25.0	-21.1	1.60
December	4.3	-9.0	18.9	-31.6	1.68
Annual	18.4	1.55	43.3	-31.6	20.1

Garrison, Utah 1600 meters(1951-1986)

Month	Daily Max. Temp (C)	Daily Min. Temp (C)	Record High Temp (C)	Record Low Temp (C)	Average Precip
January	5.5	-9.0	20.0	-29.4	1.09
February	8.8	-6.0	22.8	-28.3	1.02
March	12.7	-3.6	26.0	-20.5	2.18
April	17.8	-0.2	30.0	-12.8	1.85
May	23.3	4.4	35.0	-11.1	1.85
June	29.4	9.0	42.2	-2.8	1.17
July	33.9	13.8	41.1	1.7	1.35
August	32.2	13.0	40.0	0.6	1.83
September	26.7	7.3	36.6	5.5	1.80
October	19.7	1.4	32.2	-17.2	2.06
November	11.7	-4.2	26.6	-25.5	1.52
December	6.3	-8.4	22.2	-28.9	1.17
Annual	18.9	1.4	42.2	-29.4	18.90

Lehman Caves, Nevada 2080 meters(1941-1970)

Month	Daily Max. Temp (C)	Daily Min. Temp (C)	Record High Temp (C)	Record Low Temp (C)	Average Precip
January	5.2	-7.8	19.4	-28.9	2.64
February	6.4	-6.4	20.0	-24.4	2.72
March	8.8	-5.3	21.1	-17.8	3.43
April	10.3	-0.9	25.5	-12.2	3.25
May	19.1	3.5	28.9	-14.4	2.90
June	24.4	8.0	36.1	-10.0	2.46
July	29.9	13.6	37.7	0	2.01
August	29.6	12.8	36.1	0	2.64
September	24.1	7.9	33.9	-12.2	1.93
October	16.8	2.1	27.2	-16.1	3.78
November	9.8	-4.0	25.5	-18.9	2.92
December	5.9	-7.2	25.5	-21.1	2.90
Annual	15.8	1.4	37.7	-28.9	33.58

Ely, Nevada 1906 meters(1951-1980)

Month	Daily Max. Temp (C)	Daily Min. Temp (C)	Record High Temp (C)	Record Low Temp (C)	Average Precip
January	3.9	-12.4	20.0	-32.7	1.83
February	5.9	-9.4	19.4	-31.6	1.73
March	8.5	-7.0	22.8	-25.0	2.31
April	13.4	-3.5	25.5	-20.5	2.34
May	19.1	0.9	31.6	-13.9	2.74
June	25.3	4.7	37.2	-7.8	2.02
July	30.4	8.9	37.7	-1.1	1.65
August	29.0	8.1	36.1	-4.4	1.57
September	24.4	2.9	33.9	-9.4	1.84
October	17.8	-2.2	28.9	-19.4	1.50
November	9.5	-7.9	23.9	-26.1	1.54
December	4.9	-11.7	19.4	-33.3	1.91
Annual	16.0	-2.3	37.7	-33.3	22.91

Pioche, Nevada 1865 meters(1941-1970)

Month	Daily Max. Temp (C)	Daily Min. Temp (C)	Record High Temp (C)	Record Low Temp (C)	Average Precip
January	5.2	-6.2	17.8	-23.9	3.73
February	7.3	-4.6	21.1	-20.5	3.15
March	10.3	-2.8	26.1	-15.5	3.48
April	15.8	1.4	27.2	-11.1	3.28
May	21.4	6.0	32.7	-5.6	1.85
June	27.0	10.4	38.9	-1.1	1.02
July	31.6	14.5	38.3	7.8	2.90
August	30.0	13.8	37.2	3.3	3.18
September	26.0	10.0	35.5	-3.9	1.63
October	19.1	4.3	29.4	-7.2	2.41
November	11.0	-1.7	23.3	-15.5	3.02
December	6.2	-5.1	18.3	-20.0	4.32
Annual	17.6	3.3	38.9	-23.9	33.96

Road Report

For those who have had little experience driving the back roads of the west, it may be quite a challenge driving up and down some of the canyon roads surrounding both the north and south sections of the Snake Range. Some of the canyon roads, especially those on the west side of the South Snake Range, are among the worst and roughest this author has ever tried to negotiate in his VW Rabbit. Others, especially those out in the valleys, and which are considered county roads, are well maintained, often used, and can be driven on at or near highway speeds. The reason the county roads are so well maintained and in such good condition, is there are many active ranches scattered about on both sides of the range.

Since the author uses a VW Rabbit only, he has placed the location of trailheads on the maps so that other people with similar vehicles can also arrive at those locations. In a couple of cases, the author has placed two trailheads on a map: one for people with cars, the other for anyone with a HCV or 4WD.

For those who drive cars and who don't want to buy another vehicle just to get out in the mountains a couple of times a year, here's a simple idea on how you can easily raise the clearance of your car. The author raised his car(and especially the oil pan) up about 7 or 8 cms, by replacing the regular sized tires with some two or three sizes larger. The big tires then required him to install cargo coils and gas shocks. All these changes make the oil pan clear most rocks, and the author goes almost anywhere he wants, as long as it's on some kind of road.

Below is a list of roads one will have to use to get to the various hikes or climbs discussed in this book.

South Snake Range--Great Basin National Park

Wheeler Peak Scenic Drive This is the paved road running from Lehman Caves up to the Wheeler Peak Campground, and to the trailhead for Wheeler Peak and the Bristlecone Pine Forest. It's paved all the way, and any vehicle can make it to the campground. At present(1988), it is not kept open on a year-round basis. However it is cleared of snow up to the bottom end of the Upper Lehman Creek Campground throughout the year. The upper part of this road will likely be snowbound from late October or early November until sometime in late May or early June.

Baker Creek Road This road runs from near Lehman Caves, to the south and southwest, and into the canyon along Baker Creek. The road ends at the Baker Creek Trailhead about 7 or 8 kms from the pavement. As of 1988, this road was made of gravel and regularly maintained. It has been upgraded and could be paved anytime money is available. At present it could almost be called an all-weather road, but it's blocked off in winter and not plowed. It's felt the road bed isn't solid enough to sustain use when it's saturated, as when the winter snows melt. Thus traffic is kept off during winter and spring, until it dries out. This prevents the road from becoming deeply rutted.

Snake Creek Road The first 5 kms of this road is in very good condition. This part runs to a state fish hatchery where there are permanent residences. Above the fish hatchery, the road bed gradually deteriorates as you drive up canyon, but any car can make it up to the Snake Creek Trailhead. The road is made out of some gravel and country rock and should be drivable in wet weather(but probably not right after the winter snows melt, or after an extra heavy rain storm?).

Big Wash Road This road runs from just south of Garrison to the rim of the canyon overlooking Big Wash. When you see the sign stating 4WD's only, which is about 15 kms from Garrison, stop and park. Below, the road is washed out and for 4WD's only. Up to that point, it is a very good road for half the distance, then it slowly deteriorates; but any car can make it to the sign. Even the latter part of the road appears to be usable in moderately wet weather.

Lexington Creek Road This road begins on the highway near the Pruess Reservoir. One branch of this road begins just north of the reservoir(between mile posts 4 and 5), and runs west across the dam; another branch begins just above the lake to the south(right at mile post 6). These two branches meet after 3 or 4 kms, then head west to Lexington Creek and Lexington Arch. For the first 22 kms, and up to the point where the South Fork of Lexington joins the main canyon, the road is very good, although it probably seldom sees a grader. The road bed is made of gravel and small cobblestones, therefore is for the most part, an all-weather road. Above where the South Fork enters from the south, the road to the old Lexington Mill site is good for all vehicles, but will be slick and muddy in places in wet weather. The road up the South Fork of Lexington Creek is similar; any car can make it to the Arch Canyon Trailhead, but it could be bad news in wet weather.

Minerva--Big Springs Road This maintained gravel county road runs from Utah State Highway 21 just a few kms south of Pruess Reservoir, in a southwest direction past the old town site of Burbank, and on towards the Big Spring Ranch. This first part of the road is well maintained and used by ranchers living nearby. From just south of the Big Spring Ranch, it heads westerly and towards an old well and stock tank called The Troughs(used during winter months). From The Troughs, it heads northwest, then north to Minerva, at the end of the paved highway. This second part of the road is good and sometimes maintained, but it can become muddy during winter when snow is melting, or after heavy rains. It's nearly an all-weather road. It's used often by ranchers and can be used at near highway speeds. This is the road to take if you want to get around the south end of the South Snake Range.

Murphy and Johns Wash Road This road begins about 11 kms south of Minerva, which is at the end of the paved Minerva Highway. At that point, it runs east and into Murphy Wash. The lower part of the road is a little rough in places, but it's good for any car. In wet weather, the Murphy Wash Road will be slick and muddy. Up canyon, the road heads over a low divide and down into upper Johns Wash. This road is rougher, and cars can only go about half way up to the Highland Ridge Trailhead. It too can be muddy in wet weather. If you have a shovel and are willing to do a little "road improvement", then you might get your car to the trailhead.

The Minerva Highway This is the 25 km long paved road which first runs east from a point about 7 kms south of Majors Place on Highway 93(right at mile post 23). After a few kms, it turns south along the western face of the South Snake Range. The pavement ends at the old mill site called Minerva. Since it was built to, and ends at Minerva, the author has given it this unofficial name, the Minerva Highway.

Pole Canyon Road This road leaves the Minerva Highway at mile post 5, and runs east into the Pole Canyon which comes down the west side of Mt. Washington(not to be confused with the Pole Canyon on the north side of Eagle Peak). It is a well maintained road, and just waiting for the Wheeler Peak Mine to reopen. While it's steep near the top, any car can make it to the mine. Because it's been upgraded and made of gravel, it should be an all-weather road. Expect the upper part to be snowbound in the dead of winter.

Williams Canyon Pipeline Road This road runs from near mile post 6 on the paved Minerva Highway, up to the northeast and to the mouth of Williams Canyon. It parallels an old pipeline, which diverts water from Williams Creek down to the ranches in Spring Valley. This road runs up an alluvial fan with many cobblestones, and it's rough as hell. Cars can only go up a km, or less; HCV's can go all the way to the mouth of the canyon. There's no mud on this one; just big rocks.

Hub Mine Basin Road The original road running into the Hub Mine Basin begins at about mile post 9 on the Minerva Highway, but this one is washed out not far from the pavement. A 4WD or a HCV, plus a shovel and some road work, might get you up and over this one bad place. An alternate, and more drivable route to the Hub Basin, would be to go up Shingle Creek, then drive south along the track running next to the old West Ditch. This will take you to the Hub Mine Basin from the north. This route can be driven by any HCV, but likely not by many cars.

Shingle Creek Road This is the road running up Shingle Creek, which gives access to the west face of Wheeler Peak. It begins near mile post 11 on the Minerva Highway, and runs northeast. On hiking maps 6 and 14, it's shown to be the first road south of the pipeline. This road is rather rough in places, and people with low clearance cars may not get far. However, if people with cars go slow and easy, and occasionally stop and push rocks off the road, then it's likely you won't have trouble. This road bed is composed of cobblestones, so wet weather shouldn't effect it too much.

North Snake Range--Mt. Moriah

Eight Mile Ranch Road This road begins from between mile posts 80 and 81 on Highway 50-6(just northwest of Sacramento Pass), and runs north past Negro Creek and on toward the Eight Mile Ranch. This is a much used and well maintained gravel all-weather road, which can be used at highway speeds. Use it to gain access to the Negro Creek and Four Mile Spring Routes on the western side of Mt. Moriah.

Negro Creek Road From the Eight Mile Ranch Road to the Negro Creek Ranch(Rogers Ranch), this road is very good, seems to be regularly graded, and is, for the most part, an all-weather type road. From the ranch to the trailhead at the end of the road on Negro Creek, it is still a good road, but it was just graded for the first time in many years in 1987. It isn't used much, so it may deteriorate some with time. Parts of this road will be muddy in bad weather.

Four Mile Spring Road This is a seldom-if-ever maintained road, which runs east from the Eight Mile Ranch Road toward the Four Mile Spring area. Because of tight budgets, the BLM and Forest Service, who often times do road grading projects together, can only do a few roads each year. In 1987, cars had to be driven very carefully in order to make it to the Car-park at 2075 meters and the Four Mile Spring area. It's made of dirt and rocks. Above the spring area, and on up to the Moriah Cabin and to the 4WD Trailhead on the rim of Big Canyon, it's for powerful 4WD's. If you can get above the steep part just above the spring, then it's a pretty good road from there to Big Canyon. This high part of the road however, is only open from about the first or middle of June on through early October. During wet weather in summer, this high altitude road will be very muddy and likely impassable.

Callao Road This is the graveled county highway running north from Highway 50-6, just east of the Utah-Nevada line, towards Gandy, Partoun, Trout Creek and to Callao. It's a well traveled road(this road is exclusively in Utah, remember) and one that's maintained for driving at highway speeds. It's made of gravel and is surely a prime candidate for paving soon. This is the road to use to gain access to the east side of Mt. Moriah.

Hendrys Creek Road This is a very good and well maintained road running into Hendrys Creek Canyon. It's maintained by the BLM up to the Forest Service boundary and to the cabin and flagstone quarries of a miner named Hatch. Since it's made of gravel, it would generally be classed as an all-weather type road. This might be the best route to use if you're planning a winter climb of Mt. Moriah. The altitude at the end of the road is not as high as other trailheads, therefore it's likely one can drive up to the Hatch Cabin throughout most winters.

Hampton Creek Road This road runs from the old Robinson Ranch(now the Iverson Ranch) to the northwest and into Hampton Creek Canyon. This is a very good road, and has in the past been maintained in response to the garnet mine, located near the end of the road. It's surface is gravely, therefore is for the most part, an all-weather road. The upper half of the road will be snowbound in winter, but you can probably get to within two or three kms of the mine with a car.

Horse Canyon Road The road from the red colored ranch house on the Callao Road, up to the watering trough near the mouth of Horse Canyon is in very good condition, and likely to remain so for a long time, even through it may seldom see a grader. Above the watering trough, the road deteriorates, but most cars, driven with care, might be able to get into the canyon and to the trailhead. However, this last part is rough and rocks could be a problem for low clearance cars. It's a rocky road, and shouldn't be affected too much by wet weather.

Smith Creek Road From the Callao Road to about the mouth of Smith Canyon, this road is very good.

It doesn't get so much attention from the BLM; it just doesn't wear or wash out. Parts of it could be slick in wet weather, especially that section at the beginning of the road near the red ranch house. The upper part of the road, that part into Smith Canyon, is rocky, but was in good condition in 1987. At that time, someone had done some work on the road and perhaps laid a pipeline. The Forest Service has put up a dirt barrier about 2 kms below the end of the road, and has tried unsuccessfully to stop all traffic at that point. The reason for the barricade at that point, is that it's at the boundary of the proposed Mt. Moriah Wilderness Study Area(WSA). That point is the end of the good road. Above the barrier, it's a 4WD or HCV road to the big grove of cottonwood trees as shown on Map 42, Smith Creek.

It you intend to do a lot of traveling on the back roads of the Snake Range, here are some items to have in your car at all times. A shovel, battery jumper cable, a heavy tow rope or chain, several jugs of water, extra food, and at least a simple tool kit. Most areas aren't that far from help if you get in trouble, but go prepared anyway.

Hiking Equipment

Day Hikes

For those who may simply be inexperienced at hiking in general, or for those who haven't hiked or climbed in the western USA, here is a list of items or equipment for hiking that you may need or want, both for day hikes and for overnight backpacking trips. When day hiking, here's a list of things the author usually takes when he's out to climb Wheeler Peak or any of the other high summits.

A sturdy pair of boots, but if you're climbing or hiking on a trail only, such as the normal route to Wheeler, you can sometimes get by with a pair of running shoes. However, running shoes simply don't give enough support to the feet if you get off trails, so be careful. Serious hikers or climbers will have a pair of boots with some rigidity built in and thicker soles.

In the warm summer months, a pair of shorts or cut-off's are good, but only if it's warm weather. Remember, it's colder at the summits, and if there's a wind, which is often the case, you'll want long pants. The author always carries a pair of long pants in his day pack just in case. This also offers some padding in the pack. You'll want to wear a "T" shirt, but also have a long sleeved shirt in your pack. Depending on temps, one should also have along a light jacket or sweat shirt with hood in the day-pack as well.

In the heat of the summer, July and most of August, you can sometimes get by without a pair of gloves, but if you're heading up Wheeler Peak, it's best to have a pair at all times in your pack as a standby. If the weather becomes cloudy later in the day, as it often does, then you'll need gloves or mittens for sure.

For those of us with light skin, and especially susceptible to skin cancer, you should consider a cap or hat of some kind to protect the face and neck from the suns rays. At higher altitudes, this problem becomes even more acute. The author uses an adjustable baseball cap, with the top cut out, and a kind of "cancer curtain" sewed around the back and sides(like the French Foreign Legion caps). This type of cap stays on much better in the wind than a cowboy hat. Remember, you'll nearly always find some wind on the summits, and big hats don't do well in wind.

Besides these clothing items, here's some other odds and ends the author carries in his pack or pockets. Always have a compass, some chapstick or lip baum, a pocket knife, map, a small note pad and pen, toilet paper, camera and extra lenses, extra film, a water bottle and lunch. Some may want a walking stick of some kind. The author takes one that's been made from an aluminum shower curtain rod. It was cut and welded to form a "T", then a screw clamp was placed on top to serve as a camera stand. This also doubles as an ice ax, but not a very good cne.

If you think you'll be on snow, such as early in summer, consider taking an ice ax(or perhaps just a walking stick just described), and for those who are serious about doing some steeper snow or ice, some crampons. However, an ice ax and crampons are for difficult routes only, and won't be needed on any normal routes during summer. For early season hikes, a pair of sunglasses can be important, as well as a bandana worn around the face and nose for sun protection. Sun lotions of various kinds are good, but they sometimes leave an oily film on the face and clothing.

Overnight Hikes

Here's a list of items or equipment one might need if taking an overnight backpacking trip in the

Snake Range. This is what the author would take along. A large pack, waterproof pack cover, tent with rainsheet, sleeping bag, a foam pad of some kind(the author uses a short "Therm-a-Rest" mattress--a combination air mattress and foam pad), small kerosene stove, several lighters(no matches anymore!), large jug for water(3.78 liters)to be filled and used around camp, small day-hike water bottle(one liter), camera with lenses and film, walking stick-camera stand combination, a stitching awl and waxed thread, metal cannister with odds and ends(bandaids, patching kit for sleeping pad, wire, pens, needle and thread, etc.), small plyers, maps, small note book, reading book, chapstick, compass, toilet paper, hair brush or comb, pocket knife, lightweight raincoat, small alarm clock(or watch), candles for light, tooth brush and paste, face lotion-sun screen, cap with cancer curtain, soap, small flashlight, perhaps a heavier jacket and a lightweight mini-umbrella if the weather looks threatening. These items in addition to the clothing mentioned under day hikes.

Here's a simple list of food items the author usually takes. It may give you some ideas if you haven't done too much backpacking or camping before. Food usually includes oatmeal or cream of wheat cereal, coffee or chocolate drink, powdered milk and sugar for breakfast. Lunch usually includes cookies, candy bars or chocolate, an orange or apple, and sometimes a powdered fruit drink. Supper usually includes Ramen instant noodles, soups, macaroni, instant mashed potatoes and canned tuna fish or sardines, vienna sausages, corned beef, cheese or peanuts. Also more fruit(the kind that doesn't squash in the pack--like apples or oranges), carrots, raisin, other dried fruit, instant puddings, crackers, cookies, bread, butter, peanut butter. In addition, a plastic eating bowl and cup, spoon, knife, can opener, small cooking pot, salt and pepper, extra fuel for the stove. All of these items can be purchased at most grocery stores.

For those who have an endless budget, you can try the freeze dried foods, but you have to buy those in special stores and pay prices which are even more special. You can add your favorites to the author list above.

Winter Climbing Equipment

For winter climbing, you'll need all or most of the above, plus some special equipment to accommodate for the snow and colder temperatures. You'll need heavier boots of some kind, perhaps the expensive double boots worn in the Himalayas, or just an extra large pair of insulted hunting boots, along with more and/or thicker socks. A simple pair of rubber snow packs, especially those with rubber bottoms and leather uppers, often work fine. Snowmobile boots are extra warm, but some times the soles aren't built with traction in mind. But they would still be good none-the-less.

The author has a pair of Lowa Everest double boots, but opted for a much lighter insulted hunting boot, which was 1.5 size too large, and got along just fine. These boots worked well with both snowshoes and crampons. Most people can make successful winter climbs in the Snake Range by using boots they already have in their closet. No need to go out and spend lots of money for specialized equipment.

You'll need one pair of heavy mittens, in addition to a lighter pair of gloves. You'll want some heavy pants, perhaps a pair made out of wool, such as some military surplus trousers. You can buy these at army surplus stores or second-hand stores.

Also, a pair of expedition overboots, or gaiters. To keep boots dry during the warm afternoons, or on sunny slopes, try wrapping your feet in plastic sacks, inside the nylon overboots. If your feet are dry, they're usually warm.

Some may want a pair of long underwear underneath the trousers. Sometimes two pair of pants work just fine. A heavier(perhaps downfilled) overcoat, plus a long sleeved shirt, and a sweat shirt with a hood and pockets, will fill out the clothing requirements. There's no need to spend big money on clothes. The author often wears or uses normal winter clothing, which works fine in most cases.

For the glare from the snow, you'll want a pair of ski goggles(or some kind of sun glasses), which also protects part of the face from the sun. In winter especially, you'll want something to protect the nose and other parts of the face from the sun and sunburn. The author uses a plain bandana worn bandit-style, across the face and nose, and tied at the back of the neck, rather than oily sun creams. This also protects the underside of the chin, as well as giving protection from the wind.

On the authors winter climbs in the Snake Range, he used the bandana and a baseball cap, with a special "cancer curtain" sewn on around the sides and back, like the French Foreign Legion caps. In good weather, this combination actually eliminated the need for goggles. The main reason goggles weren't worn is that they must be removed each time a fotograph is taken. However, on one trip and after three days of perfect sunny weather in February, some slight redding occurred around the eyes. Most people would be happiest wearing a pair of ski goggles.

For sleeping, you'll want a good downfilled mummy-type sleeping bag, and even more importantly, a good sleeping pad or mattress. You'll more than likely be sleeping right on snow, so have a good one, or you wont sleep at all. The author uses a full length Therm-a-Rest pad in the winter months, and a shorty, or half length, Therm-a-Rest pad in summer.

To get around on the snow, you'll want either a pair of cross-country skis or snow shoes. Either one should work well; it's a matter of personal preference. The author has two pair of snowshoes; one is the cross-country type and long enough to reach shoulder height. If the time comes when you really need snowshoes, these are the kind to have. In deep powder, these work best.

The second pair of snowshoes are about half as long, and obviously much lighter and easier to carry. These aren't so good in the really deep snow, but if you anticipate the greater part of your trip to be on high ridges above timberline, these are likely the best pair to take along. That's because you'll almost always be carrying them in your pack on the exposed ridges. If you're doing the ridge-line running from Lincoln Peak or Mt. Washington, to Wheeler Peak, then these shorter type snowshoes are best. But if you're doing a winter climb of Mt. Moriah via the Four Mile Spring Route, the cross-country type might be best. That's because you'd have long distances to travel below timberline and where the snow isn't blown rock-hard.

Early in winter, and depending on the year, you may get by without snowshoes or skis, especially if you stay on ridge-top routes. But normally you'll need snowshoes or skis to get up to the ridges, at least from December 1 and well into March, or even later. Expect to find deep and powdery snow in the canyons; but often times rock-hard snow on the ridges rising above timberline.

If you're a cross-country skier, you should know the sport pretty well, otherwise snowshoes might be best. For example, if you're coming down the Lehman Creek Trail on skis, you'll find it steep in places, with lots of trees and low hanging branches, and some sharp turns. This particular route is for advanced skiers.

Here's a tip for those who will use snowshoes. Make and attach to your 'shoes, a kind of *snowshoe crampon.* The author used a meter-long piece of what companies who make window frames call, *one inch angle.* This is a piece of angle aluminum window frame, bent into the shape of a horseshoe, and bolted onto the bottom of the snowshoes. On steep slopes this helps a lot. You can also buy 'shoes with this type of contraption already built on, but for a heavy price.

You may also want a pair of crampons, especially if you're doing a long ridge route, and if it's late in the winter with very firm and compact snow.

See hike and *Map 38, Winter Climbing--South Snake Range,* for a more detailed account of the problems involved in winter climbing and for more information about equipment and clothes needed.

Insect Season

The discussion on insects isn't very long, because there simply aren't that many in the Snake Range. In fact, the author can't recall right now ever seeing any mosquitos on any of his hikes. Surely there will be some around, but not many. The likely season for mosquitos will be in late spring-early summer; in the months of May and June, and maybe just into July. The reason they are generally numerous at this time is because of all the moisture in the high mountain meadows just after the snow melts. However, there are very few swampy areas, which are mosquito breeding grounds, in either the North or South Snake Range, therefore a general absence of these pests.

Another reason why there are so few mosquitos around is that these mountains don't receive the amount of precipitation as do other mountains of the west, such as the Sierras, Cascades or even the Wasatch Mountains of Utah. Less moisture around, means fewer breeding places.

Other pesky insects are flies, but they seem to be few in numbers as well. In drier and warmer areas you may find a few flies, but they generally won't bother you at night or in the cooler morning hours. One place you will find flies is in or around campgrounds. That's mainly due to careless campers leaving food scraps around and not cleaning up properly. If you choose a campsite that is not normally used as such, then you'll likely have very few flies.

A general statement about insects in the Snake Range, is that there are very few, and not enough to warrant spending money on insect repellent.

Hiking Regulations in the Great Basin National Park

The bill passed by Congress to create this national park, states there will be a three year period after the inception of the park, for the National Park Service and the general public, to decide upon and put together, a utilization plan for the future use of the park. The general public means you. Since you have a vested interest in this national park, it's going to be up to you to help the NPS and the GBNP come up with a management plan for the park. A big part of this plan has to do with future regulations.

If you have an opinion as to how this brand new national park should be operated in the future, you're invited to get involved in the policy making decisions. Write to the GBNP, Baker, Nevada, 89311, and ask for a copy of the *Public Involvement Issues--Great Basin National Park, Nevada,* then you can voice an opinion and have a chance to make recommendations. However, you don't really need this PII document at all; just send any comments into the GBNP before October 27, 1989.

Because there's now a national park covering much of the South Snake Range, one must expect the area to instantly have many more visitors than ever before; and as a result, a lot more regulations to govern the congestion. During the late summer and early fall of 1987, rangers from the NPS were hard at work going around to the different entry points along the park boundary putting up signs stating several of the general rules common to all national parks. Those rules on the bulletin state: IT IS UNLAWFUL TO: **Hunt, trap or possess loaded and uncased firearms or traps; Cut, remove, or injure any tree, shrub, or foliage, or any living thing; Camp without a permit except in designated locations; Kindle a fire without a permit except in designated sites; Permit dogs, cats, and other pets to run free.**

To some, these sound like just what is needed for a national park in upstate New York, but may not be needed for a national park in the middle of the Great Basin. Surely some parts of the GBNP need this type of regulation, but maybe other almost-never-visited sites don't. It's up to you the public to get involved, so let your views be known.

Even through the management plan hasn't been created yet, there are some general rules everyone should follow, especially in congested parts of the park like along Lehman and Baker Creeks, around the Wheeler Peak Campground, and to a lesser extent along Snake Creek. First of all, just keep the place clean. You carried in food and drinks; so surely you can take out the food containers and dispose of them properly. Why not police the area you're in and pick up after the public who cares less about the place than you. Also, stay on existing roadways with your vehicle; there are enough roads already.

If you're backpacking, the two most favorable campsites in the South Snake Range are at Johnson and Baker Lakes. At the moment(1988) you *apparently* don't have to get any kind of permit to camp in these two places, but surely one day you will. So in order to postpone the inevitable, walk softly and try not to disrupt the grass, trees or bushes any more than is needed. Avoid disturbing the ground cover, don't pollute the water and pick up after yourself and others(if necessary). These are common rules to follow, no matter where you're camping, whether it be in a national park or on other public lands of the west. If everyone used common sense, there would be little need for regulatory signs posted everywhere.

Maps Available for the Snake Range

Included here is an index map showing the USGS maps presently available covering the Snake Range and the Great Basin National Park. However, an index map is hardly necessary. There are presently only 3 or 4 maps in print which can be of any real help to the hiker. For some reason, the USGS has put eastern Nevada low on their list of priorities, therefore Mt. Moriah and the North Snake Range shows up as a blank on the state index map of USGS publications(1988).

The maps that are available are these. In the South Snake Range are three good maps; Sacramento Pass, Wheeler Peak and Garrison. These maps are at 1:62,500 scale and the best available for the hiker. These three maps cover all the major peaks and access roads, but they date from the 1940's, so the road system has changed. For example, the new Wheeler Peak Scenic Drive isn't on these maps. The trails in the park are pretty much the same as shown on these maps, but some of the trails are so little used and faded, you can't follow them. Buy all three of these maps at the GBNP visitor center at Lehman Caves.

Another map covering most of the South Snake Range is the metric map Garrison, at 1:100,000 scale. This is a good map too, but it doesn't show the trails in Timber Creek and South Fork of Baker Creek. The thing it does show are all the newer roads. As far as the access roads are concerned, this

INDEX TO U.S.G.S. MAPS

is the best map. If you decide you'd like to take a trip around the south end of the range, this is the best map available which shows the entire route from Garrison to Minerva. This USGS map dates from 1979, so is rather new, at least compared to the previous three maps.

The BLM also has virtually the same metric Garrison map as the USGS, but BLM maps concentrate on land ownership. They show private land in white, BLM land in yellow, and Forest Lands in green. This is a good map, but be sure to get the one subtitled *Surface Management Status*. If you get the other Garrison BLM publication subtitled, *Mineral Management Status,* which has many mineral overlays, it's too hard to read. With a BLM map, you know who owns the land you're walking or camping on.

To travel the northern end of the South Snake Range(covering Bald Mtn. and Osceola) you can use the other metric map at 1:100,000 scale. This is the Ely map and it dates from 1977. This one happens to be one of the better maps for the North Snake Range; its only real fault, it doesn't have contour lines(1988).

To date, Mt. Moriah and the North Snake Range still does not have a decent map. The Ely metric map however does show the streams, roads and some trails rather well; the problem is, it's hard to know just where the mountains and ridges are without the contour lines.

Mt. Moriah and the North Snake Range are simply not covered by the 1:62,500 scale maps yet. Nor does any part of the Snake Range have any of the 1:24,000 scale maps(1988). However, the park rangers and the Forest Service people do have some preliminary maps at this scale, but they aren't available to the pubic. It could be years before any of these maps come out. The author got some of the elevations in this book from those preliminary maps

There's another series of maps covering the South Snake Range. These are the USGS maps MF-1343 series A, B, or C. They cover the geology and mineral resources of the South Snake Range, and are based on the Sacramento Pass, Wheeler Peak and Garrison 1:62,500 scale maps discussed above. The author likes these maps and has used them often. They not only show the trails and roads(a little dim), but the names of mines and geology formations as well.

There are two other maps of Mt. Moriah you might try. They are the Ely map at 1:250,000, and the Forest Service map simply called the Humboldt National Forest. The Ely map is at such a small scale, it lacks detail and doesn't show any trails. But it is the only map available showing any kind of contour lines on Moriah.

The Forest Service map(1:125,000 scale) shows the roads as good as any map, plus trails, but it lacks contour lines. This map covers both the north and south parts of the Snake Range, as well as other nearby mountain ranges in the Ely Ranger District. All people spending much time in this area should buy this one, as it also covers more fine climbing and camping places in the Schell Creek Range, located east of Ely. Buy this map at the Ely Ranger Station.

Still another map to get a hold of, either at the Ely Ranger Station or the visitor center at Lehman Caves, is one of the simple give-away maps showing the national park boundaries in the South Snake Range. None of the above maps have the boundaries drawn on as yet.

Introduction to the Hiking Section

Here's a brief explanation on how to use and understand the hiking section of this book. Each hike is divided into 8 sections with the same subtitles shown below.

Location and Access Where the hike is and how to reach the trailhead. Emphasis is given to people driving passenger cars.

Trail or Route Conditions A description of the trail or route, how difficult it is, if there's any bushwhacking, and if the trail is easy to find and follow. On difficult climbs, the need for special equipment is discussed.

Elevations The elevation of trailheads, destinations, peaks, lakes, campgrounds, etc.--in meters.

Best Time and Time Needed What time of year is usually the best for a given hike or climb, and how much time it should take the average person. Usually the author's time is given, but he normally walks faster than the average hiker. Many people may want to take double the author's time, and enjoy the hike more.

Water This part tells where you can find drinking water between the trailhead and the destination described. Normally the water mentioned is drinkable as is, but you'll have to use your own good judgement in some cases. Since the author was never sure of water availability, he alway carried a full bottle with him on all hikes, but often drank the water from the places he describes.

Camping Where you can camp; at or near the trailhead, or places along the way(if it's an overnight hike).

Geology An effort is made to inform the average hiker with the type of rocks one sees along a particular trail or route.

Maps What maps are needed for that particular hike, and the scale of the map. It's recommended that all serious hikers or climbers buy one or more of these, then match them with the maps in this book. This will insure a more enjoyable hike.

Highest Peaks in the Snake Range

Here's a list of the highest mountains in the Snake Range, both North and South sections. All the higher peaks in the South Snake Range are inside the boundary of the Great Basin National Park. Altitudes are in both the metric and English systems. This list includes all peaks over 3300 meters(10,827 ft.), with just a few minor exceptions. It also includes some secondary summits of the major peaks. Most people would count only one summit for Baker and Moriah; therefore would consider Pyramid Peak to be the 5th, and Quartzite Peak, the 6th, highest in the Snake Range.

1. Wheeler Peak..3982(13,063 ft.)
2. Jeff Davis Peak..3894(12,775 ft.)
3. Baker Peak(east summit)...3752(12,310 ft.)
4. Baker Peak(west summit)..3748(12,298 ft.)
5. Mt. Moriah..3673(12,050 ft.)
6. Pyramid Peak..3634(11,922 ft.)
7. Mt. Moriah(South Peak)...3603(11,821 ft.)
8. Quartzite Peak..3598(11,804 ft.)
9. Johnson Peak..3593(11,788 ft.)
10. Mt. Washington..3559(11,676 ft.)
11. Lincoln Peak...3535(11,597 ft.)
12. Bald Mountain..3524(11,562 ft.)
13. Quartzite Peak(south summit)...3524(11,562 ft.)
14. Peak 3496(south ridge of Mt. Moriah)...3496(11,470 ft.)
15. Peak 3490(southeast ridge of Mt. Moriah)...3490(11,450 ft.)
16. Peak 3478(southeast ridge of Mt. Moriah)...3478(11,411 ft.)
17. Granite Peak ....3419(11,218 ft.)
18. Central Peak...3372(11,063 ft.)
19. Peak 3372(southeast ridge of Mt. Moriah)...3372(11,063 ft.)
20. Granite(northeast summit) ....3358(11,017 ft.)
21. Granite(east summit) ....3354(11,004 ft.)
22. The(Moriah) Table(average elevation) ....3350(10,991 ft.)
23. Acrapolis Peak..3336(10,945 ft.)
24. Peak 3315(Granite--Central Peak Ridge)...3315(10,876 ft.)
25. Eagle Peak..3305(10,843 ft.)

Metrics Spoken Here!

As you can see from reading the Introduction, the metric system of measurement is used exclusively in this book. It's not meant to confuse people, but surely it will do that to some. Instead, the reason it's used here is that when the day comes for the USA to change over to metrics, the author won't have to change his books. The author feels that day is fast approaching.

In 1975, the US Congress passed a resolution to begin the process of changing over to the metric system. They did this because the USA, Burma, and Brunei were the only countries on earth still using the antiquated British System of measurement. This progressive move ended with the Reagan Administration in 1981.

Use the Metric Conversion Table on the next page for help in the conversion process. It's easy to learn and use once you get started. Just keep a few things in mind: 1 mile is just over 1.5 kms, 2 miles is about 3 kms, and 6 miles is about 10 kms. Also, 2000 meters is about 6600 feet, 3000 meters is about 10,000 feet, and 100 meters is just about the same as 100 yards. A liter and a quart are roughly the same, and a US gallon jug is about 3.75 liters.

Lunch break at the summit of Lincoln Peak.

Metric Conversion Table

1 Centimeter = .39 Inch
1 Inch = 2.54 Centimeters
1 Meter = 39.37 Inches
1 Foot = 0.3048 Meter
1 Kilometer = 0.621 Mile

1 Mile = 1.609 Kilometers
100 Miles = 161 Kilometers
100 Kilometers = 62 Miles
1 Liter = 1.056 Quarts (US)

1 Quart (US) = .946 Liter
1 Gallon (US) = 3.785 Liters
1 Acre = 0.405 Hectare
1 Hectare = 2.471 Acres

METERS TO FEET (Meters x 3.2808 = Feet)

100 m = 328 ft.	2500 m = 8202 ft.	5000 m = 16404 ft.	7500 m = 24606 ft.
500 m = 1640 ft.	3000 m = 9842 ft.	5500 m = 18044 ft.	8000 m = 26246 ft.
1000 m = 3281 ft.	3500 m = 11483 ft.	6000 m = 19686 ft.	8500 m = 27887 ft.
1500 m = 4921 ft.	4000 m = 13124 ft.	6500 m = 21325 ft.	9000 m = 29527 ft.
2000 m = 6562 ft.	4500 m = 14764 ft.	7000 m = 22966 ft.	

FEET TO METERS (Feet ÷ 3.2808 = Meters)

1000 ft. = 305 m	9000 ft. = 2743 m	16000 ft. = 4877 m	23000 ft. = 7010 m
2000 ft. = 610 m	10000 ft. = 3048 m	17000 ft. = 5182 m	24000 ft. = 7315 m
3000 ft. = 914 m	11000 ft. = 3353 m	18000 ft. = 5486 m	25000 ft. = 7620 m
4000 ft. = 1219 m	12000 ft. = 3658 m	19000 ft. = 5791 m	26000 ft. = 7925 m
5000 ft. = 1524 m	13000 ft. = 3962 m	20000 ft. = 6096 m	27000 ft. = 8230 m
6000 ft. = 1829 m	14000 ft. = 4268 m	21000 ft. = 6401 m	28000 ft. = 8535 m
7000 ft. = 2134 m	15000 ft. = 4572 m	22000 ft. = 6706 m	29000 ft. = 8839 m
8000 ft. = 2438 m			30000 ft. = 9144 m

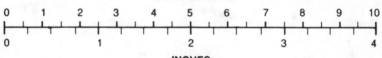

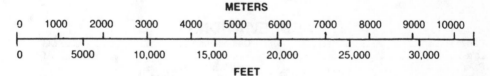

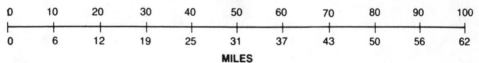

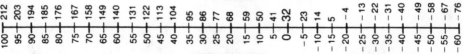

MAP SYMBOLS

Town or Community............................... ☐

Building, Ranch, or Cabin........................ ■ □

Back Country Campsite............................ ▲

Campsite(Road Access)............................ ⬟

Campground(developed)............................ ⋏

Campground(undeveloped)........................... ⋏

Visitor Center(GBNP)................................ ⛪

Landing Strip.. ✈

U. S. Highway.. 🛡50

State Highway.. (487)

Road--Maintained..................................... ═══

Road--4WD or HCV.................................... ═══

Track--Old Mining Road............................ ▬ or ▬

Trailhead Parking.................................... Ⓟ

Mile Post Markers.................................... ┼─┼
                                  72 73

Trail.. ─ ─ ─

Route, No Trail.. •••••

Peak and Prominent Ridge......................... ➤✕

Stream or Creek...................................... ⌇

Lake or Pond.. ▨

Mt. Moriah Wilderness Study Area(WSA)........ ▨

Mine, Quarry, Adit, Prospect...................... ⚒

Spring.. o

Pass.. ✕

Natural Bridge or Cave............................. ∩

Bristlecone Pine Forest............................. 🪨

Elevations in Meters................................ 3673

Ice or Permanent Snow............................. 🦴

Rock Glacier.. ⬭

ABBREVIATIONS

Canyon	C.	Campground	CG.
Lake	L.	Mine	M.
River	R.	Four Wheel Drive	4WD
Creek	Ck.	High Clearance Vehicle	HCV
Peak	Pk.	Spring	Sp.

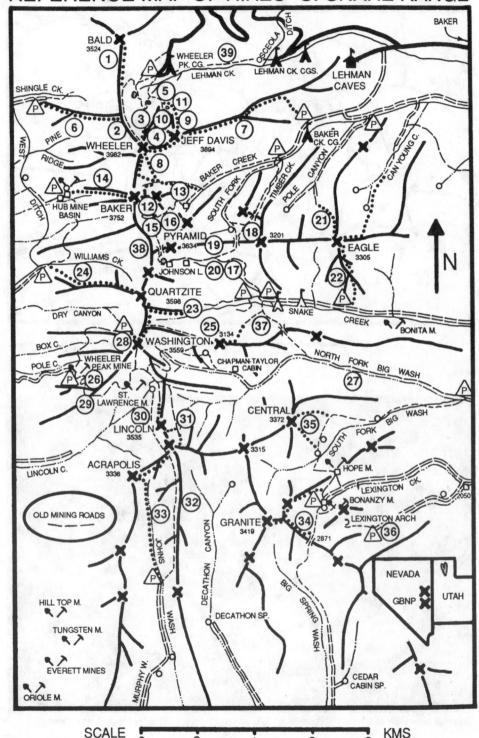

REFERENCE MAP OF HIKES--N. SNAKE RANGE

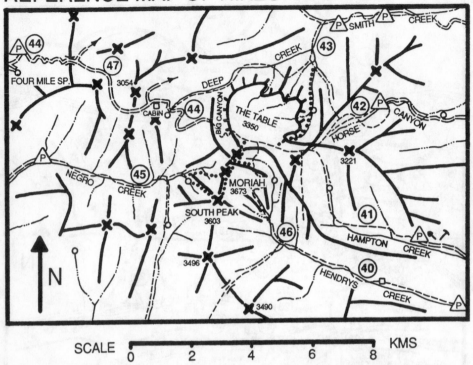

SCALE 0   2   4   6   8   KMS

Summer time view of Wheeler Cirque Basin and summit(from the Wheeler Peak Scenic Drive).

Looking down on the Wheeler Rock Glacier, from the summit of Wheeler Peak.

North Face of Baker Peak, as seen from the west, and from the Baker-Wheeler Ridge.

Bald Mountain--South Ridge Route

Location and Access Bald Mountain is at the very northern end of the South Snake Range, and the first peak north of Wheeler Peak. From Bald Mountain summit, one has one of the best views of Wheeler Peak found anywhere. Just to the northeast of the actual summit, is a small metal cabin, which houses some solar powered radio equipment. It's hidden from view, until you're right on top. At one time, and before the area received national park status, promoters in Ely had considered making a ski resort on the northern slopes of Bald Mountain. To get there, drive west out of Baker and toward park headquarters at Lehman Caves. About one km short of the caves, turn right onto the Wheeler Peak Scenic Drive. After driving about 20 kms, you'll arrive at the Wheeler Peak Campground and the trailhead.

Trail and Route Conditions The normal route to the top of Bald Mtn. begins at the Wheeler Peak CG. From the trailhead, first follow the signs and the trail toward the summit of Wheeler Peak. This trail is very good and well used. Just before you reach Stella Lake at 3185 meters, you'll turn to the northwest at a trail junction. At that point, the trail heads up-slope to the big ridge running between Bald Mtn. and Wheeler Pk. When you arrive on the ridge-top, turn north, and ridge-walk straight to the top of Bald Mountain. There is no trail along the ridge, but it's very easy walking, and you can't get lost.

Elevations Trailhead, 3033 meters; Bald Mountain summit, 3524.

Best Time and Time Needed The normal hiking season is from about mid-June until about mid-October, but it can be climbed earlier or later, depending on the weather. Each year is different. If hiking earlier or later, expect to walk in some snow. The distance from the trailhead to the summit is less than 5 kms, one-way. Strong hikers can make it up in just over an hour, but others may want two hours or more, one-way. A nice half day round-trip hike for the average hiker.

Water There is water in the campground water system, and along the first part of the trail heading out for Wheeler Peak. There's none on the ridge-top, so carry some with you if it's a warm day.

Camping Because this is a popular place, with heavy visitor use in this region, camping is permitted only in the Wheeler Peak Campground.

Geology Along the trail from the car-park, and to just above Stella Lake, you'll be walking atop *Pleistocene glacier deposits*. The whole basin was once covered by glaciers. As the trail begins to steepen along the side of the ridge to the west, you'll begin to see outcroppings of the *McCoy Creek Group* of rocks which is mostly quartzite. As you near the ridge-top, the *Prospect Mountain Quartzite* is exposed. As you walk north along the ridge and all the way to the summit of Bald Mtn., you'll be walking along this same quartzite formation.

Maps USGS or BLM maps Ely(1:100,000), or Sacramento Pass(1:62,500), or one of the geology maps MF-1343 A, B, or C(1:62,500), or Humboldt National Forest(1:125,000).

North from the summit of Wheeler. Bald Mtn, background, and up close, the Northeast Ridge.

MAP 1, BALD MTN.--SOUTH RIDGE ROUTE

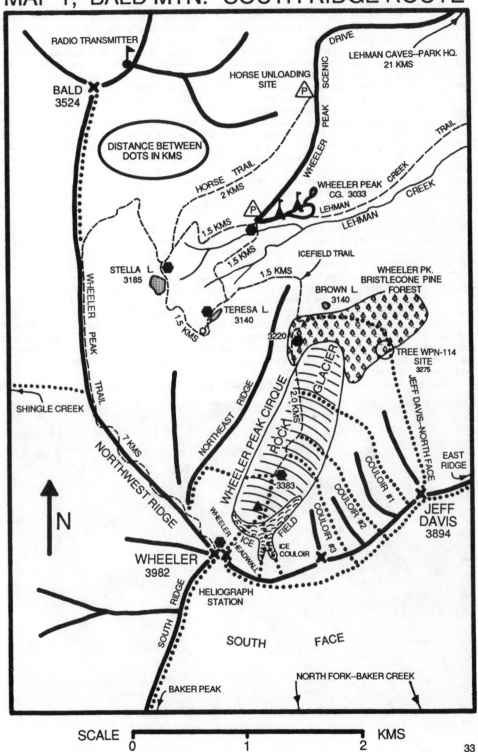

RADIO TRANSMITTER

BALD
3524

HORSE UNLOADING
SITE

LEHMAN CAVES--PARK HQ.
21 KMS

WHEELER PEAK SCENIC DRIVE

DISTANCE BETWEEN
DOTS IN KMS

TRAIL

HORSE TRAIL
2 KMS

WHEELER PEAK CREEK

CREEK

WHEELER PEAK
CG. 3033

LEHMAN

LEHMAN

1.5 KMS

WHEELER PEAK TRAIL

1.5 KMS

ICEFIELD TRAIL

1.5 KMS

STELLA L.
3185

WHEELER PK.
BRISTLECONE PINE
FOREST

BROWN L.
3140

1.5 KMS

TERESA L.
3140

3220

SHINGLE CREEK

TREE WPN-114
SITE
3275

JEFF DAVIS--NORTH FACE

NORTHEAST RIDGE

WHEELER PEAK CIRQUE

ROCK GLACIER

2.0 KMS

EAST
RIDGE

7 KMS

COULOIR #1

COULOIR #2

COULOIR #3

3383

NORTHWEST RIDGE

N

WHEELER
3982

WHEELER HEADWALL

ICE FIELD

ICE
COULOIR

JEFF
DAVIS
3894

HELIOGRAPH
STATION

SOUTH RIDGE

SOUTH   FACE

NORTH FORK--BAKER CREEK

BAKER PEAK

SCALE
0   1   2   KMS

Wheeler Peak--Normal Route

Location and Access This hike covers the route to the top of Wheeler Peak, the monarch of the Snake Range and the entire Great Basin region. The route or trail described here is the normal route. About 99% of the people who make it to the top, use this trail. For those who are beginning hikers, this is the route for you. Wheeler Peak is located in the northern end of the South Snake Range, and due east of the former Lehman Caves National Monument and Baker. To get to the trailhead, drive west out of Baker in the direction of Lehman Caves and Great Basin National Park Headquarters. About one km before you arrive at the caves, turn to the right, and head west up the Wheeler Peak Scenic Drive. It's about 20 kms to the campground, along a steep, but very good paved highway. As of 1988, this road was not plowed in winter, so when it snows, that's it for the season. Park right at the beginning of the campground, which is the trailhead parking lot.

Trail or Route Conditions From the car-park, the trail to the top of Wheeler Peak heads out in a westerly direction. In less than two kms, you'll come to a trail junction; just ahead is Stella Lake, and to the right is the trail to Wheeler. For another km or so, the trail zig zags up to the top of the ridge, which runs between Wheeler Peak, and Bald Mtn. to the north. Once on top of this ridge, the trail heads due south atop a broad ridge to the summit. In places the trail is a little difficult to see, but as the flow of foot traffic increases, the trail is becoming more obvious. Please stay on the one main trail, instead of creating a dozen un-needed ones. Further along, the trail steepens and becomes more obvious. Finally you reach the summit, which has several old shelters, some of which are the remains of an old triangulation or heliograph station.

Wheeler Peak Heliograph Station According to research done by Robert S. Waite for his 1974 Ph.D. dissertation, it was in 1881 that the U.S. Coast and Geodetic Survey began work in the Great Basin on its transcontinental triangulation and reconnaissance survey work west of the 100th Meridian and along the 39th Parallel. High mountains such as Ibapah Peak, Mt. Nebo and Mt. Belknap in Utah; and Arc Dome, Troy Peak and Wheeler Peak in Nevada, were selected as working field stations. Part of the program was to set up and experiment with a mirrored signaling device called a *heliograph*.

A heliograph or heliotrope, is a mirror set upon a tripod, with a sighting device. When the sun is out and the skies are clear, signals can be sent and seen from great distances. With a number of these devices set up on intermittent high peaks in a line running east-west, messages could be sent quickly. These stations were set up and experimented with during the 1880's, and along an east-west line from Mt. Shasta in Northern California, to the Colorado Rockies. This method of communication was called *heliography;* the operator of the device was called a *heliographer;* and the message sent was called a *heliogram.*

The first man directly involved with this station was Joseph Davis, who in August of 1881,

Winter scene of the Northwest Ridge of Wheeler Peak(the normal route up).

MAP 2, WHEELER PEAK--NORMAL ROUTE

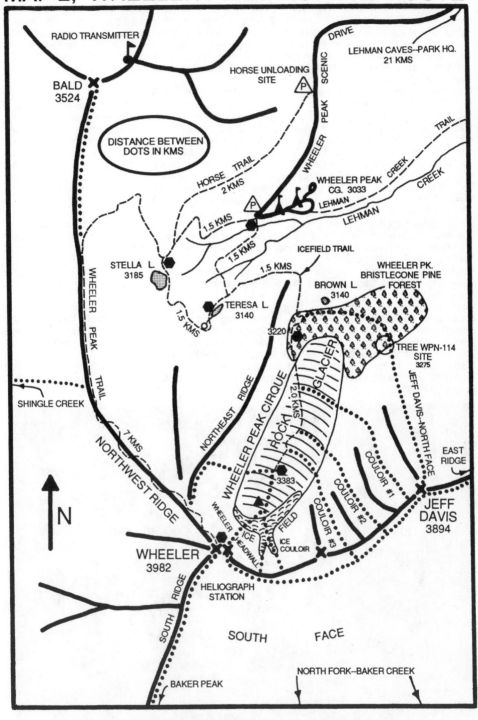

RADIO TRANSMITTER

LEHMAN CAVES--PARK HQ. 21 KMS

HORSE UNLOADING SITE

WHEELER PEAK SCENIC DRIVE

BALD 3524

DISTANCE BETWEEN DOTS IN KMS

WHEELER CREEK TRAIL

HORSE TRAIL 2 KMS

WHEELER PEAK CG. 3033

LEHMAN CREEK

1.5 KMS

LEHMAN

WHEELER PEAK TRAIL

1.5 KMS

ICEFIELD TRAIL

1.5 KMS

STELLA L. 3185

BROWN L. 3140

WHEELER PK. BRISTLECONE PINE FOREST

TERESA L. 3140

1.5 KMS

3220

SHINGLE CREEK

TREE WPN-114 SITE 3275

NORTHEAST RIDGE

WHEELER PEAK CIRQUE

ROCK GLACIER

2.0 KMS

JEFF DAVIS--NORTH FACE

7 KMS

NORTHWEST RIDGE

3383

COULOIR #1

COULOIR #2

EAST RIDGE

JEFF DAVIS 3894

N

WHEELER 3982

SOUTH RIDGE

WHEELER HEADWALL

ICE FIELD

ICE COULOIR

COULOIR #3

HELIOGRAPH STATION

SOUTH FACE

BAKER PEAK

NORTH FORK--BAKER CREEK

SCALE   KMS

0   1   2

35

climbed Wheeler Peak from the east, and set up a camp. He stayed until December of that same year. In 1882, a trail was built from Baker to the summit. A more or less permanent camp was then set up, which was used throughout the 1880's. The camp consisted of several stone huts, topped with canvas tents. Supplies were first sent to Baker by wagon train, thence by pack horse to the summit camp. During the years 1887 to 1889, two brothers, George A. and O. A. Rice were the camp keepers.

If you look closely around the base of the eastern-most stone cairn on the Wheeler Peak summit ridge, you may be able to see an inscription which reads: *"U.S. Coast and Geodetic Survey, July 4th, 1887-89, George A. Rice."* On the other side of the monument is *"O. A. Rice"*, but this author never could detect this one.

Elevations Trailhead, 3033 meters; the summit of Wheeler Peak, 3982 meters.

Best Time and Time Needed The normal hiking season along this trail is from about mid-June to about mid-October. Depending on the weather conditions for any given year, you can sometimes get to the trailhead either earlier or later than previously stated, but you'd have to expect some snow or wet conditions. Sometimes the weather is good even until the end of October, but nights can become very cold at that time in the Wheeler Peak Campground. It's about 8.5 kms from the trailhead to the summit via the Wheeler Peak Trail, and will take a strong hiker less than a couple of hours to walk it. Other hikers, and especially those who live at/or near sea level, may want 3 to 4 hours for the one way walk. For strong hikers, less than half a day round-trip; for beginners, perhaps all day for the entire hike.

Water Water is available in the Wheeler Peak Campground and along the beginning of the trail to Wheeler Peak. If you take it directly from one of the springs, it's going to be very good water. Because this area is beginning to suffer from over-use, please use the toilets at the campground if possible, to help retain the purity of the water in the creeks and springs. Once past Stella Lake, there is no more running water available. Sometimes you can get water just below snowdrifts, or from snow itself along the summit ridge.

Camping Because this is the second most popular destination point in the park, there is camping only in the Wheeler Peak Campground at the trailhead. There is no backcountry camping allowed in this immediate area.

Geology As you begin to walk up the trail, you'll be walking atop *Pleistocene glacier debris,* which covers all of the floor of this upper basin. Further along, and as you walk above Stella Lake, you pass through a narrow band of the *McCoy Creek Group* of rocks which are mostly quartzite. Just above this narrow band, and as you top-out on the ridge, you'll be walking over *Prospect Mountain Quartzite.* This same quartzite formation covers all of the upper part of Wheeler Peak.

Maps USGS or BLM maps Ely and Garrison(1:100,000), or Sacramento Pass and Wheeler Peak(1:62,500), or one of the geology maps MF-1343 A, B, or C(1:62,500), or Humboldt National Forest(1:125,000).

Stone cairn at the summit Wheeler Peak.

One of the shelters of the old Heliograph Station on Wheeler Peak.

High on the Northwest Ridge of Wheeler Peak.

Wheeler Peak—Glacier & Northeast Ridge Route

Location and Access This is one of the alternate routes to the summit of Wheeler Peak, which is the second highest peak in Nevada at 3982 meters. This route involves a hike up to and across the Wheeler Peak Rock Glacier and up what might be described as the Northeast Ridge. To get to Wheeler Peak, drive west out of Baker in the direction of Lehman Caves and Great Basin National Park Headquarters. It's 10 kms from Baker to Lehman Caves, but after about 9 kms, turn to the right and onto the Wheeler Peak Scenic Drive. This paved highway runs for about 20 kms and ends at the Wheeler Peak Campground and trailhead.

Trail or Route Conditions From the car-park, follow the trail and signs to the *south* and towards Wheeler Rock Glacier and the Bristlecone Pine Forest. This is the most used trail in the park. After a km and a half, you'll come to a trail junction. To the right about 100 meters is Teresa Lake; to the left is the Icefield Trail running into the Wheeler Peak Cirque. After another km and a half, you'll be in the bristlecone forest. Continue up the trail and into the cirque basin. The trail leads up along the middle part of the rock glacier. In the upper end of the cirque basin, the trail abruptly ends at a viewing area. From that point, head about due west and up the scree slope toward a couple of obvious gullies or couloirs. Head straight up one of these until you top-out on the NE Ridge. Once on the ridge, walk south and a little west until you meet the main Wheeler Peak Trail, thence to the top. Consider going down the Wheeler Peak Trail, and making a loop-hike out of it(or you could walk up the Wheeler Peak Trail, and go down to the glacier and finish along the Icefield Trail).

Elevations Trailhead and Wheeler Pk. Campground, 3033 meters; end of Icefield Trail, 3383; the summit, 3982 meters.

Best Time and Time Needed Normally you can make this hike from about mid-June until the middle of October, but each year is different. Before or after this time slot, you'll likely encounter some snow and cold temps. The distance from the campground to the end of the Icefield Trail, is about 5 kms. From there to the summit, it's less than two kms, but this last part is all steep. Strong hikers can do the round-trip in less than half a day; slower hikers, or those who live at or near sea level, may need nearly a full day.

Water At the campground, and in a couple of small streams you'll pass in the first km of the trail.

Camping In this heavily used area, one must camp in the Wheeler Peak Campground only. No backcountry camping is allowed in the immediate area.

Geology From the trailhead and all along the Icefield Trail, you'll be walking over *Pleistocene glacier deposits*. But once you start to climb to the NE Ridge, you'll be on the *Prospect Mountain Quartzite*. All the upper part of Wheeler Peak is composed of this formation.

Maps USGS or BLM maps Ely and Garrison(1:100,000), or Sacramento Pass and Wheeler Peak(1:62,500), or one of the geology maps MF-1343 A, B, or C(1:62,500), or Humboldt National Forest(1:125,000).

From Bald Mtn. Jeff Davis Pk, Wheeler Cirque, Northeast Ridge and summit of Wheeler(right).

MAP 3, WHEELER --GLACIER & N.E. RIDGE

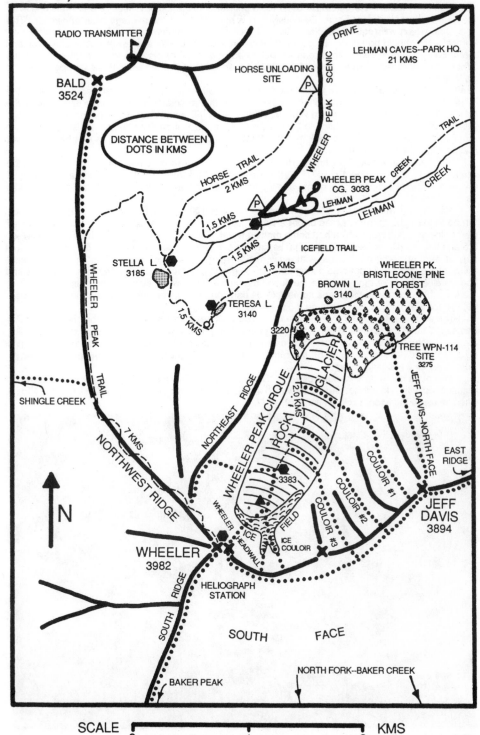

RADIO TRANSMITTER

LEHMAN CAVES--PARK HQ.
21 KMS

HORSE UNLOADING
SITE

P

BALD
3524

WHEELER PEAK SCENIC DRIVE

DISTANCE BETWEEN
DOTS IN KMS

HORSE   TRAIL
2 KMS

TRAIL

P

WHEELER PEAK
CG. 3033

LEHMAN CREEK

CREEK

1.5 KMS

LEHMAN

LEHMAN

1.5 KMS

ICEFIELD TRAIL

WHEELER PEAK
TRAIL

STELLA L.
3185

1.5 KMS

WHEELER PK.
BRISTLECONE PINE
FOREST

BROWN L.
3140

1.5 KMS

TERESA L.
3140

3220

TREE WPN-114
SITE
3275

SHINGLE CREEK

7 KMS

NORTHEAST RIDGE

NORTHWEST RIDGE

WHEELER PEAK CIRQUE

ROCK   GLACIER

2.0 KMS

JEFF DAVIS--NORTH FACE

EAST
RIDGE

3383

N

COULOIR #1

COULOIR #2

COULOIR #3

JEFF
DAVIS
3894

WHEELER
3982

WHEELER
HEADWALL

ICE
FIELD

ICE
COULOIR

SOUTH RIDGE

HELIOGRAPH
STATION

SOUTH   FACE

BAKER PEAK

NORTH FORK--BAKER CREEK

SCALE   KMS
0   1   2

39

Wheeler Peak–Northeast Face Route

Location and Access Here is still another route possibility to the top of Wheeler Peak. This one is up the near vertical Northeast Face. Obviously, this is not a route for the average hiker or climber. This is a route which will require special skills. All rock climbing equipment needed for vertical or near vertical walls should be taken. To get there, drive west out of Baker, and toward Lehman Caves and Great Basin National Park. About one km before arriving at the caves, turn to the right, and onto the Wheeler Peak Scenic Drive. This 20 km paved road ends at the Wheeler Peak Campground and trailhead.

Trail or Route Conditions From the trailhead, walk south on the Icefield Trail heading toward the Wheeler Cirque and Bristlecone Pine Forest. Follow this maintained and heavily used trail to the bristlecone forest and beyond to the Wheeler Rock Glacier. The trail ends near the head of the cirque. From there it's just a short distance to the headwall where the real climbing begins. This is perhaps the most difficult rock climb in the park and the Snake Range. If you can maintain a straight line, you should end right at the summit.

The American Alpine Club Journal, from 1953 to 1987, mentions nothing about any climbing in the Snake Range, but on June 19, 1977, Wade Mills, then of Calistoga, California, made a solo climb of this face. Here is a report of his climb, and the equipment he used or recommends, for this 600 meter vertical ascent.

Mills began with a Class 4.0 snow and ice climb of 100 meters to a ramp (A). He started left, turned to the right, then traversed under a water gully (B), with ice on top. He then climbed the wall next to the gully(left side) which had some running water. This was 60 meters, which he rated between 5.5 and 5.8. At (C) he went left into what he calls "a thin ledge--open book" at 4.0--5.5. In the area of (D), he went up some overhangs--with aid, which were wet. He made two pitches on thin horizontal holds, at 5.8. He finally got onto a long ramp (E) angling up to the left. This ramp fades in places and had ice all over. After many pitches, he got off the face just below the summit, and to the upper left of the foto. Mills mentions there was some rockfall early on in his climb, when the sun first hit the face, but that ice was hard in the cracks on the upper face.

The equipment used for this climb was as follows: 1 set of hex nuts, plus 3 tube chokes; 1 alpine hammer; 3 short ice screws; 6 thin pitons(Bugaboos Long--6 1/4" ang.); 10 quick draws; 30 snaplinks; 2 ropes, each 50 meters long--one 7mm, one 11mm; plus aid slings and Jumars. Apparently he didn't take, but could have cut 3 hours off the climb, had he taken a short ice ax and crampons. A helmet would also be a necessary item.

Mills put a name on this route, calling it "Stella by Starlight". He found no trace or sign of previous climbs or activity. He left nothing on the wall himself. He rated this solo climb as Class 5.8, A3 + Ice 9, when he made the ascent solo on June 19, 1977.

Northeast Face of Wheeler Peak, seen from the northeast(Mike Nicklas foto).

MAP 4, WHEELER PK.--NORTHEAST FACE

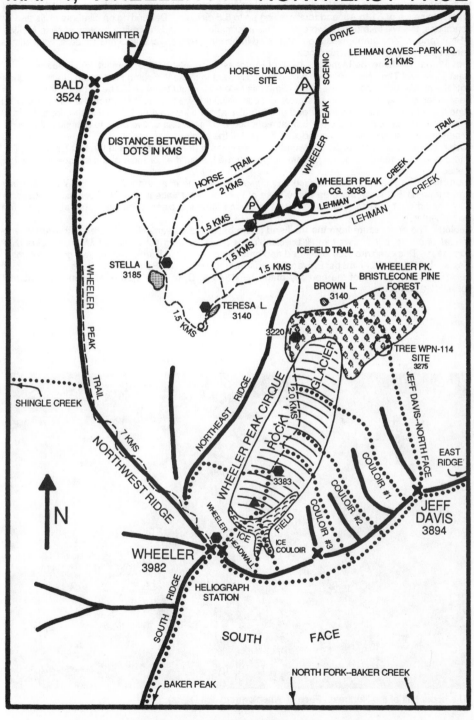

RADIO TRANSMITTER

HORSE UNLOADING SITE

LEHMAN CAVES--PARK HQ.
21 KMS

BALD
3524

DISTANCE BETWEEN
DOTS IN KMS

WHEELER PEAK SCENIC DRIVE

WHEELER CREEK TRAIL

HORSE TRAIL
2 KMS

WHEELER PEAK CG. 3033

LEHMAN CREEK

1.5 KMS

1.5 KMS

ICEFIELD TRAIL

1.5 KMS

WHEELER PK.
BRISTLECONE PINE
FOREST

STELLA L.
3185

BROWN L.
3140

TERESA L.
3140

1.5 KMS

3220

TREE WPN-114
SITE
3275

WHEELER PEAK TRAIL

SHINGLE CREEK

NORTHEAST RIDGE

WHEELER PEAK CIRQUE

ROCK GLACIER

2.0 KMS

JEFF DAVIS--NORTH FACE

EAST RIDGE

7 KMS

3383

COULOIR #1

COULOIR #2

NORTHWEST RIDGE

N

WHEELER HEADWALL

ICE FIELD

COULOIR #3

JEFF
DAVIS
3894

WHEELER
3982

ICE
COULOIR

HELIOGRAPH
STATION

SOUTH RIDGE

SOUTH   FACE

BAKER PEAK

NORTH FORK--BAKER CREEK

SCALE

0   1   2   KMS

41

On July 17, 1985, Alex Steckel and James Garrett of Salt Lake City, Utah, climbed the big couloir to the left or east side of the Northeast Face, but weren't certain if they were the first to do so. They report alpine ice of A1 to A3, and rock ranging up to 5.5 difficulty. Depending on climbers skills and ice conditions, this will take one or two days. This information reached the author by way of Mike Nicklas, GBNP ranger. The author would be interested in hearing from anyone who has made difficult climbs here or on any other peak in the range.

Elevations Trailhead, 3033 meters; base of Northeast Face, about 3425; summit, 3982 meters.

Best Time and Time Needed One would normally want to make this climb from about the first of June until the middle of October. One could climb this face earlier, but there would be snow on the Wheeler Peak Scenic Drive, making access more difficult. You'd have the most sun and the longest day on June 21. From the trailhead to the end of the trail is about 5 kms(a 1 or 1.5 hour walk); from the trails end to the summit is about another km--straight up. It will take one or two days to complete the climb, depending on which route is followed, and the skill of the climbers.

Water In the Wheeler Peak Campground or at two small year-round streams in the first km of the hike. There is always some ice at the bottom of the headwall, even if all or most of the seasonal snow has melted.

Camping The National Park Service has closed the area to camping except at the Wheeler Peak Campground. But since the area at the base of the Northeast Face is almost never visited, it seems they should over look this small corner--if everyone leaves a clean campsite. Ask about it at the visitor center.

Geology The entire route from the trailhead to the base of the headwall is covered with *Pleistocene glacial deposits,* but the wall you'll be climbing is quartzite from the *Prospect Mountain Quartzite Formation.* This quartzite rock is layered and brecciated some, but it looks reasonably good to climb.

Maps USGS or BLM maps Ely and Garrison(1:100,000), or Sacramento Pass and Wheeler Peak(1:62,500), or one of the geology maps MF-1343 A, B, or C(1:62,500), or Humboldt National Forest(1:125,000).

The upper half of the Northeast Face of Wheeler(from Jeff Davis).

The full Northeast Face of Wheeler. From summit of Jeff Davis.

The Ice Couloir, in the upper end of the Wheeler Cirque Basin.

Wheeler Peak–Ice Couloir Route

Location and Access This route to the summit of Wheeler Peak can be one of the most difficult routes on the mountain, and one which requires special skills and equipment. To get to this climb, first drive west from Baker in the direction of Lehman Caves and Great Basin National Park. About one km before arriving at the caves, turn right onto the Wheeler Peak Scenic Drive. This 20 km long paved highway ends at the trailhead and Wheeler Peak Campground.

Trail or Route Conditions You begin this climb by taking the Icefield Trail south from the trailhead. This is signposted to the Bristlecone Pine Forest. After one and a half kms, you come to a junction. Turn left and walk another 3 or 4 kms to the end of the trail in the upper part of the Wheeler Cirque Basin. From that point, walk due south across the rock glacier in the direction of the big ice couloir dead ahead. The small and shaded ice field you see is all that remains of the much larger Pleistocene Age glacier. About half way up the ice couloir, it forks, and you have a "Y" shaped gully system. You can go up either, but the one on the left or east, appears to be the easier of the two. To make it up either of these couloirs, you'll need an ice ax and crampons, and a rope. Also some ice screws and even some rock climbing gear such as pitons and nuts. Maybe the most important piece of equipment, is the helmet. Before you actually begin the climb, you'll have to sit down at the bottom of the couloir, and observe where the rocks are coming down. The author turned back out of this climb which was on the left side, because of gravel and pea-sized rocks coming down the steep ice. Falling rocks can be a big problem on this route. If the rocks are coming down one particular area, which they appear to be, then perhaps it'll be safe to proceed. The right side of the lower couloir seemed safer to the author. If it appears there's no part of the couloir free of rock-fall, try another route.

Elevations Trailhead, 3033 meters; base of ice field, 3400; top of couloir, about 3750 meters.

Best Time and Time Needed In late spring-early summer, you'll have a snow climb: in late summer-early fall, it'll be a climb over mostly solid ice. You may have more dangerous rock-fall conditions when the couloir is icy. You can make it from the trailhead to the ice field in 1 or 1.5 hours, but perhaps a full day to finish the climb.

Water At the campground, at two small streams you'll cross in the first km of the trail, and you should always find some water at the bottom of the icefield.

Camping *Officially,* people are allowed to camp in the Wheeler Peak Campground only, but for a difficult climb such as this, no one should mind if you camp at the base of the icefield. Ask about it at the visitor center.

Geology From the trailhead to the icefield, you'll be walking over *Pleistocene glacier deposits,* but all the rock above that is the *Prospect Mountain Quartzite.*

Maps USGS or BLM maps Ely and Garrison(1:100,000), or Sacramento Pass and Wheeler Peak(1:62,500), or one of the geology maps MF-1343 A, B, or C(1:62,500), or Humboldt National Forest(1:125,000).

Wheelers Icefield even has a Bergschrund or two.

MAP 5, WHEELER PEAK--ICE COULOIR

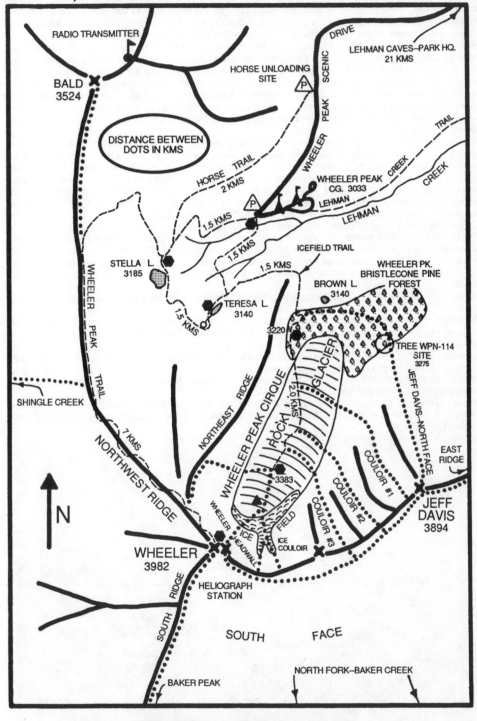

RADIO TRANSMITTER

DRIVE

LEHMAN CAVES--PARK HQ.
21 KMS

HORSE UNLOADING
SITE

P

BALD
3524

DISTANCE BETWEEN
DOTS IN KMS

WHEELER PEAK SCENIC

TRAIL

HORSE TRAIL
2 KMS

P

WHEELER PEAK
CG. 3033

LEHMAN CREEK

CREEK

1.5 KMS

LEHMAN

WHEELER PEAK TRAIL

1.5 KMS

ICEFIELD TRAIL

WHEELER PK.
BRISTLECONE PINE
FOREST

STELLA L.
3185

1.5 KMS

1.5 KMS

BROWN L.
3140

TERESA L.
3140

3220

TREE WPN-114
SITE
3275

SHINGLE CREEK

NORTHEAST RIDGE

WHEELER PEAK CIRQUE

ROCK GLACIER

2.0 KMS

JEFF DAVIS--NORTH FACE

7 KMS

3383

COULOIR #1

EAST
RIDGE

N

NORTHWEST RIDGE

WHEELER

ICE HEADWALL

FIELD

ICE
COULOIR

COULOIR #2

COULOIR #3

JEFF
DAVIS
3894

WHEELER
3982

SOUTH RIDGE

HELIOGRAPH
STATION

SOUTH   FACE

BAKER PEAK

NORTH FORK--BAKER CREEK

SCALE ──────────────── KMS
      0   1   2

45

Wheeler Peak--West Face Route

Location and Access If you don't like crowded campgrounds and trails, here's an alternate route to Wheeler Peak. This route is up from Shingle Creek on the west side of the range. To get to the trailhead or car-park, drive into Spring Valley, which is the big north-south running valley west of the range and Wheeler Peak. Drive south along the paved Minerva Highway(the one which runs from Highway 93 just south of Majors Place) towards Shonshone and Minerva. Just before arriving at mile post 11, on the big sweeping curve where the highway turns south, turn off onto the old gravel road which connects the Minerva Highway with Goody Station on Highway 50-6. After only about 100 meters, turn right and head southeast. Drive past the first road running along the pipeline. Use the second and most-used road running northeast(the one south of the pipeline). This is not a road for the average car, but cars with higher than average clearance can make it if care is taken. Just take it slow and easy. From the highway to the first campsite is about 7 kms; to the end of the road along Shingle Creek, about 8 kms.

Trail or Route Conditions From a point about half way between the two campsites, route-find up the prominent ridge to the south of the creek drainage. The lower end has cedars and sagebrush, but no bushwhacking. Further up, the ridge is open with sagebrush, and the walking very easy. Along part of the way you can use an old sheepherders track. Further up you walk through an open pine and aspen forest which is still easy walking. Just below the top of the ridge running between Bald Mtn. and Wheeler, you'll arrive at timberline. On the ridge, use the upper part of the Wheeler Peak Trail to reach the summit. You'll cross the park boundary about half way up the slope.

Elevations Valley floor, 1780 meters; upper campsite, 2375; Wheeler Peak, 3982 meters.

Best Time and Time Needed From about early or mid-June through October, but each year is different. This might make the easiest and fastest route for a winter climb up Wheeler Peak. Fast hikers can make this climb is less than a day, round-trip. The author went up in 3 hours; 5.5 hrs. for the round-trip. It will be a long day hike for slower hikers. Your time will depend partly on how far you can drive up the road.

Water Shingle Creek has good water year-round, but lookout for grazing sheep upstream in mid-summer.

Camping There are two good campsites as shown on the map. Best thing about using this route is that you'll seldom find anyone else there, and it's on public land. This means you can camp where you like and build a campfire. Please leave a clean campsite.

Geology For the first half of your hike, you'll be walking atop the various members of the *McCoy Creek Group* of rocks. This is mostly quartzite, but it also has minor beds of conglomerate, phyllite and schist. Above about 3000 meters, you'll encounter the *Prospect Mountain Quartzite*, which covers all the upper part of Wheeler Peak.

Maps USGS or BLM maps Ely and Garrison(1:100,000), or Sacramento Pass and Wheeler Peak(1:62,500), or one of the geology maps MF-1343 A, B or C(1:62,500), or Humboldt National Forest(1:125,000).

Wheeler Peak, as seen from the west and Spring Valley.

MAP 6, WHEELER PEAK--WEST FACE

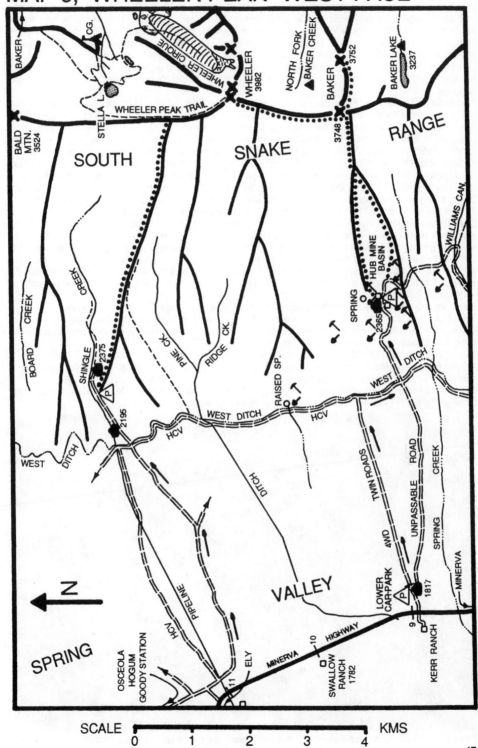

SCALE   KMS

0   1   2   3   4

Wheeler Peak--East Ridge Route

Location and Access The route covered here is the East Ridge of both Wheeler and Jeff Davis Peaks. This big hogsback actually ends right at the Lehman Caves Visitor Center. This would be one way to reach the top of these peaks from the east side of the range during winter. Here's how to get there. Drive west out of Baker toward park headquarters at Lehman Caves. You could start at the caves, but there's another starting point that's closer. About a km east of the caves, turn south at the sign pointing to Baker Ck. CG. Drive along this good gravel road for 4 or 5 kms, until you see a parking place on the left, overlooking the campground. From that point, it's only about 1.5 kms to the main ridge-top.

Trail or Route Conditions From the car-park, walk across the road in a northwest direction. Cross a fence, and head for the ridge-top via the easy-to-cross rock slope just in front of you. By using this open rock slope, you can gain the ridge-top easily, and without bushwhacking. An alternate route, would be to follow cow trails into the shallow drainage coming down from the west. If you get on the right cow trail, you can do this one without bushwhacking too. Once on the ridge, simply walk up the easiest route, staying on or near the ridge-top all the way. There will be some brush in places, but you can zig zag around it easily. Higher up, the brush turns into trees; then finally you reach timberline at about 3300 meters. Above the trees, it's very easy walking. Along this route, you'll first reach Jeff Davis, then you must descend 125 vertical meters, before making the actual ascent of Wheeler.

Elevations Car-park, 2315 meters; Jeff Davis, 3894; Wheeler Peak, 3982 meters.

Best Time and Time Needed As stated before, this is a route which could be climbed in winter, so anytime is a good time. In winter you'll either have much of the snow blown off the ridge, or you can walk along a hard wind-blown snowpack right to the summit. On a summer hike, the author made it to Jeff Davis Peak in 2 hrs. 45 min. Later, he climbed Wheeler, and did some exploring around. He finally come down the alternate route shown, all in under 8 hours. To do both peaks in one day is a lot for the average hiker. Better be in good shape to tackle both peaks in one day. In March, a long all day winter climb for a strong hiker.

Water At Lehman Caves and at the Baker Creek Campground. None on the ridge or peaks.

Camping Because of heavy traffic in the area, you must camp in the Baker Ck. CG.; or drive to a point just outside the park boundary east of the mouth of Pole Canyon. There are a number of campsites along lower Baker Creek in the cedar trees.

Geology For most of this hike, you'll be walking atop the *Prospect Mountain Quartzite Formation*(once you get above the *Pole Canyon Limestone* located right at Lehman Caves, and a short section of *granite*). See the geology cross-section of Lehman Caves later in this book.

Maps USGS or BLM map Garrison(1:100,000), or Garrison and Wheeler Peak(1:62,500), or one of the geology maps MF-1343 A, B, or C(1:62,500), or Humboldt National Forest(1:125,000).

From Eagle Peak, one sees Baker(left), then Wheeler, Jeff Davis and the East Ridge.

MAP 7, WHEELER PEAK--EAST RIDGE

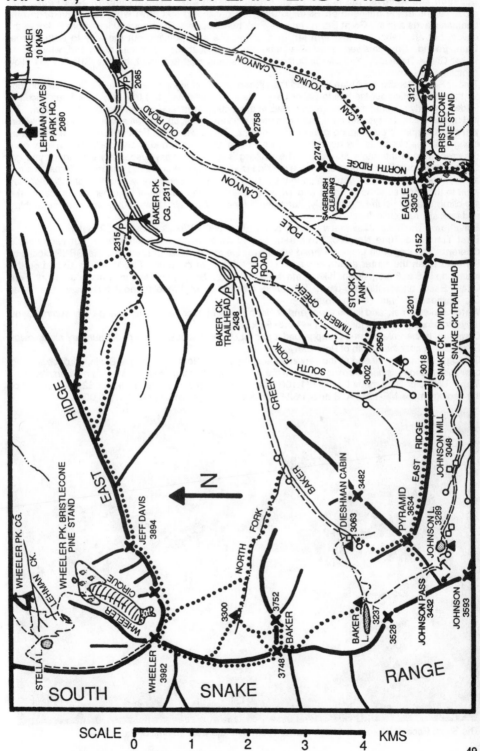

SCALE

0   1   2   3   4   KMS

Wheeler Peak--Baker Creek Route

Location and Access This is the last of several different ways you can climb Wheeler Peak. This route begins at the trailhead on Baker Creek. To get there, first drive west out of Baker toward Lehman Caves and the Great Basin National Park headquarters. It's about 10 kms from Baker to the caves, but after about 9 kms, turn left or south at the sign pointing out the way to Baker Creek Campground. Drive this very good all-weather gravel road about 7 or 8 kms to it's end, which is the Baker Creek Trailhead. You can park there in the shade next to a toilet, but the GBNP won't allow camping there anymore.

Trail or Route Conditions At the trailhead there are a couple of signs indicating two different trails; look for the one pointing out the trail to Baker Lake. Near the beginning, this trail may be a little difficult to follow. In early summer there are many cows in this grassy area, and several trails are the result. But just up the creek a ways, the right route becomes evident. Walk up the trail about 3 to 4 kms to where you cross a small creek coming down from the right. This is the North Fork of Baker Creek. Walk up along side this stream to the northwest. After a ways, the stream bed is dry, but continue in or near the creek bed in the same direction. The walking is generally easy, especially the higher you go. Once in the North Fork Cirque Basin, the walking is very easy in a scattered and mixed forest of pine, spruce, and aspen. When you're high in the basin, you have a choice of two routes: one is to go due west to the ridge separating Baker and Wheeler, thence to the summit of Wheeler; or you can make the climb straight up the moderately steep south face of Wheeler. Both routes are easy scrambles and lack any real difficulties.

Elevations Trailhead, 2438 meters; upper basin, about 3300; Wheeler Peak, 3982 meters.

Best Time and Time Needed From early to mid-June until about late October, but each year is different. You can drive to the trailhead when ever the road is clear of snow, but the GBNP blocks off the road when the winter snows come, to prevent rutting of the road. Strong hikers should do this round-trip in 6 to 8 hrs.; slower hikers, maybe 9 or 10 hrs. Some may want to camp in the North Fork Cirque Basin, and do it in two days. The author climbed Baker, Wheeler and Jeff Davis via the Baker Ck. Trailhead, in 7 hrs. 10 min., round-trip.

Water Baker Creek, and in the lower end of North Fork of Baker Ck. In late spring-early summer, you may find running water higher up in the North Fork Basin.

Camping In the Baker Creek Campground, or on BLM land just outside the park boundary along lower Baker Creek near the mouth of Pole Canyon.

Geology From the trailhead all the way into the upper part of North Fork Cirque Basin, you'll be walking over *Pleistocene glacier deposits*. Up from the basin, you'll find the *Prospect Mountain Quartzite*.

Maps USGS or BLM maps Garrison(1:100,000), or Garrison and Wheeler Peak(1:62,500), or one of the geology maps MF-1343 A, B or C(1:62,500), or Humboldt National Forest(1:125,000).

The South Face of Wheeler and Jeff Davis. From near the west summit of Baker Peak.

MAP 8, WHEELER PEAK--BAKER CK. ROUTE

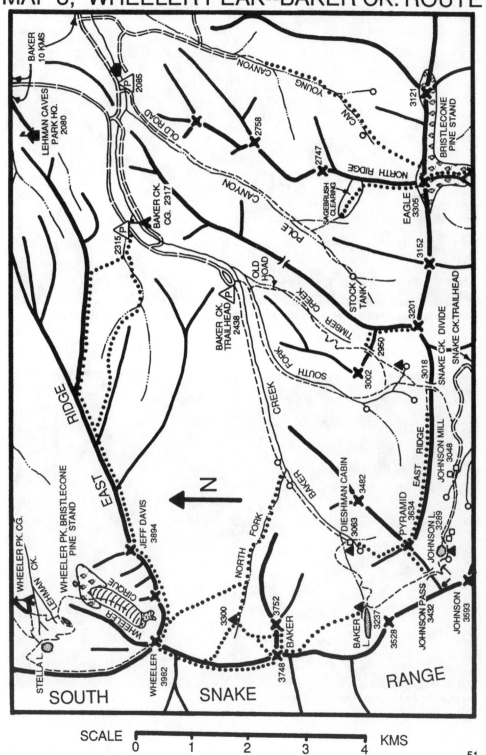

SCALE 0 1 2 3 4 KMS

From the Northeast Ridge of Wheeler, one can see the Ice Couloir and the Northeast Face.

The moat, of the Wheeler Peak Rock Glacier.

Telefoto lens view of the North Face of Jeff Davis. Northeast Ridge in center.

Looking straight up the 1st Couloir of Jeff Davis(late winter).

Jeff Davis Peak--North Face Route

Location and Access To most people, all the peaks surrounding the Wheeler Peak Cirque Basin are generally known as Wheeler Peak. But there's a name for the eastern peak, and that's Jeff Davis. At one time, this whole mountain was called Jeff Davis Peak, but then the highest summit was later named Wheeler, after the USGS surveyor. Jeff Davis stayed on the east peak. This hike describes perhaps the easiest way to reach the summit of Jeff Davis. From Baker, drive west towards Lehman Caves and Great Basin National Park headquarters, but about one km before the caves, turn right onto the Wheeler Peak Scenic Drive. This 20 km long paved highway ends at the Wheeler Peak Campground and the trailhead.

Trail or Route Conditions From the trailhead, which is at the beginning part of the campground, walk south on the trail signposted for Wheeler Peak Cirque and the Bristlecone Pine Forest. This is the most used trail in the park. In less than two kms, you come to a junction: to the right 100 meters is Teresa Lake; but turn left for a km and a half, and you'll be in the middle of the Bristlecone Pine Forest. In this general area, leave the trail and walk cross-country to the east across the lower end of the Wheeler Rock Glacier. To the east a ways is the east side lateral moraine. Climb this where it's easiest. On top of the moraine, look around for the stump and remains of tree WPN-114. This is the 4900 year old bristlecone pine cut down in 1964 for further study. It's still there along the top of the moraine, lying on it's side, at about 3275 meters altitude. From this area, head straight up slope to the south. The north face is moderately steep, but it's easy scrambling, and there are no difficult pitches. By using this route, you could ascend or descend from a loop climb of both Wheeler and Jeff Davis Peaks.

Elevations Trailhead, 3033 meters; bristlecone forest, 3200; Jeff Davis Peak, 3894 meters.

Best Time and Time Needed From mid or late June until about the middle of October would be the most pleasant time period for climbing, but in some years you could climb it earlier or later. Strong hikers could do this climb in 5 to 7 hours round-trip; slower hikers longer. The author reached the summit in 2 hrs. 15 min., then came down the 1st Couloir and explored the upper cirque basin before returning to his car. Less than 6 hrs. round-trip.

Water At the campground, at two small streams you'll cross in the first km of the trail, and at Brown Lake.

Camping Since this region is the second most popular destination point in the park, the park service requires camping in the Wheeler Peak Campground only. Backcountry camping is forbidden in this immediate area.

Geology From the trailhead to the top of the lateral moraine where tree WPN-114 once stood, you'll be on *Pleistocene glacier deposits*. Above that point the entire mountain is made up of *Prospect Mountain Quartzite*.

Maps USGS or BLM maps Ely and Garrison(1:100,000), or Sacramento Pass and Wheeler Peak(1:62,500), or one of the geology maps MF-1343 A, B, or C(1:62,500), or Humboldt National Forest(1:125,000).

Jeff Davis, as seen from near the end of the Wheeler Peak Scenic Drive.

MAP 9, JEFF DAVIS PEAK--NORTH FACE

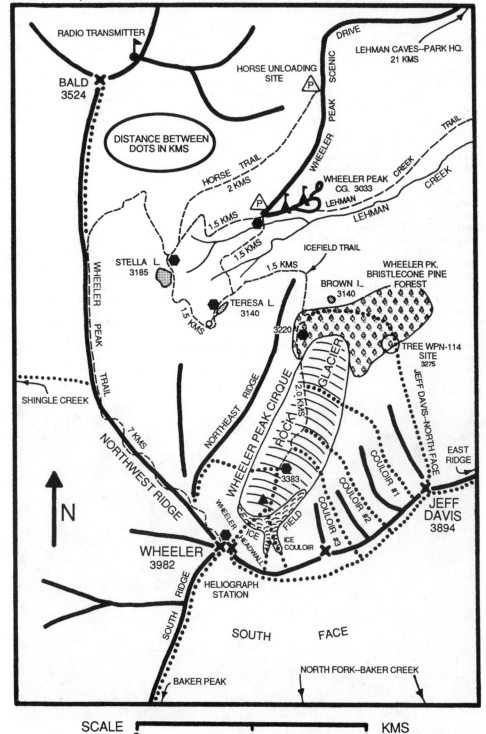

RADIO TRANSMITTER

LEHMAN CAVES--PARK HQ.
21 KMS

HORSE UNLOADING
SITE

BALD
3524

DISTANCE BETWEEN
DOTS IN KMS

WHEELER PEAK SCENIC DRIVE

TRAIL

HORSE TRAIL
2 KMS

WHEELER PEAK
CG. 3033

LEHMAN CREEK

1.5 KMS

LEHMAN CREEK

1.5 KMS

ICEFIELD TRAIL

WHEELER PK.
BRISTLECONE PINE
FOREST

STELLA L.
3185

1.5 KMS

BROWN L.
3140

WHEELER PEAK TRAIL

1.5 KMS

TERESA L.
3140

3220

TREE WPN-114
SITE
3275

SHINGLE CREEK

7 KMS

NORTHWEST RIDGE

NORTHEAST RIDGE

WHEELER PEAK CIRQUE

ROCK GLACIER

2.0 KMS

JEFF DAVIS--NORTH FACE

EAST
RIDGE

3383

COULOIR #1

COULOIR #2

COULOIR #3

JEFF
DAVIS
3894

N

WHEELER
3982

WHEELER
ICE
HEADWALL

ICE
COULOIR

FIELD

SOUTH RIDGE

HELIOGRAPH
STATION

SOUTH   FACE

BAKER PEAK

NORTH FORK--BAKER CREEK

SCALE
0   1   2   KMS

55

Jeff Davis Peak–Glacier Routes

Location and Access As you look at Wheeler Peak Massif from the north, the summit to the west is Wheeler, while the one on the east is Jeff Davis Peak. The distance between the two is far enough to make them two separate summits. This section describes several interesting routes to the summit of Jeff Davis, via the rock glacier inside the Wheeler Peak Cirque Basin. To get there, drive west out of Baker towards Lehman Caves and Great Basin National Park. About one km before the caves, turn right onto the Wheeler Peak Scenic Drive. This 20 km paved road ends at the trailhead and the Wheeler Peak Campground.

Trail or Route Conditions From the car-park, walk south on the Icefield Trail. This well used trail runs up to and through the Bristlecone Pine Forest at the bottom end of the Wheeler Rock Glacier. After the first km and a half, turn left at the junction. Continue on for 2 or 3 kms, and until you're in about the middle of the rock glacier. From that point, you can see several big gullies or couloirs coming down from near the summit of Jeff Davis. At first, these may seem very steep, and a little difficult for the average hiker, but if you're there at the right time of year, and when conditions are right, they are as easy to climb as is the North Face Route. The author has labeled them Couloir #1, #2 and #3. They are all about the same in difficulty. In late summer-early fall, you'll find all three couloirs free of snow, and very easy to climb. In late spring-early summer, they will be snow-filled from top to bottom. When they are mostly snow-filled, you'll need an ice ax and a pair of crampons, to make a safe climb. It's just steep enough to make the climb interesting.

Elevations Trailhead, 3033 meters; middle of rock glacier, 3325; summit of Jeff Davis, 3894.

Best Time and Time Needed For snow climbing, May, June and July might be the best time. September and the first part of October will be best if you prefer snow-free climbing. Winter climbing could be risky with avalanche danger. From the trailhead to the summit, should take fast hikers maybe 3 hours; when conditions are ideal. For slower people, maybe 4 or 5 hours just for the ascent. The author went from the trailhead to the summit of Jeff Davis via the North Face, in 2 hrs. 15 min., then returned via Couloir #1. On another trip, he went to the summit via Couloir #2.

Water At the Wheeler Peak Campground; at two small streams you'll pass in the first km of the trail; at Brown Lake; and sometimes in the moat of the rock glacier.

Camping Officially, camping is confined to the Wheeler Peak Campground. The reason being, this is very popular area in summer.

Geology From the trailhead all the way to the rock glacier, you're walking over *Pleistocene glacier deposits*. But above the rock glacier, all the rock you see is the *Prospect Mountain Quartzite*.

Maps USGS or BLM maps Ely and Garrison(1:100,000), or Sacramento Pass and Wheeler Peak(1:62,500), or one of the geology maps MF-1343 A, B, or C(1:62,500), or Humboldt National Forest(1:125,000).

In the upper part of the Second Couloir of Jeff Davis Peak.

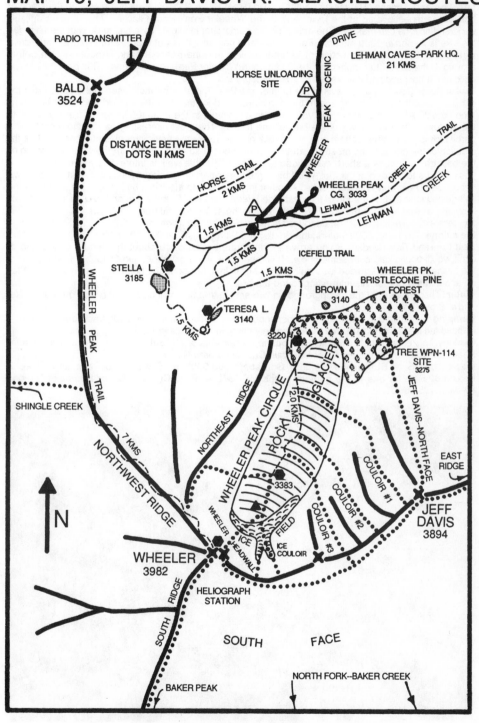

RADIO TRANSMITTER

LEHMAN CAVES--PARK HQ.
21 KMS

HORSE UNLOADING
SITE

WHEELER PEAK SCENIC DRIVE

BALD
3524

TRAIL

DISTANCE BETWEEN
DOTS IN KMS

HORSE TRAIL
2 KMS

WHEELER PEAK CG. 3033

LEHMAN CREEK

CREEK

1.5 KMS

LEHMAN

1.5 KMS

ICEFIELD TRAIL

WHEELER PK.
BRISTLECONE PINE
FOREST

STELLA L.
3185

1.5 KMS

BROWN L.
3140

WHEELER PEAK TRAIL

TERESA L.
3140

1.5 KMS

3220

TREE WPN-114
SITE
3275

SHINGLE CREEK

WHEELER PEAK CIRQUE

ROCK GLACIER

2.0 KMS

JEFF DAVIS--NORTH FACE

NORTHEAST RIDGE

EAST
RIDGE

7 KMS

3383

COULOIR #1

N

NORTHWEST RIDGE

WHEELER
HEADWALL

ICE FIELD

COULOIR #2

COULOIR #3

JEFF
DAVIS
3894

WHEELER
3982

ICE
COULOIR

HELIOGRAPH
STATION

SOUTH RIDGE

SOUTH   FACE

NORTH FORK--BAKER CREEK

BAKER PEAK

SCALE   0   1   2   KMS

The Bristlecone Pine Trail

Location and Access The most popular hike in Great Basin National Park is the walk to the stand of bristlecone pines located at the lower end of the Wheeler Peak Rock Glacier. This is not a difficult walk, and anyone can make it. The only problem some people might have, has to do with the altitude-- the hike is all above 3000 meters. For the average person this is not a problem. To get there, drive west out of Baker in the direction of Lehman Caves and the national park. About one km before arriving at the caves, turn right onto the 20 km long Wheeler Peak Scenic Drive. This paved highway ends at the trailhead and the Wheeler Peak Campground.

Trail or Route Conditions The trail to the Bristlecone Pine Forest is the most used in the park. From the car-park, take the trail running south, the one signposted for the Wheeler Icefield and the Bristlecone Pine Forest. After a km and a half, you come to a junction; to the right 100 meters is Teresa Lake; to the left less than 2 kms away is the bristlecone forest. The most interesting part of the forest is that part which is right on the bottom end of the rock glacier. Here the environment is most harsh, thus the creation of the gnarled and mostly dead trees you've heard so much about. In the area with some of the best trees, there is a short, self-guided loop trail. This little walk is interesting and informative. If you continue to the end of the trail, you'll be in the upper part of the cirque basin with some fine views of both Jeff Davis and Wheeler Peaks. Another interesting side trip might be to walk due east from the self-guided loop trail, to the top of the east-side lateral moraine. Somewhere on top of this Pleistocene moraine, is what remains of tree WPN-114. This is the 4900 year old tree which was cut down in 1964 for more extensive studies. The dead tree is lying there beside its stump.

Elevations Trailhead, 3033 meters; the Bristlecone Pine Forest, 3200-3300 meters.

Best Time and Time Needed If you arrive in the cirque basin before about the middle or late part of June, you'll be walking over some snow. It is then snow free until about mid-October. Distance from the trailhead to the self-guided loop trail is only 3 or 4 kms, or about one hours walk, maybe less. Plan on about half a day for this interesting round-trip hike.

Water There's water at the campground, in two small streams you'll cross in the first km of the hike, and at Brown Lake.

Camping Because this is the second most popular destination point in the park, backcountry camping is forbidden in the immediate area. One can only camp in the Wheeler Peak Campground.

Geology This entire hike is over old *Pleistocene glacier deposits*. But all of Jeff Davis and Wheeler Peaks are made up of the *Prospect Mountain Quartzite Formation*.

Maps USGS or BLM maps Ely and Garrison(1:100,000), or Sacramento Pass and Wheeler Peak(1:62,500), or one of the geology maps MF-1343 A, B, or C(1:62,500), or Humboldt National Forest(1:125,000).

Bristlecone pines at the bottom end of the Wheeler Peak Rock Glacier.

MAP 11, THE BRISTLECONE PINE TRAIL

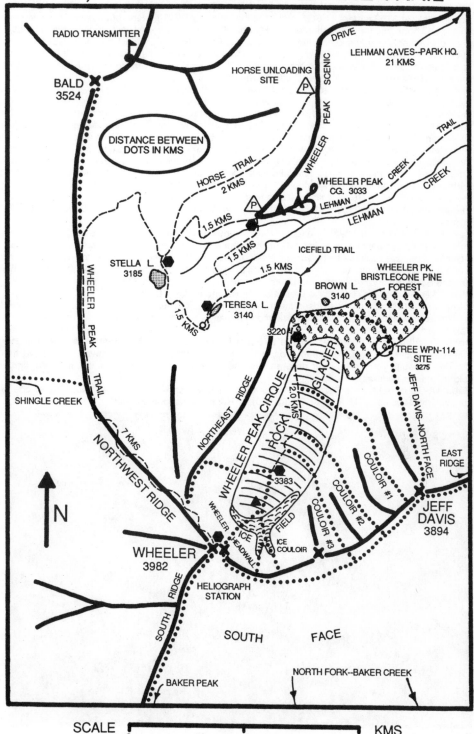

RADIO TRANSMITTER

LEHMAN CAVES--PARK HQ.
21 KMS

HORSE UNLOADING
SITE

BALD
3524

P

WHEELER PEAK SCENIC DRIVE

DISTANCE BETWEEN
DOTS IN KMS

HORSE TRAIL
2 KMS

TRAIL

WHEELER PEAK CREEK

CREEK

P

1.5 KMS

WHEELER PEAK
CG. 3033

LEHMAN

LEHMAN

ICEFIELD TRAIL

WHEELER PEAK
TRAIL

1.5 KMS

1.5 KMS

STELLA L.
3185

BROWN L.
3140

WHEELER PK.
BRISTLECONE PINE
FOREST

1.5 KMS

TERESA L.
3140

3220

TREE WPN-114
SITE
3275

SHINGLE CREEK

NORTHEAST RIDGE

WHEELER PEAK CIRQUE

ROCK GLACIER

2.0 KMS

JEFF DAVIS--NORTH FACE

7 KMS

NORTHWEST RIDGE

3383

COULOIR #1

COULOIR #2

EAST
RIDGE

N

WHEELER
3982

WHEELER HEADWALL

ICE FIELD

COULOIR #3

JEFF
DAVIS
3894

SOUTH RIDGE

ICE
COULOIR

HELIOGRAPH
STATION

SOUTH   FACE

BAKER PEAK

NORTH FORK--BAKER CREEK

SCALE

0   1   2   KMS

59

Baker Peak--Normal Route

Location and Access After Wheeler and Jeff Davis Peaks, the next highest summit in the park is Baker Peak, at 3752 meters. USGS maps list the height at 3748 meters, but this is for the western summit. On one trip, the author hurried quickly from the west peak to the east, and found it to be about 4 meters higher, according to his altimeter. To get to Baker Peak via the normal route, first drive west out of Baker towards Lehman Caves and the national park headquarters. After about 9 kms, turn left or south towards the Baker Ck. Campground. After 7 or 8 kms, you'll come to the end of this very good gravel road where is found the Baker Creek Trailhead.

Trail or Route Conditions From the car-park, take the trail running west up along Baker Creek. The sign states; Baker Lake, 5 miles(8 kms). At the beginning, the trail is a little hard to follow, because of the many cow paths in the area. Further on, the trial is easy to follow, as it's one of the most used in the park. After about 6 kms you'll come to an old cabin, which was built by early-day prospector Peter Dieshman. It's in reasonable good condition, and could be used as a shelter in an emergency. Nearby is an excellent spring and source of water. The new trail then heads out in a northwest direction(don't try to follow the trail indicated on the old USGS maps), before doing some zig zagging up the slope to Baker Lake. From the east end of the lake, head directly up the slope in a north, northwest direction. Further up, angle off to the left and towards the south ridge of Baker. This ridge takes you directly to the west summit. If you're so inclined, it's an easy 10 minute walk to the east peak.

Elevations Trailhead, 2438 meters; Dieshman Cabin, 3063; Baker Lake, 3237; Baker Peak, 3752 meters.

Best Time and Time Needed By about mid-June, you can do this hike without too much snow or wet trails, but in some years you may find lots of snow there in June. Snow begins to return by about mid-October. From the trailhead to the summit is about 9 kms. Strong hikers can be at the summit in about 3 or 3.5 hours; others maybe 4 hrs. For most it'll take all day for the round-trip climb. The author once climbed Baker, then Wheeler and Jeff Davis, returning to the car-park in 7 hrs. 10 min.

Water All along Baker Creek; at the Dieshman Cabin; and at Baker Lake.

Camping GBNP rangers have closed the trailhead for camping, but you can camp in the campground one km downstream; or you can backpack and camp anywhere along Baker Creek. The best place is Baker Lake.

Geology All the way from the trailhead to Baker Lake, you'll be walking over *Pleistocene glacier deposits*. Above the lake, you'll find *Prospect Mountain Quartzite* rocks. However, just above the Dieshman Cabin, you'll pass over an area scoured clean of debris, exposing a small area of lighter colored *granite* bedrock.

Maps USGS or BLM maps Garrison(1:100,000), or Garrison and Wheeler Peak(1:62,500), or one of the geology maps MF-1343 A, B, or C(1:62,500), or Humboldt National Forest(1:125,000).

From summit of Pyramid Peak, one sees Baker Lake, and Baker Peak, right.

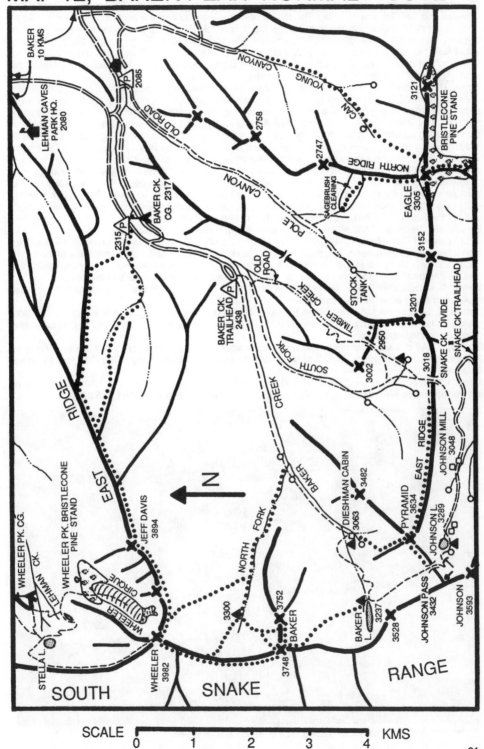

SCALE | 0 1 2 3 4 | KMS

Baker Peak--North Face Route

Location and Access The third highest summit in the Snake Range and GBNP is Baker Peak Only Wheeler and Jeff Davis are higher. The routes described here are on the North Face of Baker. Some of the most difficult climbs in the park can be found here. All routes up this broad east-west face are climbing routes with some difficulty, but some are easier than others. To get to this climb, drive west out of Baker toward the park headquarters at Lehman Caves. About one km before the caves, turn left or south, and head in the direction of Baker Creek Campground and the trailhead at the end of the road. This last 7 or 8 kms is on a good gravel road.

Trail or Route Conditions From the trailhead, walk west on the trail signposted for Baker Lake. At first there are several confusing cow trails, but after a short distance, it's one very good and well used path. After 3 or 4 kms, you'll see a small stream coming down from the basin to your right. This is the North Fork of Baker Creek. It normally has flowing water just in this lower part. At that point, walk cross-country up along the stream. The way is mostly easy, but you'll have to zig zag a bit at first, to avoid downed trees. Once inside the upper cirque basin, walking is very easy through scattered stands of fir, spruce and aspen trees. From the middle of the basin, you'll see a steep snow and ice couloir coming down from about the center of the North Face; and another to the west, which comes down from near the western peak. These couloirs appear to be of about equal difficulty. You'll need at least an ice ax and crampons. In late spring or early summer, they will be snow filled; in late summer and in the fall, the snow turns to ice, which makes things more difficult and dangerous. Climbing other parts of the North Face looks very difficult on this broken and brecciated wall.

Elevations Trailhead, 2438 meters; cirque basin, 3300; Baker Peak, 3752 meters.

Best Time and Time Needed. Climb in May or June, and you'll have snow climbing in the couloirs mentioned. By September or October, you'll be ice climbing. It's 7 or 8 kms to the base of the North Face, and can be hiked in 2-3 hours easily. Depending on ones experience and route taken, the couloirs can be climbed in a hour or two, or half a day, depending on conditions at the time.

Water All along Baker Creek, and in the lower end of the North Fork. In late spring-early summer, you should find some water in the upper basin.

Camping Camping is forbidden at the trailhead, but Baker Creek Campground is not far away. You could also camp down stream a ways just outside the park boundary near Pole Canyon. One can camp anywhere in the upper basin.

Geology All the way from the trailhead to the base of the North Face, you'll be walking over *Pleistocene glacier deposits,* but all of Baker and Wheeler Peaks are made of the *Prospect Mountain Quartzite.*

Maps USGS or BLM maps Garrison(1:100,000), or Garrison and Wheeler Peak(1:62,500), or one of the geology maps MF-1343 A, B, or C(1:62,500), or Humboldt National Forest(1:125,000).

From the top of Wheeler, looking down on the North Face of Baker.

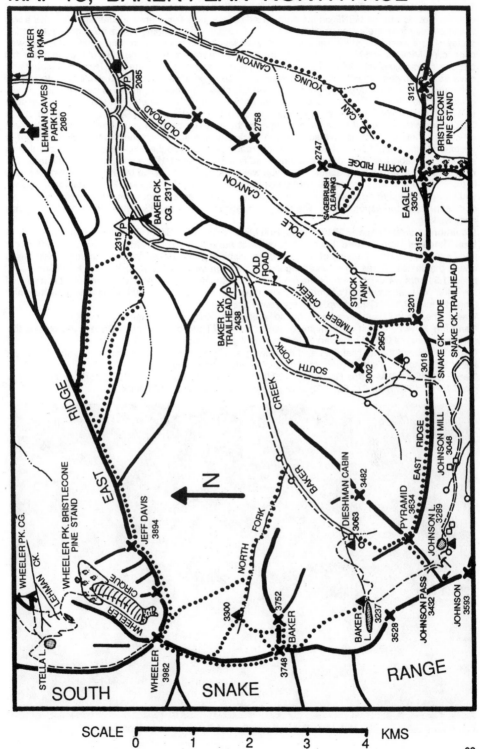

SCALE

0   1   2   3   4   KMS

Baker Peak--West Face Route

Location and Access For those who would like to climb Baker Peak, but do not want to get involved with the crowds and the GBNP on the eastern side of the mountain, here's a different route. It's a way to climb Baker from the never-used West Face. To reach the beginning of this hike, drive into Spring Valley on the west side of the range. Make your way to the north-south running Minerva Highway, connecting Minerva and Major's Place. There are several ways to reach the base of the mountain, but this one seems simplest. Just south of mile post 9, and directly east of the Kerr Ranch, turn east and drive as far you can. In only 300-400 meters you'll come to a washout, where you'll have to stop. If you have a HCV or 4WD, you might get around this place. Further up, the road isn't so bad. Or you could head for Shingle Creek, and drive south on the road along side the West Ditch. You'll need a HCV to use the West Ditch route. Hikers with cars will end up at the Lower Car-park(1817 meters).

Trail or Route Conditions If you're beginning near the Kerr Ranch, then you'll be walking an old road, which in the upper parts, is divided into twin tracks. When you reach the West Ditch, turn right or south, and after a km, turn east again. This old road takes you into the Hub Mine Basin, where there's a couple of usable cabins and many old mine adits and prospects. From the cabins, continue on the road to the east, until it turns south. Then you walk straight up one of the two not-so-prominent ridges in front of you and which come straight down from the west peak of Baker. By careful route-finding, you can get up either ridge without bushwhacking. Further up the mountain, brush gives way to an open spruce, fir and aspen forest. The last part is above timberline. It's a little steep, but all relatively easy walking.

Elevations Lower Car-park, 1817 meters; Hub Mine Basin, 2365; Baker Peak, 3752 meters.

Best Time and Time Needed Each year is different, but usually from late May or early June, until about late October. If you're thinking of doing a winter climb of either Baker, Wheeler or Jeff Davis, this is one of the easiest routes. It's something like 7 kms from the Lower Car-park to the Hub Mine Basin; about 1.5 hours walking. Then it's maybe 3 hrs. more to the summit. Any way you look at it, it's an all day hike. You can save a lot of time if you can drive into the basin. The author made it to the summit in 3 hrs. 22 min.; 7 hours round-trip, from the Lower Car-park.

Water At a spring in Hub Mine Basin, but no where else locally. Have some in your car.

Camping Anywhere east of the highway, which is all BLM public land. Both trailheads are outside the park boundary(the GBNP boundary is half way up the mountain).

Geology Above the alluvial flats and the mining area, you'll see outcroppings of *granite*, but above about 2950 meters, it's the *Prospect Mountain Quartzite Formation.*

Maps USGS or BLM maps Garrison(1:100,000), or Wheeler Peak(1:62,500), or one of the geology maps MF-1343 A, B, or C(1:62,500), or Humboldt National Forest(1:125,000).

Old miners cabins, in the Hub Mine Basin. West face of Baker in the background.

MAP 14, BAKER PEAK--WEST FACE ROUTE

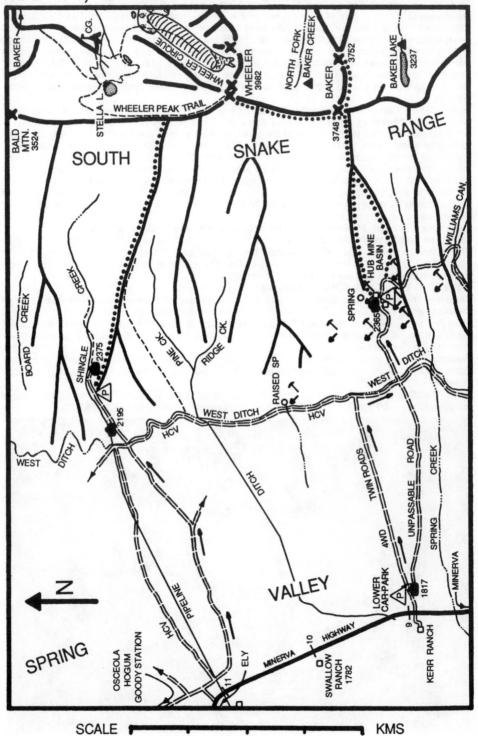

SCALE

KMS

0   1   2   3   4

Baker Lake Hike--Baker Creek Route

Location and Access The southern Snake Range has a number of high mountain cirque basins which are of interest to hikers. One of the most beautiful and more isolated of these is the basin which holds Baker Lake. Baker Lake is located at the head of Baker Creek, about one km due south of Baker Peak, and one km northwest of Pyramid Peak. There are several ways to reach this lake, including a route in from Snake Creek and Johnson Lake, but the normal route is up along Baker Creek. To get there, take the highway west out of Baker toward Lehman Caves and the national park. Drive about 9 kms, then turn south in the direction of Baker Creek Campground. After about 7 or 8 kms along a heavily used and very good graveled road, you'll arrive at Baker Creek Trailhead, which is at the end of the road.

Trail or Route Conditions. From the car-park, locate and follow the trail heading west along Baker Creek. In the beginning, there are several cow trails, but after a ways, the trail is easy to follow. It heads up canyon along the north side of the creek, passing several springs about half way up to the lake. After about 6 kms, you'll come to the Peter Dieshman Cabin, sitting next to upper Baker Creek. From there, the trail heads in a northwest direction, before doing some zig zagging up the slope before arriving at the lake. This last part of the route(2 kms) is not located where the USGS maps shows it to be. They have built a new trail since those old maps were printed. Just a few meters before the lake, you come to a sign pointing out the trail running south to Johnson Lake. In Baker Lake, you'll find trout, although it's not a deep body of water. To the south and west are vertical walls, making one of the best scenes in the park.

Elevations Trailhead, 2438 meters; Dieshman Cabin, 3063; Baker Lake, 3237 meters.

Best Time and Time Needed Winter snows will cover much of the ground around the lake until mid-June, but each year is different. Snow again begins to fall around mid-October. It's 8 kms from the trailhead to the lake; or about 2 hours walking for fast hikers, longer for others. It will also take longer if you're carrying a large pack and planning to camp.

Water Along Baker Creek all the way to the lake.

Camping The best place to camp is at Baker Lake, but one can also camp at the Dieshman Cabin, or anywhere along Baker Creek. The NPS has closed the trailhead to camping, but you can drive one km down the road and camp in the Baker Creek Campground. Or drive further east and camp just outside the GBNP boundary near the mouth of Pole Canyon along lower Baker Creek(but if camping there, don't use the creek water).

Geology From the trailhead to the lake are *Pleistocene glacier deposits,* but just above the Dieshman Cabin you'll pass some exposed *granite* bedrock. Above the lake, all the rocks are *Prospect Mountain Quartzite.*

Maps USGS or BLM maps Garrison(1:100,000), or Garrison and Wheeler Peak(1:62,500), or one of the geology maps MF-1343 A, B, or C(1:62,500), or Humboldt National Forest(1:125,000).

Baker Lake, one of the finest scenes in the GBNP.

MAP 15, BAKER LAKE HIKE--BAKER CK.

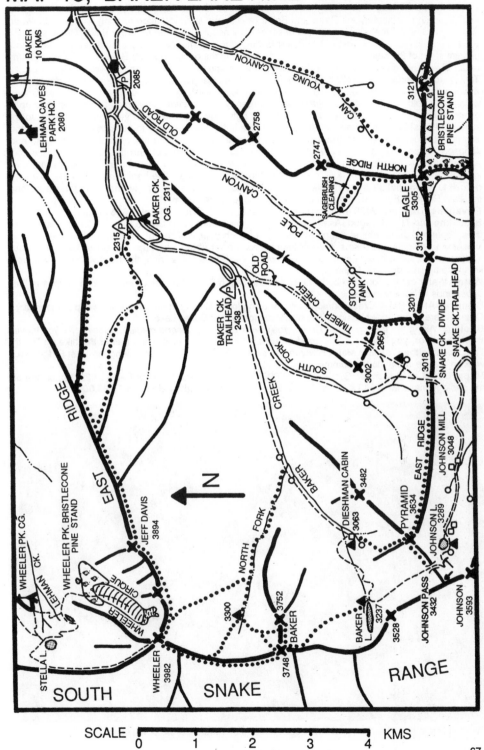

BAKER 10 KMS

LEHMAN CAVES PARK HQ. 2080

P 2085

OLD ROAD

BAKER CK. 2317

P 2315

BAKER CK. CG. 2317

BAKER CK. TRAILHEAD 2438 P

OLD ROAD

CANYON

POLE

YOUNG CANYON

NORTH RIDGE

2758

2747

SAGEBRUSH CLEARING

EAGLE 3305

BRISTLECONE PINE STAND

3121

3152

3201

STOCK TANK

TIMBER CREEK

SOUTH FORK

2950

3002

3018

SNAKE CK. DIVIDE

SNAKE CK. TRAILHEAD

EAST RIDGE

JOHNSON MILL 3048

DIESHMAN CABIN 3482

3063

PYRAMID 3634

JOHNSON L. 3289

RIDGE

EAST

JEFF DAVIS 3894

BAKER CREEK

NORTH FORK

N

WHEELER CIRQUE

WHEELER PK. BRISTLECONE PINE STAND

WHEELER PK. CG.

LEHMAN CK.

STELLA L.

WHEELER 3982

3300

3752

BAKER

3748

BAKER L. 3237

JOHNSON PASS 3432

3528

JOHNSON 3593

SOUTH   SNAKE   RANGE

SCALE 0 1 2 3 4 KMS

Pyramid Peak--Baker Creek Trail

Location and Access The 4th highest peak in the South Snake Range is Pyramid Peak. This one is located south of Wheeler, Jeff Davis and Baker Peaks, and is on the ridge running east-west between Baker and Snake Creeks. This section describes the access route up from the Baker Creek side. To get to the trailhead, drive west out of Baker towards the park headquarters at Lehman Caves. About one km short of the caves, turn left or south, and drive in the direction of the Baker Creek Campground on an all-weather gravel road. After 7 or 8 kms, you'll come to the end of the road and the trailhead.

Trail or Route Conditions Probably the easiest and least complicated way to the top of Pyramid, is to walk up the trail toward Baker Lake. After about 6 kms, you'll reach the old Peter Dieshman Cabin, which still could be used for a shelter in an emergency. From there, one could head south and up a minor canyon, but shortly thereafter, veer to the right or west, and climb the northwest ridge to the summit. It's steep, but a walk-up all the way. This is the shortest way to the summit. However, the normal route up, is to walk all the way to Baker Lake, then south in the direction of Johnson Lake and Johnson Pass. From the pass, walk up a gentle slope to northeast and the summit. This is the easiest route on the mountain. A third possibility; from the trailhead, take the trail running south and into South Fork of Baker Creek. It's signposted to Johnson Lake. The beginning of this trail is a little difficult to follow, but it's there. Walk up South Fork to the Snake Ck. Divide, thence to the west along the East Ridge of Pyramid. Stay on the forested ridge to the summit.

Elevations Trailhead, 2438 meters; Dieshman Cabin, 3063; Pyramid Peak, 3634 meters.

Best Time and Time Needed As with most other high summits in the Snake Range, you can climb here from about mid-June until about mid-October, but each year is different. The shortest route, via the Dieshman Cabin, is 7 or 8 kms, and will take a strong hiker about 3 hrs. up. Via Baker Lake, it's about 11 kms to the summit, or 3 to 4 hours, one-way. Via Snake Ck. Divide, the distance is about 7 or 8 kms, and again 3 or 4 hrs. to the top.

Water Water can be found in both Baker and the South Fork of Baker Creeks, and in springs in the upper ends of both canyons.

Camping At the Baker Creek Campground, or along lower Baker Creek just outside the park boundary. Or anywhere in the upper basins. The nicest campsite is at Baker Lake.

Geology Along the trail up Baker Creek, you'll walk atop *Pleistocene glacier deposits*. As you leave the valley floor, you'll see the *Prospect Mountain Quartzite*. For the first half of the hike up South Fork, you see the *Prospect Mtn. Quartzite*, but then in the upper basin and along the East Ridge, you walk on *granite* nearly to the summit.

Maps USGS or BLM maps Garrison(1:100,000), or Garrison and Wheeler Peak(1:62,500), or one of the geology maps MF-1343 A, B, or C(1:62,500), or Humboldt National Forest(1:125,000).

Pyramid Peak, from the east, and from near the head of Timber Creek. A fall scene.

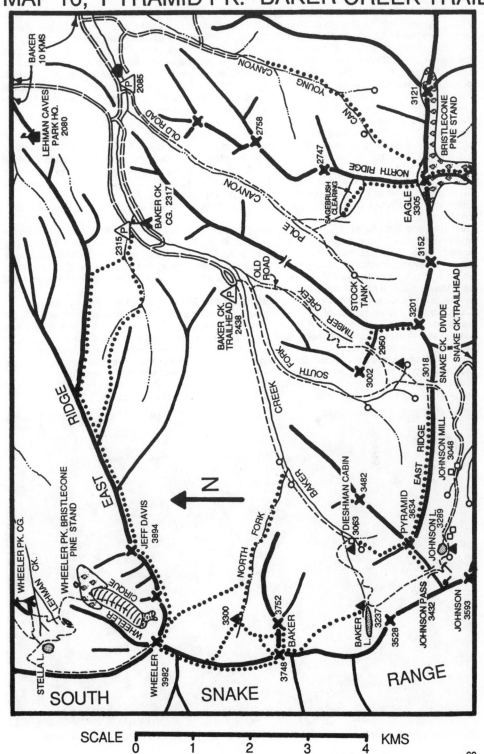

SCALE
0   1   2   3   4   KMS

Pyramid Peak--Snake Creek Trail

Location and Access One of the funnest climbs in the range is the walk to the summit of Pyramid Peak. Pyramid is located south of Wheeler, Jeff Davis and Baker Peaks, and is the 4th highest peak in the range(5th in the Snake Range) at 3634 meters. There are basically two access routes to this mountain; one from Baker Ck., the other from Snake Creek. This section describes the route in from the Snake Ck. Trailhead. To get there, drive along the highway linking Baker, Nevada, and Garrison, Utah. At a point about 3 kms northwest of Garrison, and about 10 kms southeast of Baker(right at mile post 1), turn south on the main access road to Snake Ck. Follow the signs up this very good gravel road and soon you'll turn west and pass the fish hatchery on your left, or south. After another 16 or so kms, you'll be at the Snake Ck. Trailhead. All cars can make it to the trailhead.

Trail or Route Conditions From the trailhead you walk up the old wagon(now 4WD) road to the northwest. In 1987, some vehicles still could and were using this track, but may soon be closed to all vehicles. Stay on this one track until you pass the old Johnson Stamp Mill on your left. After another 1.5 kms, you'll see two well preserved cabins on your left. From there it's just a short walk to Johnson Lake. The trail heads to the west side of the lake, finally zig zagging up the steep slope past Johnson's Mine and cable-way to Johnson Pass at 3432 meters. From there you walk up the gentle slope to the northeast to the summit of Pyramid Peak. An easy walk all the way.

Elevations Trailhead, 2500 meters; Johnson Lake, 3289; Johnson Pass, 3432; and Pyramid Peak, 3634 meters.

Best Time and Time Needed The summer hiking season would be from about mid-June until around the middle of October. From the trailhead to Johnson Lake is about 7 kms. From the lake to the summit, another km or two. This means the average hiker could climb Pyramid in about 2.5 or 3 hours, one way. However, there are interesting things to see at Johnson Lake(see Map 20, Johnson Lake Hike), so plan on a full day for this hike. The author did this one, which included a climb to Pyramid and Johnson Peaks, in 6 hrs. 20 min., round-trip.

Water In Snake Creek and at several points along the way, including the lake and nearby spring.

Camping There are a number of fine campsites at or near the trailhead, and all along the road up to the trailhead. Also at Johnson L., but this is a popular place, and soon may have some restrictions applied as a result. If you camp there, take good care of the place, and carry out all garbage.

Geology From the trailhead up to Johnson L., the valley was once covered by Pleistocene glaciers, but the old road passes over outcroppings of *granite* bedrock all the way to the lake and to just above Johnson Pass. The upper part of Pyramid Peak is made of *Prospect Mountain Quartzite*.

Maps USGS or BLM maps Garrison(1:100,000), or Garrison and Wheeler Peak(1:62,500), or one of the geology maps MF-1343 A, B, or C(1:62,500), or Humboldt National Forest(1:125,000).

From the summit of Johnson Peak. Wheeler, Jeff Davis, Pyramid Peaks, and Johnson Lake.

MAP 17, PYRAMID PK.--SNAKE CK. TRAIL

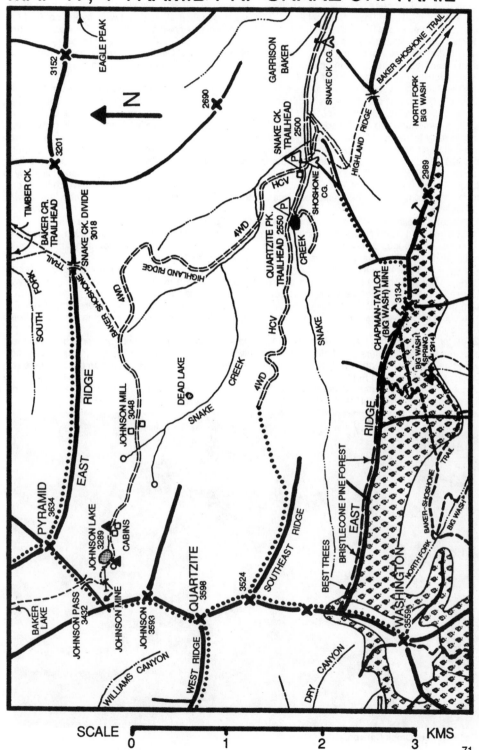

SCALE

0   1   2   3   KMS

Timber Creek--South Fork of Baker Creek Loop

Location and Access Here's a nice half-day hike for people who just want to walk in some of the canyons of the Great Basin National Park. This is a description of trails up two canyons not far from Lehman Caves or the Baker Creek Campground. The canyons are the South Fork of Baker Creek and Timber Creek. Both canyons are to the southwest of the Baker Creek Trailhead. To get there, drive west out of Baker towards park headquarters at Lehman Caves. One km before the caves, turn left or south, and head in the direction of Baker Ck. Campground on a good all-weather gravel road. After 7 or 8 kms, you'll arrive at the trailhead at the end of the road.

Trail or Route Conditions At the trailhead, look for the sign pointing out the way to Johnson Lake via South Fork of Baker Ck. Walk due south across the creek, then veer to the right or west. The first part of this track is a little indistinct--but it's there. It used to be an old wagon road of some kind. The trail stays between the two creek beds for a couple of kms, then heads up South Fork. In this canyon the trail is easy to see and follow. At the head of the canyon, you come to a large open meadow. There the trail veers to the left or east, then splits. One heads south to Snake Ck. Divide; the other curls to the east, where in half a km it intersects the trail coming up Timber Creek. Continuing on, you then cross a low divide and start down Timber Creek. In places the trail is indistinct, but is generally easy to follow. In the bottom end of Timber Canyon, you again encounter an old wagon road, which leads out to the trailhead. It might be easier to locate the trails if you did this hike going up Timber and down South Fork.

Elevations Trailhead, 2438 meters; the pass between Timber and South Fork, 2950 meters.

Best Time and Time Needed This loop-hike could be used from sometime late in May until early November. The loop distance is about 10 kms, and could be done in 2.5 or 3 hours, but many would rather do it at a slower pace and take about half a day, round-trip.

Water There's year-round water in both creeks, but there are cattle in the upper meadows of South Fork, so caution should be taken with the creek water. Take it from springs if you can, or carry it. Lower Timber Creek also has a flow in the bottom end(as well as cattle).

Camping Camp at the Baker Creek Campground a km below the trailhead, or anywhere along the trails. You could also drive down Baker Ck. and camp just outside the park boundary near the mouth of Pole Canyon.

Geology You'll find the *Prospect Mountain Quartzite* in the lower ends of both canyons, but from the pass marked 2950 meters, and half way down South Fork, you're on top of a *granite* intrusion. In the upper meadows of South Fork, you may observe some old glacier debris which came down the east face canyon of Pyramid Peak.

Maps USGS or BLM maps Garrison(1:100,000), or Garrison and Wheeler Peak(1:62,500), or one of the geology maps MF-1343 A, B, or C(1:62,500), or Humboldt National Forest(1:125,000).

Trail in Timber Creek Canyon.

MAP 18, TIMBER CREEK--SOUTH FK. LOOP

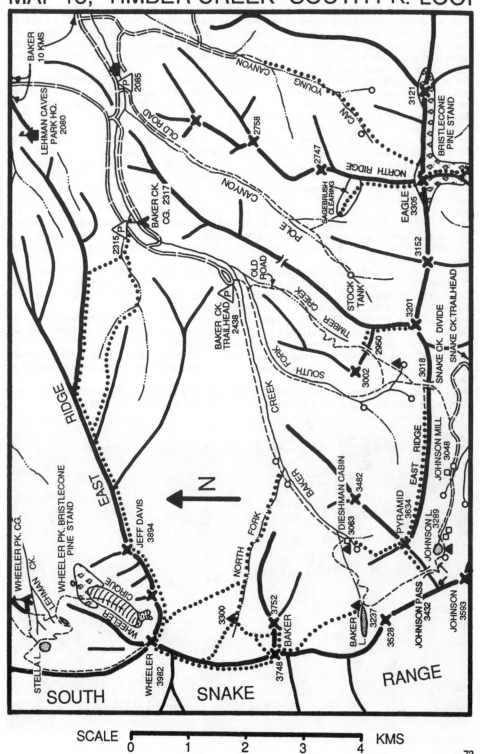

SCALE

0   1   2   3   4   KMS

Johnson Lake--Baker Creek Loop Hike

Location and Access The hike discussed here is one of the more popular in the Great Basin National Park. It involves making a loop-hike from the end of the road on Baker Creek, up one of the two forks of Baker Ck., and down to Johnson Lake. To get to the beginning of this hike, first drive west out of Baker in the direction of park headquarters at Lehman Caves. About one km before arriving at the caves, turn south onto a good gravel road signposted for Baker Ck. Campground. After 7 or 8 kms, you'll come to the end of the road which is the Baker Ck. Trailhead.

Trail or Route Conditions From the car-park, you have a choice of going up Baker Creek, or its South Fork(another alternate would be to go or return via Timber Ck.), then use the other trail on the return trip. For simplicity, let's start up Baker Ck. From the car-park, take the trail running to the west up Baker Ck. and in the direction of Baker Lake. After about 6 kms, you'll pass the old cabin built by Peter Dieshman. Two more kms and you arrive at Baker L., one of the prettiest places in the park. From near the lake head south towards Johnson Lake. The high point on the trial will be Johnson Pass, at 3432 meters. From there, you could easily climb Pyramid Pk., then head down to Johnson L. and the ruins of the tungsten mining operation there. Read more about this mine under Map 20. There are many good campsites around the lake, and one fine spring nearby. Just east of the lake, are two old cabins. From there you walk eastward on the remains of an old wagon road. After 1.5 kms, you'll pass other ruins, which include the Johnson Mill. After another km or so, and as you continue to descend an old road, watch carefully to the left to locate the sign and trail heading up to Snake Ck. Divide. From the divide, you can go down South Fork or Timber Ck. to the trailhead. This route is signposted at several places and is generally easy to follow.

Elevations Trailhead, 2438 meters; Baker Lake, 3237; Johnson Pass, 3432; Johnson L., 3289; Snake Ck. Divide, 3018 meters.

Best Time and Time Needed From about mid-June until late in October. Each year is different. From the Baker Ck. Trailhead, it's 10 kms to Johnson L. via Baker L.; or 8 kms via the South Fork of Baker Ck. Thus the round-trip hike is 18 kms. This can be done easily in one full day, or one could camp one night at Johnson or Baker Lake, and do the trip in two days.

Water Baker Ck. and South Fork; at Baker and Johnson Lakes; and near the Johnson Mill.

Camping Best at Baker or Johnson Lakes, but Johnson L. is a popular place, so tread lightly and keep the place clean. Soon the GBNP will surely put camping restrictions on both lakes.

Geology All along Baker Ck. and to near Johnson P. are *Pleistocene glacier deposits.* Same around Johnson L. Over both passes, you'll see *granite* rock, but the upper part of Pyramid is *Prospect Mtn. Quartzite.*

Maps USGS or BLM maps Garrison(1:100,000), or Garrison and Wheeler Peak(1:62,500), or one of the geology maps MF-1343 A, B, or C(1:62,500), or Humboldt National Forest(1:125,000).

High meadow at the head of South Fork of Baker Creek.

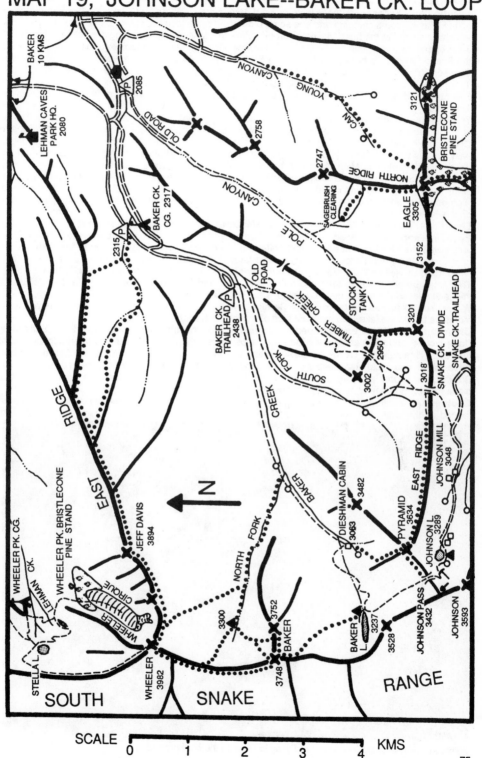

BAKER 10 KMS

LEHMAN CAVES PARK HQ. 2080

2085

YOUNG CANYON

BRISTLECONE PINE STAND

3121

OLD ROAD

2758

2747

NORTH RIDGE

EAGLE 3305

BAKER CK. CG. 2317

2315

POLE CANYON

SAGEBRUSH CLEARING

3152

OLD ROAD

STOCK TANK

3201

SNAKE CK. DIVIDE

SNAKE CK. TRAILHEAD

BAKER CK. TRAILHEAD 2438

TIMBER CREEK

2950

3002

3018

SOUTH FORK

CREEK

BAKER

RIDGE

EAST

EAST RIDGE

JOHNSON MILL 3048

N

JEFF DAVIS 3894

DIESHMAN CABIN 3482

PYRAMID 3634

JOHNSON L 3289

WHEELER PK. BRISTLECONE PINE STAND

3063

WHEELER PK. CG.

LEHMAN CK.

WHEELER CIRQUE

NORTH FORK

3300

3752

BAKER

BAKER L. 3237

JOHNSON PASS 3432

JOHNSON 3593

STELLA L.

WHEELER 3982

3748

3528

SOUTH

SNAKE

RANGE

SCALE

0   1   2   3   4   KMS

75

Johnson Lake Hike–Snake Creek Trail

Location and Access For those who may not be mountain climbers, but would rather just hike to an alpine lake, do some camping and see some old mining relics instead, this might be for you. It's a hike to Johnson Lake at the head of Snake Creek. Near this lake are several tungsten mining sites which were operating earlier this century, and which now offer an interesting look into the mining history of the Snake Range. To get there, drive along State Highway 487, the link between Baker, Nevada, and Garrison, Utah. About 10 kms southeast of Baker, and 3 kms northwest of Garrison(right at mile post 1), turn south on a good gravel road signposted for Snake Ck. It's about 5 kms to the Snake Ck. Fish Hatchery, and another 16 or so kms to the end of the good road, where is found the Snake Ck. Trailhead.

Trail or Route Conditions From the trailhead(which has the ruins of an old cabin at the corner) you walk in a northwest direction on an old former wagon road. This track is used today by some 4WD's and ORV's, but hopefully will be closed to vehicles soon, to make this a hiking trail only. The walking is easy on this track all the way to Johnson Lake. About 1.5 kms before arriving at the lake is the old Johnson Concentrating Mill. About 200 meters before the lake are a couple of cabins still in pretty good condition. One of these cabins could still be used in an emergency. The trail then heads around to the south, then west side of the lake, before zig zagging up the slope to Johnson Pass and beyond. High on the slope west of the lake is the Johnson Tungsten Mine, with a cable-way still in place. More on this later.

Elevations Trailhead, 2500 meters; Johnson Mill, 3048; Johnson Lake, 3289 meters.

Best Time and Time Needed The normal hiking season for this walk would be from about early June until about late October, but each year is different. Early in the season, you'll surely find snow banks and some wet ground around the lake, and later in the season you may have an early season snowstorm as well as frigid nights. From the Snake Ck. Trailhead to Johnson Lake, is about 7 kms. This could be done in less than two hours, one-way, and four hours round-trip. But there's lots of things to see, so it's best to plan to make it a full day hike.

Water You'll find good water in Snake Creek above the trailhead, and at several places as you walk along the trail to the lake. On the west side of the lake is a very good spring.

Camping There's an undeveloped campground near the trailhead, once called the Shoshone Campground, and there are many good little campsites along Snake Creek as you approach the end of the road. Hopefully the GBNP will allow visitors to continue to use these sites in the future, and not close them. You could also camp anywhere along the trail to the lake, and of course at Johnson Lake. But the lake shores are fragile, and it's a popular place, so tread lightly and take good care of this place. Surely one day camping restrictions will be imposed on the place.

Geology All of this upper basin was once covered with glaciers. The *Pleistocene glacier deposits* extend all the way from Johnson Lake to about the Snake Ck. Trailhead. However, the old road

Johnson Lake, with the lower part of Pyramid Peak in the background.

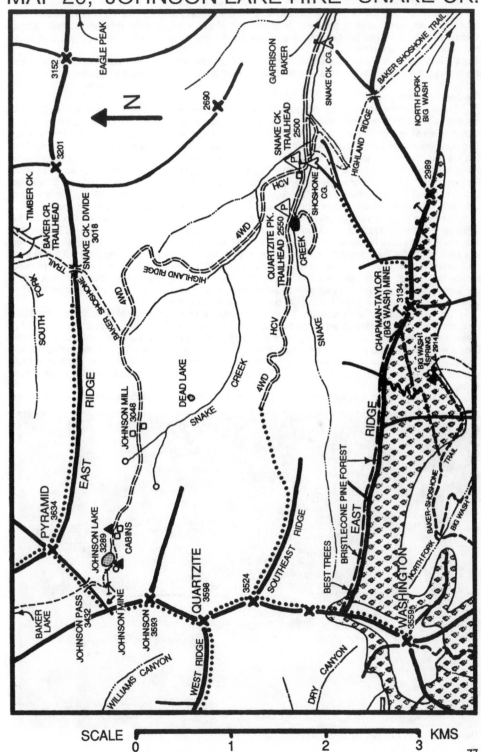

SCALE

0   1   2   3   KMS

roughly parallels the northern edge of the glacial till. Along the way to the lake you will see outcroppings of *granite,* which is below the *Prospect Mountain Quartzite.* From the lake looking north at Pyramid Peak, you see *granite* up to about half way, with the *Prospect Mtn. Formation* above that. Johnson Peak, southwest of the lake, is composed of this same *granitic intrusion,* called *Quartz Monzonite.* The Johnson Tungsten Mine is situated in the granite rocks, which are cut by quartz veins that contain tungsten minerals.

Maps USGS or BLM maps Garrison(1:100,000), or Garrison and Wheeler Peak(1:62,500), or one of the geology maps MF-1343 A, B, or C(1:62,500), or Humboldt National Forest(1:125,000).

The Johnson Mine

Throughout the years since the end of last century, there have been miners scouring these mountains looking for gold and silver or any other precious metals. Since early on, tungsten has been known to exist in the Snake Range, but there was no need for it until World War I. That's when tungsten became an important commodity. Tungsten is used to harden steel, so with the arrival of the first big war, the nation needed it badly in the weapons industry. According to Waite's dissertation on the Snake Range, there came to be six small tungsten stamp(concentrating) mills in these mountains. Four were on the northern or western slope; at Willow Patch Spring, Willard Creek, Williams Creek and at Minerva(there was another mill at Goody Mill or Station, which worked in the 1950's). On the east side, two mills were set up; one in Upper Snake Creek, the other in upper Lexington Creek.

The mining operation in Upper Snake Creek began with a man named Alfred Johnson. He built a cabin early in the 1900's(Wayne Gonder of Garrison believes it was built in 1907 or 1908?) near the lake which now bears his name. He apparently was the first to mine tungsten in this drainage. That was back in 1913. The tungsten ore was of very high quality, which may have offset the difficulties of the operation. Because the principal mine was at about 3400 meters, the altitude made the working season very short. Then there was the rugged and difficult terrain, which made transportation costly and time consuming. There was apparently another attempt to open a mine somewhere at the head of Baker Creek just over the pass, but the ore quality there wasn't so good.

This is how the operation worked. There was a cable-way or tramway set up at the mouth of the main mine which extended down to an outcropping just above the lake(this can still be seen today above and to the west of Johnson Lake). Ore was lowered down to the bottom terminal in large barrels. Then it was put on the backs of mules, and taken to the stamp or concentrating mill somewhere down the canyon a ways. Waite mentions it was located at 2200 meters originally, but later on, another mill was set up about 1.5 kms below the lake. There it was ground and crushed, and the excess rock removed.

After concentrating, the ore was taken by wagon to Frisco, Utah. Frisco is now an old ghost town

The old Johnson Mill, not far below Johnson Lake.

not far west of Milford in the southwestern part of Utah. From there it was shipped by rail to a smelter in Salt Lake City. After the First World War, the mine was shut down, but later on, in the late 1920's and early 1930's, efforts were made to revive the operation. After a devastating snowslide in the early 1930's, the mine was closed forever.

Much of this old operation can still be seen today. The mill located east of the lake, is still there, and still in relatively good condition. This mill, according to Wayne Gonder, was built in about 1928-30. He says it was used for a short period of time, then had to shut down forever after the snowslide wiped out the operation just above the lake. The mill is a rather large log structure, but about ready to fall. Nearby is another cabin, which looks as if it were a shelter for mules. If you look longer than did the author, you might find more at this lower site.

Another site just east of the lake features one old tumbled down cabin, and just beyond, two more log cabins. One has a corrigated metal roof, which still keeps out most of the rain. It's wet inside, indicating it leaks pretty bad, so don't count on sleeping there. This larger structure has two rooms, and appears to have been a mess cabin for workers. Beside it is a rubbish pile of rusty tin cans, bottles and other articles. This is an historic site, so please leave it as is. Near to this large cabin is another cabin in fairly good condition, but without a roof.

The miners attempted to enlarge the lake, by building a low dam across the southeast side, but it seems to have failed, as the dam leaks like a sieve. The dam is still clearly visible.

The next site is perhaps the most interesting. This is the lower cable-way terminal. It's on the west side and on a granite outcropping overlooking the lake. There you will find a large flathead Beaver motor, with a hand crank, and several other pieces of equipment. The author thought the motor may have been used to pump water up to the mine or was used to power the cable-way, but Wayne Gonder says it was brought in during the last stages of the operation, to run a concentrating mill there, very near the mouth of the mine.

All the equipment at the bottom of the cable-way was once inside a building or shelter of some kind. But in the early 1930's, a massive snowslide roared down the slope from the area around the mine, taking much of the operation with it. Some of the lumber, logs and other relics may still be seen in the bottom of the lake when the water is low, and along the western side of the lake.

Just above the motor and other machinery, the cable is still in place. Still attached to the cable, is part of the contraption which brought the ore down from the mine. Apparently the barrels were attached to this pulley system.

From the lower cable-way terminal, you walk up slope along the still very good trail to the old mine entrance, which is now covered with debris. Near the former tunnel entrance, is what remains of another log cabin. Above the main entrance, are several other tunnel openings. It appears you might be able to get into one, but there's loose rock everywhere, so beware.

Meadows, pines, old cabins, and Johnson Peak in the background.

One of the better cabins near Johnson Lake.

Johnson Lake, and some of the remains of the old mining operation.

An avalanche in the early 1930's, wiped out the building which housed this mining equipment(Johnson Tungsten Mine).

The cable-way, still in place at Johnson Lake.

Eagle Peak--Pole Canyon Route

Location and Access This hike is to the top of Eagle Peak, due south of Lehman Caves and the Baker Ck. Campground. The attractions are the fine view of Wheeler Peak, and a big bristlecone pine stand covering the top of the mountain. It can be climbed from the south ridge, but this section describes the route from the north and Pole Canyon. To get to the trailhead, drive west out of Baker towards the park headquarters at Lehman Caves. About a km before the caves, turn south onto a good gravel road signposted for Baker Ck. Campground. Go about 3 kms, then turn east and follow the road along the north side of lower Baker Ck. In about one km, look for a little-used road crossing the creek to the south. This is the starting point.

Trail or Route Conditions From the car-park on Baker Ck., walk up this seldom used old road into Pole Canyon. The road gradually fades, but it makes a good trail. As you go up canyon, keep an eye ahead and to the left; that's Eagle Peak in front of you. Higher up, look again to the left and you'll see a big clearing(sagebrush covered) coming down from the North Ridge. Walk up this easy slope. At the ridge-top is a fence, which runs south part way up to the summit. Follow the fence up. When it ends, continue on the North Ridge to the summit. Most of the trees you'll see on the south face are bristlecones. So as not to back-track, head down into Can Young Canyon on one of several routes. From the springs shown on the map, and on down, you'll have to route-find along the easiest way, until you reach the trail and the end of the old road. From there back to your car, is an easy road-walk.

Elevations Trailhead, 2085 meters; Eagle Peak, 3305.

Best Time and Time Needed In most years, you could make this climb from the first part of June until late October. Count on about 3 or 3.5 hours to reach the summit, making it an all day hike. The author made it to the summit in 2 hrs. 8 min. The round-trip time for him was 6 hrs. 20 min., for the loop-hike suggested. He spent some time exploring in the bristlecones.

Water Lower Pole Canyon has water(if the cattle haven't muddied it up too much), and there's a spring and stock tank in upper Pole C. At the head of Can Young C., are several places where water flows for short distances. For camping at the trailhead, better fill your water bottles at Lehman Caves.

Camping At Baker Ck. Campground, or just to the east of the trailhead on BLM public land just outside the national park boundary.

Geology For the first couple of kms, you'll walk along beds of *Pole Canyon Limestone*. The next two kms show *Prospect Mtn. Quartzite.* Above the quartzite is *granite,* then again near the summit, narrow bands of *Prospect Mtn. Quartzite* and *Pioche Shale*. Right at the summit and covering all the south face, is *Pole C. Limestone* again. The bristlecones thrive on limestone soils.

Maps USGS or BLM maps Garrison(1:100,000), or Garrison(1:62,500), or one of the geology maps MF-1343 A, B, or C(1:62,500), or Humboldt National Forest(1:125,000).

The South Ridge of Eagle Peak has lots of bristlecone pines.

MAP 21, EAGLE PK.--POLE CANYON ROUTE

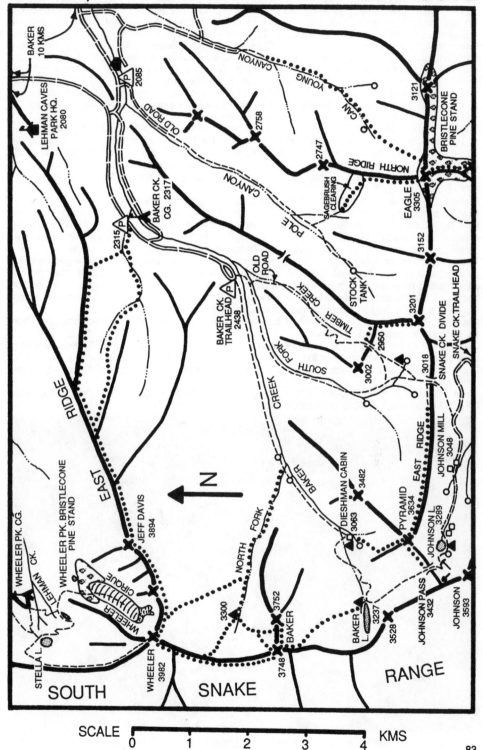

BAKER 10 KMS

LEHMAN CAVES PARK HQ. 2080

P 2085

OLD ROAD

BAKER CK. CG. 2317

2315 P

2758

YOUNG CANYON

YOUNG CAN.

3121

BRISTLECONE PINE STAND

NORTH RIDGE

2747

CANYON

SAGEBRUSH CLEARING

EAGLE 3305

POLE CANYON

3152

BAKER CK. TRAILHEAD P 2438

OLD ROAD

STOCK TANK

TIMBER CREEK

CREEK

3201

SNAKE CK. DIVIDE

SNAKE CK. TRAILHEAD

SOUTH FORK

2950

3002

3018

RIDGE

CREEK

JOHNSON MILL 3048

EAST

BAKER

DIESHMAN CABIN 3063

3482

EAST RIDGE

PYRAMID 3634

JOHNSON L. 3289

N

JEFF DAVIS 3894

WHEELER PK. CG.

WHEELER PK. BRISTLECONE PINE STAND

LEHMAN CK.

WHEELER CIRQUE

NORTH FORK

3300

3752

BAKER

BAKER L. 3237

JOHNSON PASS 3432

JOHNSON 3593

3528

STELLA L.

WHEELER 3982

BAKER

3748

RANGE

SOUTH

SNAKE

SCALE

0   1   2   3   4   KMS

83

Eagle Peak--South Ridge Route

Location and Access Eagle Peak at 3305 meters, is the highest summit on the big ridge running east from Pyramid Peak. This ridge is the one you see to the south of Lehman Caves and the Baker Ck. Campground. One reason for climbing this mountain is that it has one of the more fotogenic bristlecone pine stands in the Snake Range. To get there, drive along Nevada Highway 487, between Baker, Nevada, and Garrison, Utah. About 10 kms southeast of Baker, and about 3 kms northwest of Garrison(right at mile post 1), turn south onto a good gravel road signposted for Snake Creek. After about 5 kms, you'll see the fish hatchery on your left. From there, drive about 10 more kms to the old Bonita Mine. To the left, you can see an old dredge. From the dredge, continue on for about two more kms, until you're at the base of the South Ridge. From your vehicle, and as you approach the car-park, observe the prominent ridge coming down the mountain. It's prominent up towards the top, but branches out into several indistinct ridges near the bottom.

Trail or Route Conditions There is no trail on Eagle Peak, but the way up the South Ridge is easy with no bushwhacking. From the car-park, choose either of the two or maybe three little ridges you see above you. Get on top of one of these, as the ridge tops seem to have less brush than in the gully bottoms. Higher up and as the smaller ridges merge into one, walking is easier, as there are no trees or brush the along the way. When you reach the bristlecones, the route is then in an open forest right to top.

Elevations Trailhead, about 2275 meters; the summit of Eagle Peak, 3305 meters.

Best Time and Time Needed Because this is a south ridge approach, you could likely do this climb from around the first or middle of May, without finding snow on the route. The season with no snow, normally lasts until late October. Most hikers can do this climb in 2 or 3 hours to the top; 4 or 5 hours round-trip. The author made the summit in 1 hr. 40 min., the round-trip taking 2 hrs. 40 min.

Water There will be other campers along the creek above the car-park, so have some good water in your car, or get it from the creek higher up in the canyon near the Snake Ck. Trailhead. Near the car-park, there is no water in Snake Ck. The water goes into a pipeline for several kms in this section, because it used to sink into the ground. Further down, the water is returned to the stream bed, where it makes its way to the fish hatchery, then on to Garrison where it's used to irrigate farm land.

Camping From the car-park, you'll have to look up or down canyon a ways for a good campsite. There are good places near the Bonita Mine.

Geology Along the South Ridge, from bottom to top, you'll be walking atop the *Pole Canyon Limestone*. Look carefully at the limestone at the summit, and you'll see it's slightly crystallized, or marbleized. Bristlecone pines love limestone soil, that's the reason there are so many of them on the upper south face.

Maps USGS or BLM maps Garrison(1:100,000), or Garrison(1:62,500), or one of the geology maps MF-1343 A, B, or C(1:62,500), or Humboldt National Forest(1:125,000).

Bristlecone pines, and the steep southwest face of Eagle Peak.

MAP 22, EAGLE PEAK--SOUTH RIDGE

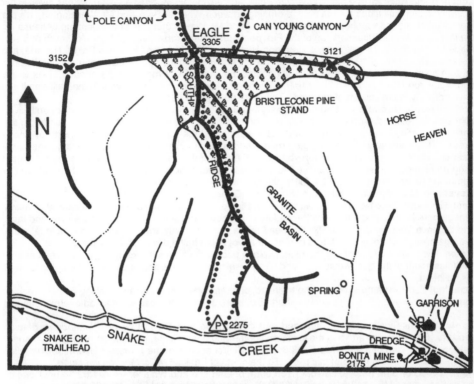

POLE CANYON

CAN YOUNG CANYON

EAGLE
3305

3152 X

3121

N

SOUTH

RIDGE

BRISTLECONE PINE
STAND

HORSE

HEAVEN

GRANITE

BASIN

SPRING

GARRISON

SNAKE CK.
TRAILHEAD

SNAKE

CREEK

P 2275

DREDGE

BONITA MINE
2175

SCALE

0   1   2   3   KMS

Old bristlecone pine, on the south face of Eagle Peak.

Quartzite Peak--Snake Creek Route

Location and Access The name Quartzite Peak, at 3598 meters, is a name the author has given to one of the high summits along the main ridge running between Wheeler Peak and Mt. Washington. It's the high point about half way between Pyramid Peak and Mt. Washington. It gets this name because it's the last peak on this ridge made up of the *Prospect Mountain Quartzite* rock. All peaks south of it are made up of limestone. To get there, drive along Highway 487, which runs between Baker, Nevada, and Garrison, Utah. About 10 kms southeast of Baker, and 3 kms northwest of Garrison(right at mile post 1), turn south onto a good gravel road signposted for Snake Ck. From there it's about 22 kms to the end of the good road and the Quartzite Pk. Trailhead. About any car can make it to the trailhead if you drive carefully in the last km of the road. There are no signs at this car-park.

Trail or Route Conditions You could easily head up to Johnson Lake, then ridge-walk south over Johnson Pk. and to Quartzite, but here's the shortest way to the top of the fifth highest summit in the park. From the Quartzite Pk. Trailhead, walk west along the rough 4WD track just north of Snake Creek. This is some kind of old logging road, and isn't used anymore. This old track zig zags to the west and up the gentle slope. When you reach the end of the track, just head west to the prominent ridge running southeast from Quartzite Pk. The walk through the forest is easy, as is the climb up the Southeast Ridge. From Peak 3524, follow the ridge northwest to the main summit.

Elevations Quartzite Pk. Trailhead, 2550 meters; Quartzite Peak, 3598 meters.

Best Time and Time Needed As with all other high peaks of the Snake Range, the normal climbing season here is from mid-June until the middle of October. In some years, it can be earlier and later. The distance from the Quartzite Pk. Trailhead to the summit is only about 5 kms, and should take the average hiker only a couple of hours to reach the top; about half a day for the round-trip climb.

Water The trailhead is normally the highest place people drive to in this canyon, so the creek at that point has some of the best water you'll find. The creek water comes from springs not far to the west of the trailhead.

Camping You can camp at or near the trailhead, or at any one of many locations along Snake Creek as you drive up canyon. Since it's such a short hike, there seems little need to make an overnight hike of it.

Geology While walking along the road and through the forest, you'll be on *Pleistocene glacier deposits*. But when you arrive at the lower end of the Southeast Ridge, you'll be on *granite* for a short distance. One third of the way up Peak 3524, you'll first encounter the *Prospect Mountain Quartzite*. All of Quartzite Peak is made of this rock. To the south of Peak 3524, is *Pioche Limestone*.

Maps USGS or BLM maps Garrison(1:100,000), or Garrison and Wheeler Peak(1:62,500), or one of the geology maps MF-1343 A, B, or C(1:62,500), or Humboldt National Forest(1:125,000).

Looking north at Wheeler and Baker(in background). East face of Quartzite in center of foto.

MAP 23, QUARTZITE PK.--SNAKE CK.

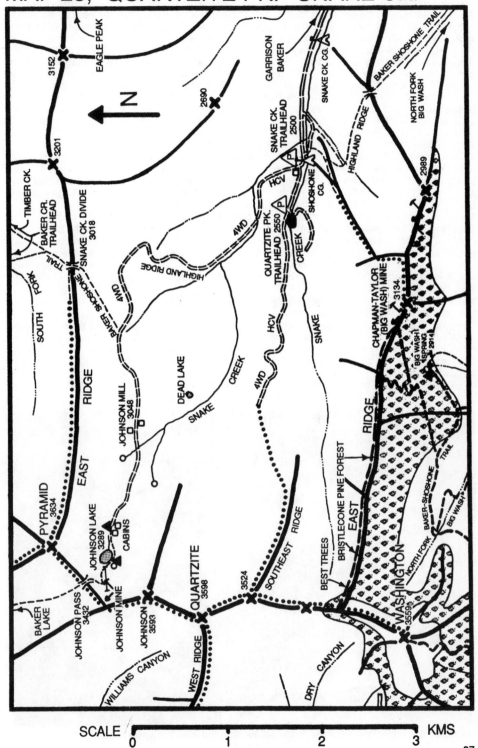

EAGLE PEAK

3152

2690

N

3201

TIMBER CK.

BAKER CR. TRAILHEAD

SNAKE CK. DIVIDE 3018

SOUTH FORK

EAST RIDGE

BAKER SHOSHONE TRAIL

4WD

HIGHLAND RIDGE

4WD

JOHNSON MILL 3048

DEAD LAKE

SNAKE CREEK

SNAKE

PYRAMID 3634

JOHNSON LAKE 3289

CABINS

BAKER LAKE

JOHNSON PASS 3432

JOHNSON MINE

JOHNSON 3593

QUARTZITE 3598

WEST RIDGE

WILLIAMS CANYON

3524

SOUTHEAST RIDGE

GARRISON BAKER

SNAKE CK. CG.

HIGHLAND RIDGE

SNAKE CK. TRAILHEAD 2500

HCV

SHOSHONE CG.

QUARTZITE PK. TRAILHEAD 2550

CREEK

SNAKE

HCV

4WD

BRISTLECONE PINE FOREST

BEST TREES

DRY CANYON

EAST RIDGE

BAKER SHOSHONE TRAIL

NORTH FORK BIG WASH

2989

CHAPMAN-TAYLOR (BIG WASH) MINE 3134

BIG WASH SPRING 2911

WASHINGTON 3559

NORTH FORK BAKER-SHOSHONE TRAIL

BIG WASH

SCALE

0   1   2   3   KMS

Quartzite Peak--West Ridge Route

Location and Access The route discussed here is the climb up the West Ridge of Quartzite Peak, the 5th highest summit in the GBNP, at 3598 meters. Quartzite is the name given the peak by the author, because it's the most southerly mountain in the South Snake Range which is composed of quartzite rock. To the south of Quartzite Peak, all mountains are made of limestone. To do this hike, head for the west side of the South Snake Range, and into Spring Valley. The road you'll want to get on is the paved Minerva Highway running south along the western side of the mountains to Minerva. You can turn south from Highway 50-6 at a place called Goody Station near Osceola; or you can turn south at Majors Place, at the junction of Highways 93 and 50-6. Just south of this junction(mile post 23) turn east on the Minerva Highway. Drive to a point just south of mile post 6, which is just north of the Kirkeby Ranch and airstrip. Then turn to the east and onto a very rough road which parallels a pipeline. With a HCV, you can drive to near the mouth of Williams Canyon; but for those with cars, drive as far as you can and walk from there. Cars will be lucky to make it up one km.

Trail or Route Conditions From the upper trailhead, continue up along the ditch into Williams Canyon, staying on the south side of the creek. Walk into the canyon 200-300 meters, and look up to your right. You should see a big rocky slope, free of trees and brush. Get on this rock slope and head up and in a southeast direction. Above the rock slope, you'll walk into the forest, but if you stay on or near the ridge-top, there's virtually no bushwhacking and the walking is easy. Ridge-walk this prominent West Ridge all the way to the summit of Quartzite Peak.

Elevations Lower car-park, 1890 meters; upper trailhead, 2150; Quartzite Peak, 3598 meters.

Best Time and Time Needed It should be easy to make this climb from about June first, on through October. The south side of the ridge should be free of snow for most of this time. Strong hikers should be able to make this climb in 4 to 5 hours, and maybe 7 or 8 hours round-trip, from the lower car-park. Since it's 5 kms from the highway to the upper trailhead, you can save about one hour of walking each way, if you have a HCV. The author walked from the lower car-park to the summit in 3 hrs. 3 min., and 6 hrs. round-trip.

Water Carry some in your car, otherwise there's good water in Williams Creek on a year-round basis. You can't get any water from the pipeline.

Camping There are good campsites near the upper trailhead, or in the cedars near the highway. All areas east of the Minerva Highway are BLM or Forest Service lands and public domain, so you can camp anywhere. You don't reach the park boundary until about half way up the ridge.

Geology Above the upper trailhead and all the way to the summit, you'll be walking on *Prospect Mountain Quartzite.*

Maps USGS or BLM maps Garrison(1:100,000), or Wheeler Peak(1:62,500), or one of the geology maps MF-1343 A, B, or C(1:62,500), or Humboldt National Forest(1:125,000).

Quartzite Peak(upper left) and West Ridge; Mt. Washington in far background.

MAP 24, QUARTZITE PEAK--WEST RIDGE

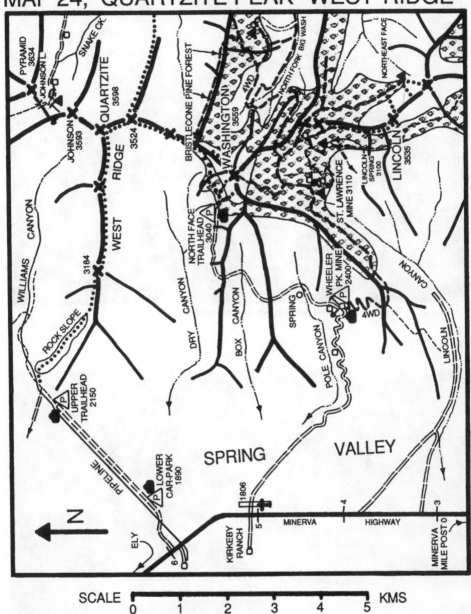

SCALE

0 1 2 3 4 5 KMS

Looking at Mt. Washington, from Spring Valley and the northwest.

From the South Summit of Quartzite, looking south at Mt. Washington.

ACCESS MAP--WEST SIDE ROUTES TO QUARTZITE, WASHINGTON, LINCOLN PEAKS.

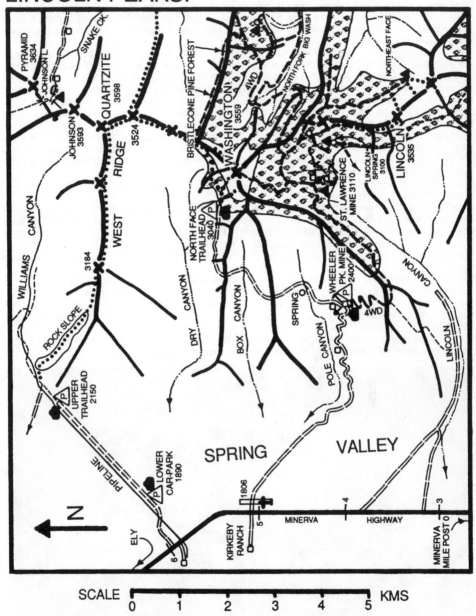

Mt. Washington--Snake Creek Route

Location and Access The climb featured here is to Mt. Washington, which is located on the main north-south ridge of the South Snake Range, and at the head of Snake, Big Wash, Lincoln, Pole and Dry Canyons. It can be approached from any of these canyons, but this route is from the east side of the range and from the Snake Ck. Trailhead. To get there, drive along Nevada State Highway 487, running between Baker, Nevada, and Garrison, Utah. About 10 kms southeast of Baker, and 3 kms northwest of Garrison(right at mile post 1), turn south onto a good gravel road signposted for Snake Creek. Drive 5 kms and you'll see a fish hatchery on your left. Drive another 16 kms and you'll arrive at the Snake Ck. Trailhead. Depending on the route you want to take, park at either of the two car-parks shown on the map.

Trail or Route Conditions You could start at the Quartzite Pk. Trailhead, walk west up the old track to the Southeast Ridge of Quartzite Pk., then south to the summit of Washington. This route is better described under Quartzite Pk. Or try a not-so-normal, but easy route, which might be called the East Ridge Route. From the Snake Ck. Trailhead, walk south across the creek, then southeast on an old track. After maybe 200 meters, turn southwest and walk along this same old track up a minor ridge. After about a km, the track ends just beyond a huge ponderosa pine. From there, route-find up the forested slope to the southwest until you're on top of the East Ridge. Then ridge-walk west. Soon you'll pass some of the diggings of the Chapman-Taylor or Big Wash Mine. From there, you will have a very faint old vehicle track to follow right on the ridge-top. This track ends north of Washington and just west of one of the best bristlecone pine groves in you'll ever see, and maybe the most fotogenic in the range. From there simply walk south to the summit.

Elevations Snake Ck. Trailhead, 2500 meters; Chapman-Taylor(Big Wash) Mine, 3100; Mt. Washington, 3559 meters.

Best Time and Time Needed This route can be climbed from about mid-June until mid-October, but snow conditions each year are different. The distance to the top via this East Ridge Route is about 8 or 9 kms. The average hiker can make it to the summit in about 3 or 3.5 hours, and 5 or 6 hours, round-trip. More time for others. Some may want to spend time in the bristlecone pine stand.

Water The only water source is right at Snake Ck. Trailhead. This water comes from springs not far up stream.

Camping At or near the trailhead or anywhere along Snake Ck. as you approach the car-park.

Geology As you walk up the north slope toward the top of the East Ridge, you'll be walking on *granite*, but once on the ridge-top, and all the way to the top of Washington, you'll be on the massive *Pole Canyon Limestone Formation*. Most of the Southeast Ridge of Quartzite Peak is made of *Prospect Mountain Quartzite* rock.

Maps USGS or BLM maps Garrison(1:100,000), or Garrison and Wheeler Peak(1:62,500), or one of the geology maps MF-1343 A, B, or C(1:62,500), or Humboldt National Forest(1:125,000).

Summit of Washington, from the stand of bristlecones on the upper end of the East Ridge.

MAP 25, WASHINGTON--SNAKE CK. ROUTE

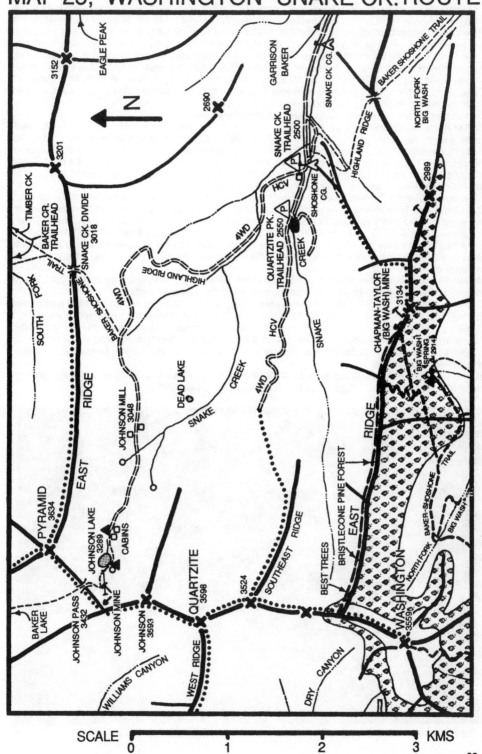

SCALE

0   1   2   3   KMS

Mt. Washington--Pole Canyon Trail

Location and Access Mt. Washington, is located on the big main north-south ridge which runs south from the Wheeler Peak area. This section describes the normal route to the top of Washington, via Pole Canyon(not to be confused with the Pole Canyon near Eagle Peak and Lehman Caves). To get to the beginning of this hike, first head for Spring Valley on the west side of the range. One way is to drive south from Majors Place, located at the junction of Highways 93 and 50-6. Not far from there, turn east(at mile post 23) onto the paved Minerva Highway running south to Shoshone and Minerva. Or you could turn south from Highway 50-6, at a place called Goody Station, which is near Osceola. Drive along the Minerva Highway to mile post 5, which is right next to the Kirkeby Ranch and airstrip. From there drive up a very good gravel road to where it ends, at the Wheeler Pk. Mine. You have the owners permission to park and camp there, but don't leave a mess behind.

Trail or Route Conditions From the trailhead at the Wheeler Pk. Mine, there's actually an old 4WD road running upon the mountain, but it takes a tough vehicle which can make tight turns, to make it up. As a result, nowadays it serves as a good trail. When you arrive at the upper cabin of the St. Lawrence Mine, turn north and follow the old road up hill. After another km, you'll come to a fork in the road. Head left, and straight for the summit. You can follow this same old track all the way from the trailhead to the top. It's obviously an easy walk, and you can't get lost.

Elevations Wheeler Pk. Mine, 2400 meters; St. Lawrence Mine, 3110; Mt. Washington, 3559 meters.

Best Time and Time Needed All of the higher part of this route to the summit is on the south face or slope, so in some years you could climb this mountain from the first of June, on through late October. It's about 7 kms to the St. Lawrence Mine, then another 2 kms to the top. Most will take 2 to 3 hours to the mine, then another hour to the summit. The author made it to the St. Lawrence Mine in 1 hr. 25 min., and 2 hrs. 10 min. to the top. You'll probably want to visit the mine on this hike, so plan on a full, but easy day-hike.

Water There's a small flow of water coming out of the Wheeler Pk. Mine which tasted OK, but it's best to carry some in your car. There's none on the mountain after the snow melts.

Camping At the Wheeler Pk. Mine, or somewhere along the road to the mine. It's all public land east of the highway, including the Wheeler Pk. Mine site. The St. Lawrence Mine is on patented private land.

Geology The Wheeler Pk. Mine tunnel begins at about the contact point between the *Prospect Mtn. Quartzite* and the *Pioche Shale*(the host rock for the tungsten and beryllium minerals at the mine). As you walk up the old road to the summit, all you'll see is the massive *Pole Canyon Limestone,* for which this mountain is famous.

Maps USGS or BLM maps Garrison(1:100,000), or Wheeler Peak(1:62,500), or one of the geology maps MF-1343 A, B, or C(1:62,500), or Humboldt National Forest(1:125,000).

The 4WD road running through tall bristlecones, on the southwest side of Washington.

MAP 26, WASHINGTON--POLE CAN. TRAIL

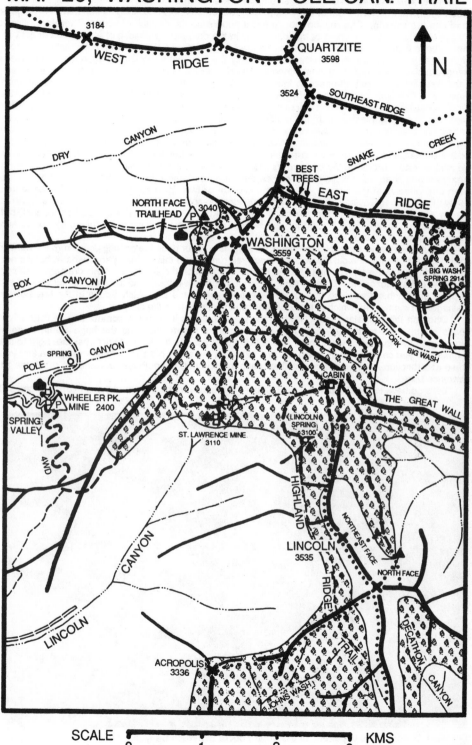

N

3184
WEST RIDGE
QUARTZITE 3598
3524 SOUTHEAST RIDGE
DRY CANYON
SNAKE CREEK
BEST TREES
EAST RIDGE
NORTH FACE TRAILHEAD
3040
WASHINGTON 3559
BIG WASH SPRING 2914
BOX CANYON
NORTH FORK BIG WASH
SPRING CANYON
POLE
CABIN
THE GREAT WALL
WHEELER PK. MINE 2400
4WD
SPRING VALLEY
LINCOLN SPRING 3100
ST. LAWRENCE MINE 3110
HIGHLAND
LINCOLN 3535
NORTHEAST FACE
RIDGE
NORTH FACE
LINCOLN CANYON
TRAIL
DECATHON CANYON
ACROPOLIS 3336
JOHN'S WASH

SCALE

0   1   2   3   KMS

Mt. Washington--Big Wash Trail

Location and Access One of the longest hikes in this book is the one to the top of Mt. Washington via the North Fork of Big Wash. One reason this hike is so long, is that there isn't a good road into the canyon. The reason there's not a good road, is the lack of water. Therefore, there's always been very little ranching or mining activity in the drainage. Because of a minimum of activity, there's been little reason to build or improve a road or trail into Big Wash. One of the main attractions of this hike is there are very few visitors. It's surely the loneliest and wildest part in the South Snake Range. It also has some of the best scenery. The North Fork of Big Wash has big cliffs, which makes it the deepest and most attractive in the range. To get to the starting point, drive to the southern outskirts of Garrison, and on the right you'll see a road signposted for the Big Wash Ranch and the North Fork of Big Wash. The first half of the way is on a very good gravel road, then after the turnoff to John Osborne's Big Wash Ranch, the road deteriorates some, but any car can make it. The car-park or trailhead is on top of a hill where you see a sign reading, *"Notice--Hazardous Road, 4WD only"*. Half a km beyond is a big washout, and for 4WD's only. From Garrison to the car-park is about 15 kms.

Trail or Route Conditions From the car-park, walk down hill to the creek, then up the North Fork via an old mining road. Further up the canyon, it's called on some maps, the *Baker-Shoshone Trail*. For the most part this is an easy walk, but in places the road has been totally washed out, so there haven't been any vehicles in the canyon, beyond the first km or two, for many years. At the big bend just below the Chapman-Taylor Cabin, the road completely disappears, due to floods which poured down a narrow section of the canyon in the early 1980's. Above the cabin, the old trail or road all but disappears for several kms along the very bottom of the canyon. It's been ruined by floods and avalanches, but it's there.

About a km above the cabin(which has no roof), is a minor drainage coming down from the right or north. Old maps show the old *Baker-Shoshone Trail* running up this drainage somewhere, but it's not visible today. However, if you head for the little minor ridge on the west side of this drainage, you can locate an old bulldozer track running straight up the ridge to a rather good track about half way up the slope to the north. If you use this route, it will take you to the Big Wash Spring at the head of the drainage just mentioned, which is the only year-round waterhole in the canyon.

Once on this mid-slope track, walk to the west again as it follows a contour line. Eventually it heads south, then northwest, and up a minor canyon, before reaching the huge South Face of Washington. At that point you can go straight up the slope, via the easiest way possible, right to the summit. Or you can walk to the west a ways, following the same old track. After less than a km, you arrive at a junction--turn north and uphill to reach the summit; or south and downhill, to reach the St. Lawrence Mine.

Let's go back to the Chapman-Taylor Cabin. If you stay in the bottom of the canyon, you can still

Big Wash Spring, in the upper end of the North Fork of Big Wash Canyon.

MAP 27, WASHINGTON--BIG WASH TRAIL

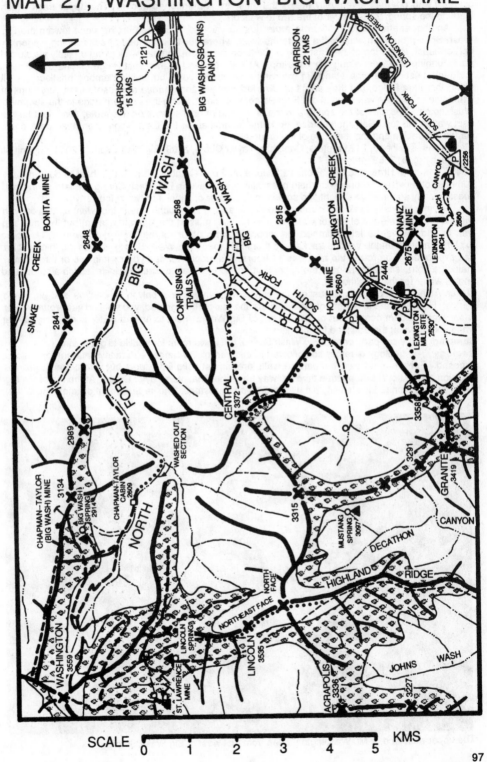

follow one of the old tracks up the right hand fork as you near the end of the canyon. This route, covered with deadfall, eventually meets the other track mentioned above. The upper track which leads to the spring, is the easier of the two to walk on.

Another alternative to this *"normal route"* just mentioned, is to head up the slope toward the Big Wash Spring, but then walk half a km to the west, where you'll find another track running diagonally up(northeast) to the top of the East Ridge. Once on this ridge, you can walk along a faintly visible old track running due west along the ridge-top. At the west end of this East Ridge, is one of the most fotogenic bristlecone pine stands in the range. Actually, you'll be walking among bristlecones all along this East Ridge, but they aren't so dwarfed, twisted and gnarled as those on the very brink of timberline. From the west end of the East Ridge, walk south along the northern ridge to the summit of Washington. Because of the spring and the fine stand of bristlecones on this route, this might be the best way to the top. Still another idea; go to the summit along the East Ridge, then head back down via the old track along the east side of the mountain.

Elevations Trailhead, 2121 meters; Chapman-Taylor Cabin, 2609; Big Wash Spring, 2914; summit of Mt. Washington, 3559 meters.

Best Time and Time Needed From early June until mid-October. It might be best to do it in early summer, otherwise, the only waterhole possibility you'll have is Big Wash Spring. In late spring and possibly early summer, you might find some running water at a place or two in the canyon.

For most people, to do this climb in one day is asking too much. The author went up this canyon with no prior knowledge of trail or water conditions, and missed the summit by a km(but the intention was to find routes--he later climbed the mountain from other routes). He did however, do some exploring around on the various tracks, and thankfully found Big Wash Spring. It was the thirstiest he has ever been. The round trip hike was 11 hours. It's recommended you try it in two or three days, making a camp somewhere near the spring(but not so close as to disturb wildlife, which also depend on this water for their livelihood!).

Water As has already been discussed, the only permanent water supply in the canyon is at Big Wash Spring. However, at the bottom of the hill where the car-park is located, you will find year-round water in the small stream coming out of South Fork of Big Wash. Best to have a water supply in your car when you arrive at the trailhead for this hike.

Camping At the car-park, or near Big Wash Spring, but leave room for wildlife to get a drink,

Geology The geology is rather complicated in this part of the range, with many different formations exposed. For the most part, the canyon walls are almost solid limestone, but with a small *granite* intrusion on the north side about a third the way up to the Chapman-Taylor Cabin. At the top of the big East Ridge and on to the summit, is the *Pole Canyon Limestone*. The large amount of limestone in this

The upper east face of Mt. Washington, seen from just west of Big Wash Spring.

region is the primary reason for so many bristlecone pines.
Maps USGS or BLM maps Garrison(1:100,000), or Garrison and Wheeler Peak(1:62,500), or one of the geology maps MF-1343 A, B, or C(1:62,500), or Humboldt National Forest(1:125,000).

Bristlecone pines on the East Ridge of Mt. Washington.

Winter winds blow most of the snow off the South Face of Washington.

Mt. Washington--North Face Routes

Location and Access The climb discussed here is to the top of Mt. Washington via one of several routes up the difficult North Face. Here's how to get there. First head for the west side of the range and Spring Valley. From Majors Place, at the junction of Highways 93 and 50-6, turn south. After about 7 kms, turn east(at mile post 23) onto the Minerva Highway running to Shoshone and Minerva. Or you can turn south from Highway 50-6, at a place called Goody Station, just west of Osceola, and from between mile posts 72 and 73. Drive toward Minerva, but turn east off the highway near mile post 5, which is next to the Kirkeby Ranch. Drive this good gravel road about 8 kms to the Wheeler Pk. Mine, which is at the end of the good road in Pole Canyon. Park at the mine. If you have a tough HCV or a 4WD, then you could drive on up to the end of the fairly good road to the North Face Trailhead.

Trail or Route Conditions For those without a HCV or 4WD, park at the Wheeler Pk. Mine, and walk 5 or 6 kms to the end of the road at the bottom of the North Face. The face has some cliffs and some steep gullies or couloirs, or just some fairly steep slopes toward the east side of the face. If you intend to do some real challenging climbing, then go prepared with all the normal rock climbing equipment. You could find some interesting snowgully climbing in early summer before all the snow and ice melts. This access road would also be an easy way to reach the ridge north of Washington, the one running to Quartzite Pk. To do this, head up and to the east, along the bottom of the steep face, but stay in the trees. This would be the shortest and easiest route to the fine stand of gnarled bristlecones at the beginning of the East Ridge of Washington or to Quartzite Peak.

Elevations Wheeler Pk. Mine, 2400 meters; North Face Trailhead, 3040; Washington, 3559 meters

Best Time and Time Needed If you want this to be a relatively snow-free climb, you'll have to wait until late August or September, but for snowgully climbing, May or June might be good. It'll take 1.5 hours to walk to the North Face Trailhead from the mine. If you're going to the bristlecones on the East Ridge, then add another 1.5 hours.

Water There's a small stream of water coming out of the mine, and it tasted OK, but it's best to have water in your car. One km from the mine, there's a small spring just below the road.

Camping You have the owners permission to camp at the Wheeler Pk. Mine, but keep the place clean. Or you can camp anywhere along the 4WD road to the North Face Trailhead.

Geology From the Wheeler Pk. Mine along the road to the North Face, you'll be on about the contact point of the *Prospect Mtn. Quartzite*(below) and the *Pioche Shale*. The lower part of the North Face is the *Pioche Shale*, while the steep upper part is the massive *Pole Canyon Limestone*.

Maps USGS or BLM maps Garrison(1:100,000), or Wheeler Peak(1:62,500), or one of the geology maps MF-1343 A, B, or C(1:62,500), or Humboldt National Forest(1:125,000).

The North Face of Mt. Washington.

MAP 28, WASHINGTON--NORTH FACE

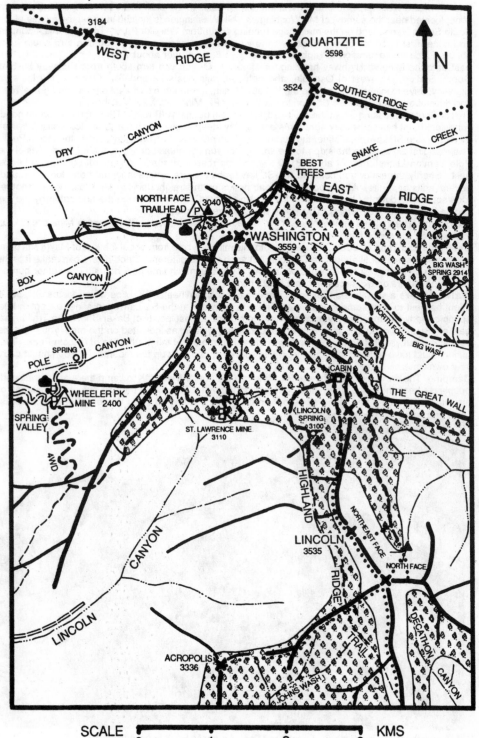

SCALE

KMS

0 1 2 3

101

St. Lawrence Mine Hike

Location and Access One of the most interesting hikes in the park is the one to the St. Lawrence Mine, located near the summit of Mt. Washington. Mt. Washington is located in about the middle of the South Snake Range, and on the main ridge running south from Wheeler Peak. To get to this mountain and mine, first head for Spring Valley on the western side of the range. You can turn south from Majors Place at the junction of Highways 93 and 50-6, then after about 7 kms(at mile post 23), turn east onto the Minerva Highway heading for Minerva. Or you can turn south from Highway 50-6 at Goody Station, just west of Osceola, and between mile posts 72 and 73. Once on the Minerva Highway, drive to mile post 5, next to the Kirkeby Ranch. From there turn east onto a good gravel road and drive about 8 kms up Pole Canyon to the Wheeler Pk. Mine. Park there at the mine.

Trail or Route Conditions From the trailhead, walk south up the 4WD road. This road is in pretty good condition, but it has some very tight turns and is very steep in places. It makes a nice walking trail all the way to the St. Lawrence Mine, the summit of Washington and allows easy access to Lincoln Peak. The road first zig zags up the slope to the south, then runs northeast on top of the inclined beds of the Pole Canyon Limestone. At about 3100 meters, the road then tends to level off some, and heads east. Shortly thereafter you come to the St. Lawrence Fissure, where is located one log cabin and several adits or shafts. At that point, one road heads north straight uphill to Mt. Washington; another runs south and downhill to the main mine workings about 150 meters from the first cabin(by the zig zagging roads, it's 300 meters). This lower site is where you want to go.

Elevations The trailhead at the Wheeler Pk. Mine, 2400 meters; upper St. Lawrence Mine site, 3170; the lower St. Lawrence Mine site, 3110 meters.

Best Time and Time Needed You can walk to this mine anytime from about the last of May(it sits on a south facing slope) until about late October, but each year is different. Good hikers can make it to the St. Lawrence in about 2 hours, while others might want as much time as 3 hours. The author hurried and made it there on two occasions, in 1 hr. 25 min.

Water There's a small stream of water coming out of the Wheeler Pk. Mine which tastes OK, but it might be best to take some in your car. There is no water at the St. Lawrence Mine, except in late spring or early summer, but if you can follow the old and almost indistinct Baker-Shoshone Trail to the east of the upper mine site, then follow the road south a ways, as indicated on the map, you'll find the very small, but year-round Lincoln Spring at the western base of the north ridge of Lincoln Peak. The miners must have gotten their water from this spring, or carried it up the mountain? You should carry your own water.

Camping The owners of the Wheeler Pk. Mine told the author it was OK to camp there at the trailhead, but please keep the place clean, and don't go into the mine. The author met the owners coming out of the mine, where they had found some poisonous gases building up. The Wheeler Peak Mine site is

One of several cabins at the St. Lawrence Mine. Acrapolis Peak in background.

MAP 29, ST. LAWRENCE MINE HIKE

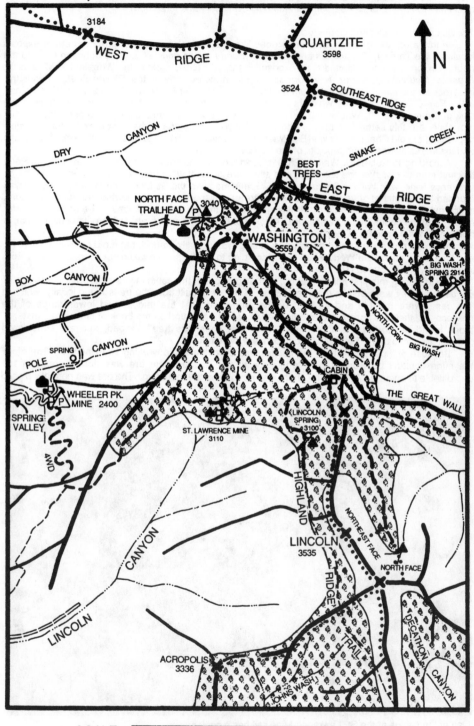

WEST RIDGE
3184

QUARTZITE
3598

3524 SOUTHEAST RIDGE

N

DRY CANYON

SNAKE CREEK

BEST TREES

EAST RIDGE

NORTH FACE TRAILHEAD
P
3040

WASHINGTON
3559

BIG WASH SPRING 2914

BOX CANYON

NORTH FORK BIG WASH

SPRING CANYON

POLE

CABIN

THE GREAT WALL

WHEELER PK. MINE 2400
P

SPRING VALLEY

4WD

LINCOLN SPRING 3100

ST. LAWRENCE MINE
3110

HIGHLAND

NORTHEAST FACE

LINCOLN
3535

NORTH FACE

LINCOLN CANYON

RIDGE TRAIL

DECATHON CANYON

ACROPOLIS
3336

JOHNS WASH

SCALE

0   1   2   3   KMS

actually on Forest Service land, while the claims at the St. Lawrence Mine are patented private land. **Maps** USGS or BLM maps Garrison(1:100,000), or Wheeler Peak(1:62,500), or one of the geology maps MF-1343 A, B, or C(1:62,500), or Humboldt National Park(1:125,000).

The St. Lawrence Mine and Geology

In this area, the geologic sequence goes like this. A long way under ground, but not exposed locally, is the Tertiary, Cretaceous and Jurassic *granite* rocks you see around Johnson Lake to the north. On top of the granite, and seen exposed in the cliffs to the north of the Wheeler Pk. Mine, is the *Prospect Mountain Quartzite*. Next formation up from the quartzite is the *Pioche Shale*. This is the host rock for the tungsten and beryllium minerals in the Wheeler Pk. Mine. On top of the Pioche Shale is the *Pole Canyon Limestone,* which is about 600 meters thick. This is the formation which forms the bulk of the massive Mt. Washington. The big grey cliffs you see on the west and north face of this mountain, are this same formation. The Pole Canyon Limestone is the host rock for the tungsten deposits of the old Chapman-Taylor(Big Wash) Mine located at the head of the North Fork of Big Wash, and the lead-zinc and silver deposits of the St. Lawrence Mine.

According to Robert S. Waite's Ph.D. dissertation on the Proposed Great Basin National Park, the first man to discover the lead-zinc and silver ore body at what has been known since as the St. Lawrence Mine, was William Bacon in 1890. Sometime later, the St. Lawrence Mining Company was founded and a total of seven mining claims were established on the big north-south running fissure, which extends from the summit of Mt. Washington to the south about 3 kms. The primary area for mining is at the south end of this fissure. Altitude of the claims, which are still in private ownership, is from about 2900 up to 3559 meters.

No exact dates are known as to when mining was actually started, but it did operate until 1910, and then again during the World War I era. According to Waite, the ore taken out averaged about 75% lead and 1.7 kg (60 ounces) of silver per ton.

It was during this first mining period, that all or most of the cabins were built(Shirley Robison of Ely believes they were built in the late 1880's). They were built from the trees found locally, which in this case, were the tall and straight bristlecone pines. At the middle and lower range of the bristlecones, they are not twisted and gnarled, as are those found on the brink of timberline. Instead, those found at around the 3000 meter level are "christmas tree" shaped, and are considered commercially valuable. Several of the cabins are still standing.

Because of the high altitude, the access was difficult and the working season short. Therefore the mine couldn't be worked very long each year. Although the ore was rich, it was just too unprofitable to operate. At that time, there was no road up the mountain. The ore was normally placed

One of the cabins at the St. Lawrence Mine still has a cook stove.

in sacks and put on the backs of mules for the journey down the mountain. At one time they even tried tobogganing the ore off the mountain. Not much happened there in the early days of mining.

Between World War I and 1948, there was random workings at the St. Lawrence, mainly just to keep up the claims. But then with a few surplus 4WD army jeeps available to the public for the first time, someone began thinking of building a road to the mine. In the summer of 1948, according to Waite, several men by the names of Hulse and Cottino of Pioche, and Shirley Robison of Ely, build the jeep or 4WD road up Mt. Washington to the mine for the first time.

With this new road, mining once again started up in the fall of 1948, and enough lead-zinc and silver ore was jeeped out of the mine to fill four railway cars. The contents of the ore was about 30% lead and about .5 kg(18 ounces) of silver per ton. Shortly after the spring of 1949, the price of lead declined, and the operation stopped for good.

This is obviously an interesting place to visit. At the upper site, you will now find one old cabin, and nearby, almost at the cabin doorstep, are a couple of shafts which are caved in. The author never did explore above this site, but you might find something if you take the time to look.

From the upper site, walk due south and down the exposed fissure about 150 meters. Along the way you'll see evidence of mining activity, including several ore heaps. It's easy to tell the ore from the host rock. The host rock is the Pole Canyon Limestone, which is typically grey in color. The ore heaps are composed of rock which is a deep dark brown color. Two very distinct rocks.

At the lower site are three cabins still standing, but barely. They could give you some shelter, but shouldn't be trusted very far. There's also the remains of another cabin on the ground. One of the cabins still has an old cook stove inside.

From where the cabins stand, walk to the east just a few paces and you'll see some of the actual mining relics. There's an old garbage dump, with lots of old rusty tin cans, and other items lying about. From the cabin area, walk downhill about 75 meters, to see several old tunnels where most of the mining actually took place. The mine tunnel which seems to have been used the most, is at the very bottom end of the fissure, and on the edge of the big limestone canyon to the south. There's a steel cable(from 1948) strung up in some trees, but the author couldn't tell if any mining took place down inside the canyon. This site easily compares to the Johnson Mine as far as interesting old mining artifacts are concerned. Please don't forget, the land immediately around the mine is still privately owned. It's likely no one will care if you visit the place, but leave everything as is and in place. Help protect this historic site.

Old mining equipment at the St. Lawrence Mine.

Lincoln Peak–Pole Canyon Route

Location and Access The climb featured here is the normal route to Lincoln Peak, the most southerly of the big alpine peaks in the South Snake Range. If you follow the high ridge line south from Wheeler Peak, you will eventually come to Lincoln. To make it to the starting point, first head for Spring Valley, which is to the west of the range. If you're coming from the west or south, head for Majors Place, at the junction of Highways 93(from Las Vegas) and 50-6. Turn south and drive 7 kms, and turn east(at mile post 23) onto the Minerva Highway heading for Shoshone and Minerva. Or you can turn south from Highway 50-6, at Goody Station, which is west of Osceola and between mile posts 72 and 73. Once on this highway running to Minerva, drive to mile post 5, near the Kirkeby Ranch. Turn east and drive 8 kms up Pole Canyon to the trailhead at the Wheeler Pk. Mine.

Trail or Route Condition From the trailhead, you will first walk south and up a steep 4WD road, which has some very tight turns. Very few vehicles can make it up this road, so it makes a nice route to hike on. After a couple of kms, you'll turn to the northeast, and walk into the bristlecone pine forest with big straight trees. After 7 kms of walking, you reach the upper part of the St. Lawrence Mine. From there you can walk due east along the old hard-to-find Baker-Shoshone Trail toward the cabin shown on the map. Or you could walk uphill on the same road, and circle around finally arriving at the cabin just mentioned. From the cabin, head south on another old vehicle track which ends 1.5 kms from the summit of Lincoln. At the roads-end, ridge-walk south to the top, a very easy walk all the way.

Elevations Trailhead, 2400 meters; St. Lawrence Mine, 3170(upper part); Lincoln Peak, 3535 meters.

Best Time and Time Needed From about mid-June until the middle of October, but on either end of this time period, expect some snow or wet trails. If you go directly to the summit of Lincoln, it should take the average person about 3.5 or 4 hours, one way. The author can't remember exactly how long it took to reach the top, but on one trip he first climbed the peak via this route, then back-tracked and walked to the base of the North Face of Lincoln, and finally to the St. Lawrence Mine for awhile, then to the trailhead in 8 hrs. 25 min.

Water There's water coming out of the Wheeler Pk. Mine, which tastes good, but it might be best to carry water in your car, as well as in your pack for this hike. Also at Lincoln Spring near the base of Lincoln's north ridge, but this spring has a very small discharge.

Camping At the trailhead, or at or near Lincoln Spring.

Geology You start out walking along the *Pioche Shale,* then the *Pole Canyon Limestone,* where the St. Lawrence Mine is found. After the mine you pass along the *Corset Spring Shale, Johns Wash Limestone* and the *Lincoln Pk. Formation.* Near the summit you reach the *House Limestone.*

Maps USGS or BLM maps Garrison(1:100,000), or Wheeler Peak(1:62,500), or one of the geology maps MF-1343 A, B, or C(1:62,500), or Humboldt National Forest(1:125,000).

From the summit of Lincoln Peak; the North and Northeast Face of Lincoln.

MAP 30, LINCOLN PK.--POLE CAN. TRAIL

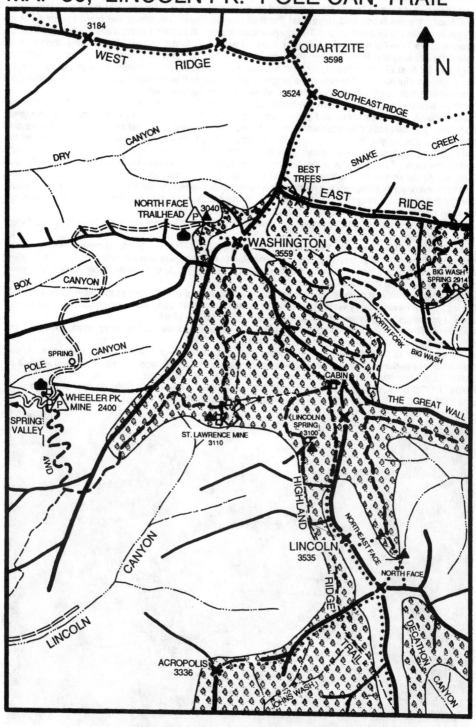

N

3184

WEST RIDGE

QUARTZITE 3598

3524 SOUTHEAST RIDGE

DRY CANYON

SNAKE CREEK

BEST TREES

EAST RIDGE

NORTH FACE TRAILHEAD

P 3040

WASHINGTON 3559

BIG WASH SPRING 2914

BOX CANYON

NORTH FORK BIG WASH

SPRING CANYON

POLE

CABIN

THE GREAT WALL

WHEELER PK. MINE 2400

P

LINCOLN SPRING 3100

SPRING VALLEY

ST. LAWRENCE MINE 3110

4WD

HIGHLAND

LINCOLN 3535

NORTHEAST FACE

NORTH FACE

RIDGE TRAIL

DECATHON CANYON

LINCOLN CANYON

ACROPOLIS 3336

JOHNS WASH

SCALE

0   1   2   3   KMS

107

Lincoln Peak--Northeast Face Routes

Location and Access The climbs described here are some of the more challenging climbs featured in this book. It's the North and Northeast Face of Lincoln Peak. Lincoln is the most southerly of the alpine peaks in the Snake Range. The normal approach route is from Spring Valley, west of the range. From Major's Place at the junction of Highways 93 and 50-6, turn south for about 7 kms, then east(at mile post 23) onto the Minerva Highway running south to Shoshone and Minerva. Or turn south from Highway 50-6 at Goody Station, located just west of Osceola, and between mile posts 72 and 73. Once on this highway to Minerva, drive to mile post 5, next to the Kirkeby Ranch. Turn east into Pole Canyon and drive 8 kms to the Wheeler Pk. Mine, which is the trailhead.

Trail or Route Conditions From the trailhead, walk south and up the very steep 4WD road running toward the St. Lawrence Mine, and to the base of the north ridge of Lincoln. At the upper St. Lawrence Mine site, you can walk due east along the indistinct Baker-Shoshone Trail to the cabin at the base of the north ridge; or you could continue up the road north, then east, and finally down(south) to the cabin just mentioned. From the cabin, continue southeast on another track for about a km. Look for a fork in the track. Take the one to the right, which will put you at the very base of the Northeast Face of Lincoln. At the end of the track, pick out the route best for you and you're skill levels. You can find a relatively easy scrambling route directly to the summit(via the Northeast Face), or you can walk south, and try the very difficult and vertical North Face of the southern peak of Lincoln. This one looks tough on solid limestone, and you'll need all the rock climbing gear to do it.

Elevations Trailhead, 2400 meters; St. Lawrence Mine, 3170(upper mine site); base of Northeast Face, 3100 meters.

Best Time and Time Needed From about mid-June until mid-October, but for a completely snow free climb, you'll have to wait until August or September. The average climber will need 3 to 4 hours to reach the base of the face, but more if a large pack is taken. If you choose a difficult face route, you'll need more than one day for this round-trip hike.

Water Water runs out of the Wheeler Pk. Mine(and it seems good), and at the hard-to-find Lincoln Spring. You'll have to carry water to the North Face, or make an early summer climb, and plan to melt snow if you're camping there. Water could be a problem on this climb.

Camping The owners of the Wheeler Pk. Mine told the author it was OK to camp at the trailhead, but please keep it clean. Or beneath the face or near Lincoln Spring.

Geology Most of the northern part of Lincoln Peak is composed of *Lincoln Peak Limestone*. At the very base of the North Face are some *Pleistocene glacier deposits*, and just above that is a band of *Notch Peak Limestone*. The top of the mountain is the *House Limestone*.

Maps USGS or BLM maps Garrison(1:100,000), or Wheeler Peak(1:62,500), or one of the geology maps MF-1343 A, B, or C(1:62,500), or Humboldt National Forest(1:125,000).

Dead ahead is the headwall, or North Face, of Lincoln Peak.

MAP 31, LINCOLN PEAK--NORTHEAST FACE

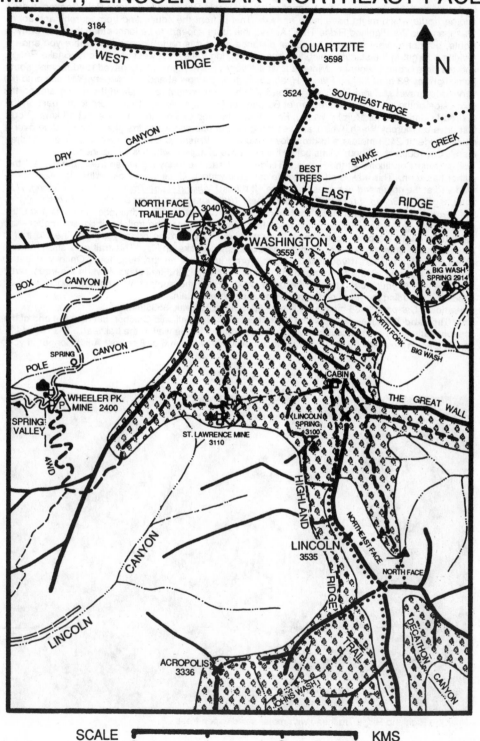

N

3184

WEST RIDGE

QUARTZITE
3598

3524

SOUTHEAST RIDGE

DRY CANYON

CREEK

SNAKE

BEST TREES

EAST RIDGE

NORTH FACE TRAILHEAD
P 3040

WASHINGTON
3559

BIG WASH SPRING 2914

BOX CANYON

NORTH FORK BIG WASH

SPRING CANYON

POLE

CABIN

THE GREAT WALL

WHEELER PK. MINE 2400
P

LINCOLN SPRING 3100

SPRING VALLEY

4WD

ST. LAWRENCE MINE
3110

HIGHLAND

NORTHEAST FACE

LINCOLN
3535

NORTH FACE

RIDGE

CANYON

TRAIL

LINCOLN

DECATHON CANYON

ACROPOLIS
3336

JOHNS WASH

SCALE   KMS
0   1   2   3

Lincoln Peak--Highland Ridge Trail

Location and Access While the normal route up Lincoln Peak would be from Pole Canyon, there's another route which might have more appeal. This is from the south, and from Murphy and Johns Wash, and via the Highland Ridge Trail. At first, this route appears to be longer than the Pole Canyon Route, but not by very much. The actual distance along this route depends on where you end up parking. To get to the starting point, first head for Spring Valley just west of the South Snake Range, and the area around Minerva. Minerva is at the very southern end of the paved road running south from Highway 93 near Majors Place. Head south from the now abandoned Minerva Mill site onto the very good gravel Minerva-Big Springs Road which is the normal route taken if heading around the south side of the range in the direction of Burbank or Garrison. After 11 kms, turn to the east on the dirt road signposted for Murphy Wash. From there until the end of the road, is about 16 kms. You'll first drive up Murphy Wash, where are several good springs and water troughs. Then you go over a minor divide at 2423 meters and drop down into Johns Wash. Cars can make it another km, then there's one rough spot about 2 kms below the big grove of aspens which is the trailhead.

Trail or Route Conditions At the Highland Ridge Trailhead are many big aspen trees, the biggest the author has seen. This makes a fine place to camp(no water). Once there look for the sign east of the road and at the upper end of this aspen grove. It reads:_Highland Ridge Trailhead_ *Lincoln Spring, 7(11 kms); Big Wash Spring, 11(18 kms); Snake Creek, 18(29 kms); and Baker Creek, 23(37 kms).*

From the trailhead sign, head north and northeast and into a minor drainage. In the first km, the trail zig zags up the steep slope to the ridge-top. You'll likely lose the trail, but it doesn't matter--just head up through the pines to the top. Easy walking. Once on the ridge, you'll see the old trail in places, and in other places trail markers on trees, shaped like an "i". This trail runs straight north along the ridge-top, so if you lose it, don't worry; just stay on the ridge-top. Once you get to timberline, just stay on the top of the ridge. Near the summit, the trail stays down in the trees, but if Lincoln Peak is your goal, stay on the ridge crest. From the summit, you have a fine view in all directions, including the north and northeast face of the mountain.

Elevations Car-park, 2438 meters; trailhead, 2545; Lincoln Peak, 3535 meters.

Best Time and Time Needed Anytime from about mid-June until mid-October, but near the end of the season, early snow storms could prevent you from driving all the way to the trailhead. The round-trip hike to Lincoln Peak will be an all day walk, somewhere between 6 or 8 hours. A little longer, if your

Near the Highland Ridge Trailhead with meter-sized aspen trees.

MAP 32, LINCOLN PK.--HIGHLAND RIDGE TR.

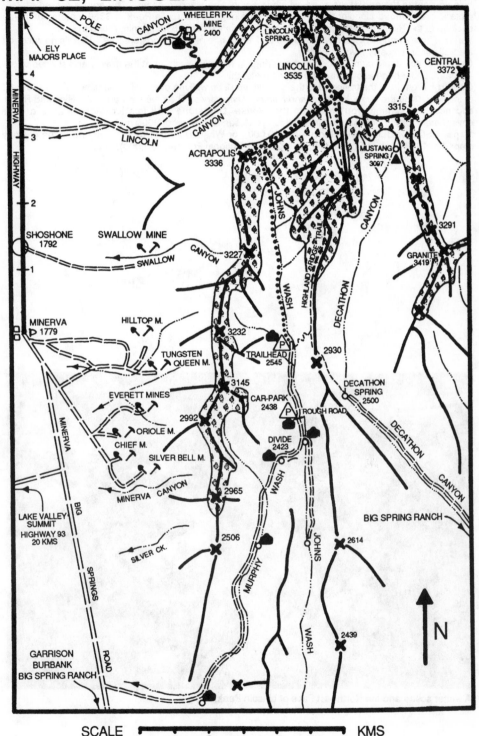

POLE CANYON

WHEELER PK. MINE 2400

LINCOLN SPRING

ELY MAJORS PLACE

LINCOLN 3535

CENTRAL 3372

3315

MINERVA HIGHWAY

LINCOLN CANYON

ACRAPOLIS 3336

MUSTANG SPRING 3097

SHOSHONE 1792

SWALLOW MINE

SWALLOW CANYON 3227

JOHNS

3291

GRANITE 3419

HILLTOP M.

HIGHLAND RIDGE TRAIL

DECATHON CANYON

MINERVA 1779

TUNGSTEN QUEEN M.

3232

TRAILHEAD 2545

P

WASH

2930

DECATHON SPRING 2500

3145

EVERETT MINES

CAR-PARK 2438

P ROUGH ROAD

DECATHON CANYON

MINERVA

2992

ORIOLE M.

CHIEF M.

SILVER BELL M.

DIVIDE 2423

BIG SPRING RANCH

MINERVA CANYON

2965

BIG SPRINGS ROAD

LAKE VALLEY SUMMIT HIGHWAY 93 20 KMS

SILVER CK.

2506

2614

JOHNS WASH

MURPHY WASH

N

2439

GARRISON BURBANK BIG SPRING RANCH

SCALE 0 1 2 3 4 5 6 KMS

111

vehicle won't make it to the upper trailhead. A shovel and a little road work on the one bad spot might help you get to the end of the road, which is a very fine place to camp. The author parked at 2438 meters, and climbed Lincoln; then went down the ridge to Acrapolis Peak at 3336 meters; later went back up to the Highland Ridge; and finally back to his the car in 8 hrs. 7 min. round-trip.

Water There's none at either trailhead, so tank up at one of the springs enroute. There's no water on the trail either, so carry a water bottle.

Camping You could camp at one of the springs in Murphy Wash, or at the grassy and shaded upper trailhead, under huge aspen trees up to one meter thick.

Geology Right from the trailhead to the summit, you'll be walking over solid limestone. For the first 2/3 of the way it'll be the *Juab, Wahwah and Fillmore Limestones*. Then the top part of the Highland Ridge and near the summit, you'll walk on the *House Limestone*. All this limestone makes a good environment for the bristlecone pines, which you'll see above about 3000 meters.

Maps USGS or BLM maps Garrison(1:100,000), or Wheeler Peak(1:62,500), or one of the geology maps MF-1343 A, B, or C(1:62,500), or Humboldt National Forest(1:125,000).

A winter scene and the Northeast Face of Lincoln Peak.

Descending the North Ridge of Lincoln Peak.

From the north, one can see the Northeast Face of Lincoln Peak.

Acrapolis Peak–Johns Wash Route

Location and Access The hike emphasized here is to Acrapolis Peak, but it can also be another route to the top of Lincoln Peak, via Johns Wash to the south. Acrapolis Peak, 3336 meters, is the prominent summit you see to the south from the St. Lawrence Mine. It's the highest point on a long north-south limestone ridge, between Johns Wash and Spring Valley. At the western base of this ridge, is one of the regions more prominent mining areas, the Shoshone District. While you can climb Acrapolis from the trailhead in Pole Canyon, this is the normal route. To get to the trailhead in Johns Wash, read about the access route under the hike, *Lincoln Peak--Highland Ridge*. Higher clearance cars, with care, should make it all the way to the trailhead at the end of the road, but normal cars may have to stop at the car-park marked 2438 meters.

Trail or Route Conditions From the trailhead, which is the beginning of the Highland Ridge Trail, you can walk up Johns Wash a ways on a very primitive track, a recent extension of the canyon road. Beyond where vehicles have been, there will be deer and livestock trails heading up the canyon. This valley has no running water, but there are still some nice stands of aspen and meadows. There is deadfall in places, but no serious obstacles anywhere along the way to the head of the wash where you look down into Lincoln Canyon. At that divide, veer left or west, and head straight up the bristlecone forested slope to the summit of Acrapolis. Or, from the pass, go northeast up a steep ridge toward the Highland Ridge, thence to the top of Lincoln Peak. An interesting all day hike, would be to combine the Johns Wash access route, with the Highland Ridge Trail, and take in both peaks.

Elevations Trailhead, 2545 meters; Acrapolis Peak, 3336; Lincoln Peak, 3535 meters.

Best Time and Time Needed This hike can be made from the first of June until mid-October, but in some years, you can have early season snow storms, which would make it difficult to reach the trailhead(parts of the road in Murphy and Johns Wash are made of dirt). Most hikers could climb Acrapolis and return in about 6 hours, but to combine it with Lincoln, will make a long day-hike of maybe 8 to 10 hours for some.

Water There is no water at the trailhead or in upper Johns Wash. Tank up at one of the several springs in Murphy Wash on the way to the trailhead.

Camping At the trailhead is one of prettiest groves of aspens you'll ever see. Some trees are a meter in diameter. This makes a nice grassy campsite, but because it lacks water, you may want to camp at one of the springs in Murphy Wash.

Geology The rocks you see right along the bottom of Johns Wash are from the *Johns Wash Limestone*. From the pass to the summit of Acrapolis, you walk atop *Notch Peak Limestone*. Most of the upper part of Lincoln Peak is made of the *House Limestone*. Because of the limestone soils, the bristlecones grow well here.

Maps USGS or BLM maps Garrison(1:100,000), or Wheeler Peak(1:62,500), or one of the geology maps MF-1343 A, B, or C(1:62,500), or Humboldt National Forest(1:125,000),

One can see Acrapolis Peak from near the summit of Lincoln Peak.

MAP 33, ACRAPOLIS PEAK--JOHNS WASH

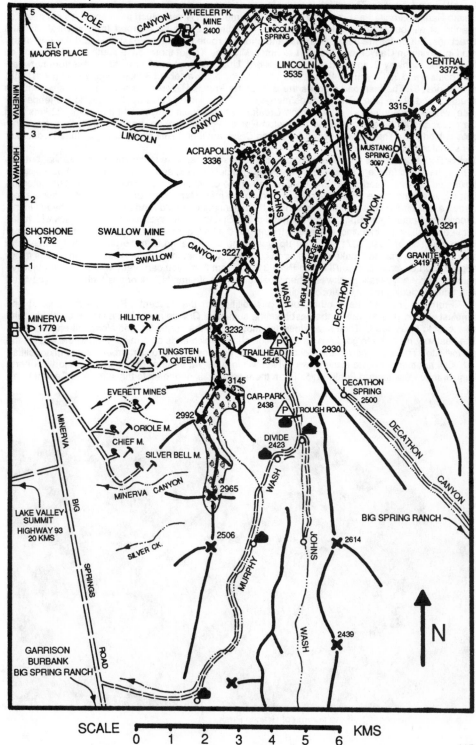

SCALE
0 1 2 3 4 5 6 KMS

Granite Peak--Eastern Routes

Location and Access This climb is to the top of one of the lesser known high summits of the South Snake Range, Granite Peak, at 3419 meters. This mountain is very much misnamed; it's not made of granite at all, but is solid dolomite instead. Granite Pk. can be climbed from several different directions, but by far the easiest, fastest and shortest route is from the east side and the end of the road in Lexington Canyon and the old Lexington Mill site. To get there, drive south out of Garrison on Utah State Highway 21 in the direction of Milford, Utah. After about 7 kms, turn west from between mile posts 4 and 5. Or you could continue south on the highway about 3 more kms, and turn west right at mile post 6. The first road crosses the dam of the Pruess Reservoir; the second turns west at the southern end of the lake. These roads merge after 3 or 4 kms. Drive up this road to the fence and gate, where the South Fork of Lexington Creek meets the main canyon. At that point, 22 kms from Garrison, and at the site of the old Lexington Ranch, you must open, pass through, then close the gate behind you. Then drive west up Lexington Creek another 8 kms or so, to the trailhead located at the site of the old Lexington Mill.

Trail or Route Conditions There are two or more routes you can take to the summit of Granite, but this is how the author made the trip. From the spring, miners shack, and the two old school buses at the Lexington Mill site, head south and up the road in the direction of the Bonanzy Mine. Just after the first big sweeping curve on the road(as shown on the map), turn south on a side road. After a short distance and on the right side of a clearing is the beginning of an old road or track which heads in the direction of Cedar Cabin Spring near the head of Big Spring Wash. Walk south on this track which has some deadfall and is indistinct in places. If you lose the trail, don't worry; just head south anyway, and in the direction of Pass 2871. Further up, you come to a clearing with the pass straight ahead. At about that point, you can make out the ridge coming down from the right or west. Climb up this minor ridge a short distance and you'll be on Peak 3163. From there you can pretty well see your objective ahead; simply ridge-walk northwest, then west to the top of Granite. All of this high ridge is covered with trees, including many bristlecone pines.

From the top, you have other route possibilities for the descent. Perhaps the easiest and simplest way down is to walk to the east from the summit of Granite about half a km. From there head northeast to Peak 3358. Then head down the mountain to the northeast, and along the easiest route. The best way might be to go down an avalanche chute, which ends on a minor road to the west of the old mill site. The upper part of this descent is steep, and you'll have to skirt around some minor cliffs.

Still another alternate route down, which will include yet another climb, would be to walk north from Granite Peak toward Peak 3315. From there ridge-walk northeast to the summit of Central Peak,

The North Ridge coming off the summit of Granite Peak.

MAP 34, GRANITE PEAK--EAST. ROUTES

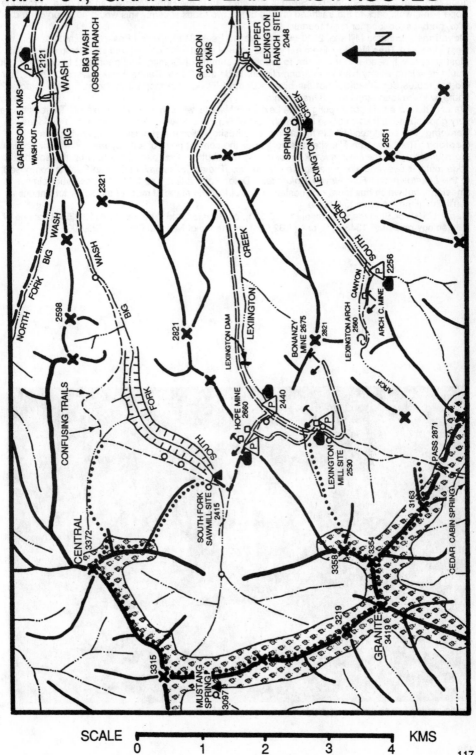

SCALE

0   1   2   3   4   KMS

then down to the east or the southeast. At the bottom of the east face, make your way to the very good spring at the old South Fork Sawmill site, then up to the Hope Mine via an old road. From the Hope Mine, walk back to the trailhead on one of the two roads shown. This would be a very long day hike, perhaps too long for most mortals.

Elevations Lexington Mill site, 2530 meters; Granite Peak, 3419; Central Peak, 3372 meters.

Best Time and Time Needed From early June on until about mid-October, and still later in some years. Most people will need about 3 hours to reach the summit of Granite, and another 2 hours down. It would be a long all day hike for a strong climber to do the Granite-Central Peak traverse. The author did the routes described(but not the hike to Central Peak). He made it to the summit in exactly 2 hours, with the round-trip being 3 hrs. 25 min.

Water There is a very good spring at the Lexington Mill site, which has now been piped. There is also a very good spring at the site of the old South Fork of Big Wash Sawmill site. No water on the ridges.

Camping The Lexington Mill site makes a fine campsite, which is just outside the park boundary.

Geology The Lexington Mill site, sits very near the contact point of a *porpyhritic quartz monzonite stock(granite)* and the *Lincoln Peak Limestone*(to the south). That part of the hike up the southeast ridge route, is over and along the *House Limestone*. The actual summit of Granite Peak is composed of the *Laketown and Fish Haven Dolomites*. Dolomite is a limey sedimentary rock very similar to limestone, but which has more magnesian. Central Peak is made of most of the same formations as you'll find along the route to Granite.

Maps USGS or BLM maps Garrison(1:100,000), or Garrison and Wheeler Peak(1:62,500), or one of the geology maps MF-1343 A, B, or C(1:62,500), or Humboldt National Forest(1:125,000).

Cattle graze near an old miners cabin at the Lexington Mill site.

The eastern parts of Granite Peak, with Wheeler and Jeff Davis far away.

Old school bus at the site of the old Lexington Mill(Lexington Canyon).

Central Peak--South Fork of Big Wash Route

Location and Access Central Peak gets this locally known name because it sits between the North and South Forks of Big Wash. This mountain is due west of Pruess Reservoir, due north of Granite Pk. and east of Lincoln Pk. There are basically two trailheads which can be used to climb this summit. To reach the trailhead on Big Wash, read the route description on Map 27. To get to the trailhead with the easiest route to the top, drive to the Lexington Mill site at the head of Lexington Creek. Read the access route description on Map 34.

Trail or Route Conditions From the Big Wash Trailhead, walk down the road to the valley floor and head west. At the fork of the canyon, turn left, and enter the South Fork on the left(south) side of the stream. There's an old vehicle track at first, then after a ways, it's just a cow trail. Further on, the track leaves the canyon bottom for a benchland above the gorge part of South Fork. Soon there will be an area with many trails--but don't worry, they all seem to come together further on. In the vicinity of the "confusing trails", look for a route up through the trees on the east face of Central. It gets steep, but it's not difficult. The other route, perhaps the easiest and the fastest way to the top, is via Lexington Creek and the old mill site there. From the good campsite at the head of Lexington, drive back down the road half a km, and attempt to drive to the area of the Hope Mine, but people with cars may have to walk from the canyon bottom. From the Hope Mine, you'll walk down an old road or track to the old sawmill site. There's a big spring and a boiler to mark the spot. From there you can head straight up the southeast ridge, but there may be more bushwhacking there than you'd like. Perhaps it's best to walk north on the South Fork Trail to just east of the summit, then route-find up the east face. For really fit hikers, you might try ridge-walking from Central to Granite, and come down the eastern route of that peak to the Lexington Mill site.

Elevations Big Wash Trailhead, 2121 meters; Lexington Trailhead, 2440; sawmill site, 2415; Central Peak, 3372.

Best Time and Time Needed From early June through late October. Plan on a full day climb from the Big Wash Trailhead. From a trailhead near the Hope Mine, it'll likely take the average person 5 or 6 hours round-trip.

Water At the Lexington Mill site, South Fork sawmill site, and in the lower end of South Fork.

Camping A good, but dry camp can be made at the Big Wash Trailhead, but the best campsite is at the Lexington Mill site.

Geology The gorge in the bottom of South Fork is the massive *Pole Canyon Limestone*, whereas the bottom half of Central Pk. is made of the *Lincoln Pk. Limestone*. From there to the summit, you'll pass through the *Johns Wash Limestone, Corset Spring Shale, Notch Peak Limestone,* and at the summit, the *House Limestone*.

Maps USGS or BLM maps Garrison(1:100,000), or Garrison and Wheeler Peak(1:62,500), or one of the geology maps MF-1343 A, B, or C(1:62,500), or Humboldt National Forest(1:125,000).

Fall scene at the old sawmill site in South Fork of Big Wash.

MAP 35, CENTRAL PEAK--S. F., BIG WASH

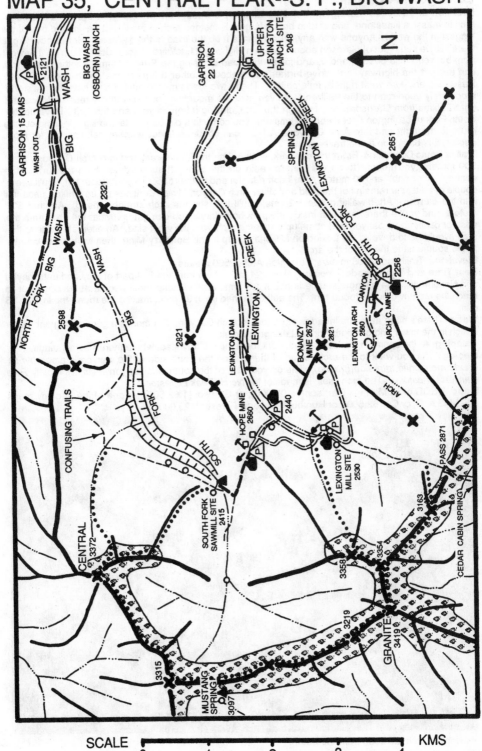

Lexington Arch Hike

Location and Access Lexington Arch is located in the South Fork of Lexington Creek. It is a huge arch in massive limestone, and said to be the largest limestone arch in the Great Basin, and one of the biggest in the world. Anyone with any car can make it up the road to the trailhead. Here's how to get there. Drive south out of Garrison about 7 kms on Highway 21, toward Milford, Utah. Turn right or west from between mile posts 4 and 5, and follow that road crossing the Pruess Dam. Another place you can turn off the highway is to drive further south about another 3 kms to the south end of Pruess Reservoir, and turn west right at mile post 6. These two roads merge after 3 or 4 kms, then it's one moderately good road to the trailhead. As you near the mountain you'll eventually reach a fence and gate(22 kms from Garrison). Go through the gate, closing it behind you, and turn left. Drive up the South Fork of Lexington Creek about 3 kms until you come to a dirt barricade and sign pointing out the route to the right and into Arch Canyon. A HCV can continue about another half km, but for most people, this barricade is the trailhead.

Trail or Route Conditions From the car-park, walk up the track due west and into Arch Canyon. After 500 meters, you'll come to an old miners cabin on the right. It surely dates from the turn of the century. After another 100 meters, you'll come to the end of the road. To your upper left, you'll see a couple of adits, the remains of the gold and silver Arch Canyon Mine. Continue on up a hiker-made trail into the canyon. After walking about 2 kms, you'll first see the arch straight ahead. Another 500 meters, and you're there, and just inside the park boundary. You can get up under the arch from the east, or continue up canyon and come up under the arch from the west side. An alternate route to the arch, would be to drive to the Lexington Mill site, go up to the Bonanzy Mine, then walk cross-country to the southeast to the top of the arch.

Elevations Trailhead, 2256 meters; Lexington Arch, 2560 meters.

Best Time and Time Needed You can likely get to this hike from the first part of May and until maybe mid-November. The hiking distance is about 2.5 kms, and will take most people about one hour to reach the arch; two hours round-trip. The author hurried up in 35 min.; making the round-trip in 1 hr. 15 min.

Water There's none at the trailhead or anywhere in Arch Canyon. But there's a good spring and water trough in the lower end of South Fork of Lexington Creek.

Camping At the spring in the lower South Fork, or at the dry trailhead, where there's some shade.

Geology As you walk to the arch, some of the rock on the north side of the canyon is a *porphyritic quartz monzonite intrusion(granite),* while on your left, or the south side canyon walls, it's mostly *Pole Canyon Limestone.* The arch itself, is made of the *Notch Peak Limestone.*

Maps USGS or BLM maps Garrison(1:100,000), or Garrison(1:62,500), or one of the geology maps MF-1343 A, B, or C(1:62,500), or Humboldt National Forest(1:125,000).

Lexington Arch, as seen from the south.

MAP 36, LEXINGTON ARCH HIKE

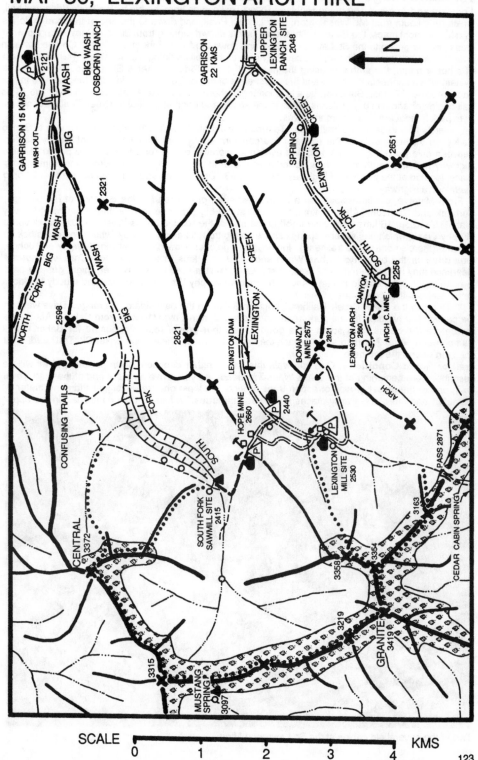

SCALE

0   1   2   3   4   KMS

123

Highland Ridge--Baker & Shoshone Trail

Location and Access The name Highland Ridge Trail comes from the big high altitude ridge and trail, which runs south from Mt. Washington, over Lincoln Peak, and down to the end of the road in Johns Wash. On most maps, the Baker & Shoshone Trail is shown running from Lincoln Canyon on the west side of the range, up to the St. Lawrence Mine, and down the North Fork of Big Wash. On one trail sign near the Snake Creek Trailhead, it states the name of the trail as being the Shoshone Trail. So for lack of a better name, the author is using the name, Highland Ridge--Baker & Shoshone Trail, on a trail system which connects the north and the south ends of the range. This makes the longest hike in this book, at about 37 kms. But it can be a little longer or shorter, if you use an alternate route or two. This trail begins(or ends) in upper Johns Wash in the south, and ends at the Baker Creek Trailhead, not far from park headquarters at Lehman Caves.

Here's how to get to the trailheads. To reach the Johns Wash Trailhead, make your way to Spring Valley on the west side of the range. You can turn south from Highway 50-6 at Goody Station, between mile posts 72 and 73, and first use an all-weather gravel road to reach the paved Minerva Highway heading south to the now abandoned site of Minerva. Or you can turn south from Majors Place, located at the junction of Highways 50-6 and 93. Drive 7 kms and turn east at mile post 23 onto the Minerva Highway.

From Minerva, continue south on a good all-weather gravel road in the direction of Big Springs, Burbank and Garrison. After 11 kms, turn east at the big sign and drive in the direction of Murphy Wash. It's about 16 kms from this turnoff to the end of the road in Johns Wash. You'll first drive up Murphy Wash, which has several springs and watering troughs along the way, where you can stock up on water(there's none at the trailhead). Finally, you'll go over a low divide between Murphy and Johns, then drive up the bottom of Johns Wash another 3 or 4 kms to the trailhead. Cars with normal clearance may not make the last 2 kms. A shovel and a little *road work* however, might get you past the one rough spot, and to the trailhead. The road in Murphy Wash will be slick and muddy in places during wet weather conditions.

To reach the Baker Creek Trailhead, begin in Baker on the east side of the range. Drive west on the paved road heading for the park headquarters at Lehman Caves(10 kms from Baker). About one km before the caves, turn south on a good all-weather gravel road signposted for Baker Creek Campground. After 7 or 8 kms you'll reach the end of the road, which is the Baker Ck. Trailhead. You can start or end the trip here.

Trail or Route Conditions One can walk this trail in either direction, north or south, but it will be described here beginning at the Johns Wash Trailhead. As you arrive near the end of the road, you'll be in one of the nicest groves of aspen trees around. At least one tree is bigger than one meter in diameter, and there are grassy places in between the trees. A fine, but dry campsite. In the upper

Two of the several old cabins at the St. Lawrence Mine.

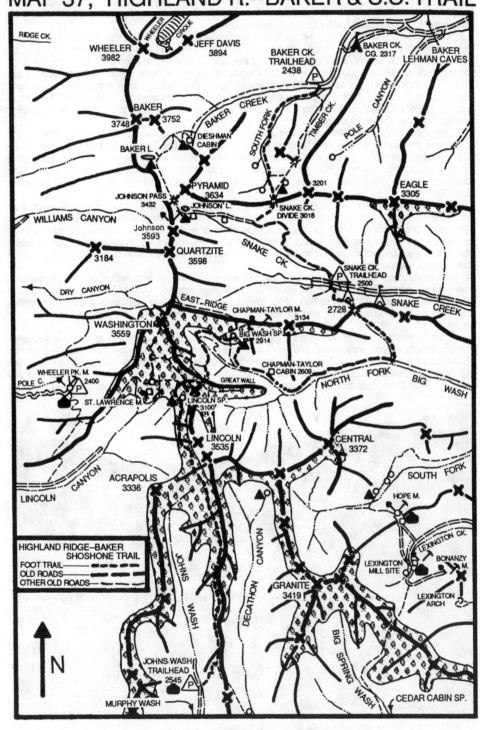

RIDGE CK.

WHEELER
3982

JEFF DAVIS
3894

BAKER CK.
TRAILHEAD
2438

BAKER CK.
CG. 2317

BAKER
LEHMAN CAVES

BAKER CREEK

BAKER
3748   3752

SOUTH FORK

TIMBER CK.

POLE   CANYON

DIESHMAN
CABIN

BAKER L.

PYRAMID
3634

JOHNSON PASS
3432

JOHNSON'S L.

3201

SNAKE CK.
DIVIDE 3018

EAGLE
3305

WILLIAMS   CANYON

Johnson
3593

3184

QUARTZITE
3598

SNAKE   CK.

DRY   CANYON

EAST-RIDGE

CHAPMAN-TAYLOR M.
3134

SNAKE CK.
TRAILHEAD
2500

SNAKE   CREEK

2728

WASHINGTON
3559

BIG WASH SP.
2914

CHAPMAN-TAYLOR
CABIN 2609

NORTH   FORK   BIG   WASH

WHEELER PK. M.
POLE C.   2400

ST. LAWRENCE M.

GREAT WALL

LINCOLN SP.
3100

LINCOLN
3535

CENTRAL
3372

SOUTH   FORK

ACRAPOLIS
3336

HOPE M.

LINCOLN   CANYON

LINCOLN

LEXINGTON CK.

BONANZY
M.

LEXINGTON
MILL SITE

JOHNS   WASH

DECATHON   CANYON

GRANITE
3419

LEXINGTON
ARCH

HIGHLAND RIDGE--BAKER
SHOSHONE TRAIL
FOOT TRAIL
OLD ROADS
OTHER OLD ROADS

N

BIG   SPRING   WASH

JOHNS WASH
TRAILHEAD
2545

MURPHY WASH

CEDAR CABIN SP.

SCALE   0   1   2   3   4   5   6   7   KMS

end of the last stand of aspens, look carefully to your right, or east. The sign stating, _Highland Ridge Trailhead_, is off the road 8 or 10 meters, and a little hard to see. The sign reads: _Lincoln Spring 7(11 kms); Big Wash Spring 11(18 kms); Snake Creek 18(29 kms); and Baker Creek 23(37 kms)._ The vehicle track actually goes further up the canyon a ways.

The trail heads to the right, then north and northeast into a minor drainage of the long Highland Ridge emanating from Lincoln Peak. At first you can follow the trail easily, but further up, it's lost in the pines. But don't worry, just head straight up this little canyon to the ridge-top. Once on the ridge, you can pick up the trail again, but it's never very easy to follow. In some places you can actually see the trail; in other places you can see the markers on trees. This trail was built in the 1920's, and hasn't been used much since. It stays right on the ridge-top nearly all the way to Lincoln Peak. As it nears Lincoln, it tends to stay down in the trees on the west side of the mountain. If you want to climb Lincoln, just stay on the ridge-top.

Beyond Lincoln Peak, the trail stays down in the trees, a mixture of Englemann spruce, and bristlecone and limber pines. Not far before you arrive at Lincoln Spring, the trail turns into an old mining exploration track. This short little section of trail-road, the author hasn't seen. Lincoln Spring will be on your right, looking north. It doesn't put out much water, and it might be hard to locate, but it flows year-round. Don't miss this one, as it's a pretty good walk(7 kms) to the next waterhole, Big Wash Spring.

From Lincoln Spring, you'll be walking along an old miners track first to the west a ways, then north, then it veers back to the east. About 1.5 kms from the spring, is a 4-way junction with the remains of an old cabin nearby. Going south from there, is another old track which you take to climb the north ridge of Lincoln; going north is the track which heads up Mt. Washington, then it circles around to the south and to the St. Lawrence Mine, which is on the west side of a minor canyon on the south face of Washington.

The easiest way to reach the St. Lawrence Mine from the 4-way, is to walk due west. In the area where the old mining track veers to the south, you walk west instead. The old Baker-Shoshone Trail is there somewhere, but it's hard to find. Best to just forget the trail, and just walk towards the setting sun. Cross over the little canyon, and not far beyond, will be a north-south running road and cabins of the mine.

Back to the trail. From the 4-way, the tract running east, or southeast, is the one you take. Watch carefully as you walk along and you'll see trail markers on some trees. At this point the old Baker-Shoshone Trail was used as a guide for the still later-built miners track. Soon the trail veers left and zig zags down the steep slope to the north and into the head of North Fork of Big Wash. If you were to stay on the miners track, you would end up at the North Face of Lincoln, or along the big ridge

This sign is at, or very near, the Snake Creek Trailhead.

running east of the 4-way junction labeled the "Great Wall".

As you head down the trail into North Fork, look ahead for still another old track which circles around the eastern flanks of Washington. Use this track instead of trying to follow the old trail and tree markers. Eventually this track turns east and runs along the south face of the big East Ridge of Washington(see Map 27, Mt. Washington-Big Wash Route). Further on, you'll come to another junction. The track running to your upper left goes to part of the Chapman-Taylor(Big Wash) Mine on the ridge-top. But stay on the track running straight ahead. This track ends at the Big Wash Spring. Make sure you stock up on water at this spring, because you're next water stop is at Snake Creek.

This part of the old 1920's built Baker-Shoshone Trail is supposed to pass right by the spring, but the author never saw it. From the spring, the trail is shown on maps as running down a little drainage to the south. At the canyon bottom, it turns left or east, and heads down canyon. But the easiest way to reach the canyon bottom, is to back-track from the spring about a half km, and follow a faint old bulldozer track down the minor ridge to the west of the drainage where the trail is supposed to be. Take either the old trail(if you can find it) or the miners track, but just get down into the bottom of North Fork. There you can barely see in places, still another old track or trail, running to the mouth of North Fork of Big Wash to the east.

As you walk down North Fork, look for the old roof-less Chapman-Taylor Cabin on your left. The cabin will not give you shelter, but it could be a campsite(no water). Continue down canyon. Soon you'll pass down a steep narrows section of the canyon, where there is no sign of any trail or track. Finally, about two kms from the cabin, you'll pass through an area of avalanche debris, then what remains of the old track in North Fork. From that point on down it's a pretty good trail(in places), and relatively easy walking.

About half way down North Fork of Big Wash, you'll see the ridge on your left(north) pull back into a minor canyon. This is where the next part of the trail is. The author hasn't been in this short section, but all the maps show a trail being there. Look for it right in the bottom of the drainage. The author has been up to the ridge-top at Pass 2728 meters from the Snake Creek side, but on the south side of the pass, he missed the trail in the open sagebrush slope. Surely you'll have to do some route-finding in this 2 km section of the hike up to the Pass 2728.

When you arrive on the ridge-top at 2728 meters, you can then pick up a good trail heading down to Snake Creek. You'll arrive at Snake Creek right where the Snake Creek Trailhead is found. At that point you'll see another sign pointing out the way to the south. It reads:_Shoshone Trail_; Big Wash 3(5 kms); Lincoln Spring 12(19 kms); and Murphy Wash Road 19(30.4 kms).

The next leg of the journey is along another old mining track, but one which presently(1988) gets some 4WD vehicle use. After about 4 kms, watch carefully on your right for the trail heading for the

An old Beaver, flathead motor, just above Johnson Lake.

Snake Creek Divide and the South Fork of Baker Creek. In 1987, the sign at that junction faced the west and was high and half hidden in a pine tree. Hopefully someone from the GBNP can return to this spot, remedy the problem, and make the sign more visible.

Once on this trail, you'll walk east and northeast angling up the slope to the ridge-top, and the divide between Snake and Baker Creeks. Shortly after you begin down the other side, you arrive at another signposted junction. One trail heads down Timber Creek; the other down South Fork of Baker Creek. South Fork trail might be the best. Either way you go, you'll have some water just below the divide. After you walk down the good trail in South Fork, and as you're very near the Baker Creek Trailhead, you'll see several cow trails. It would be easier to locate the trailhead if coming down the canyon(south to north), than to find the right trail as you leave this trailhead and walk south or up South Fork Canyon.

There's an alternate route and trail for this last section of the hike, which is probably the best route to take. Instead of going up toward Snake Ck. Divide, and down either the South Fork or Timber Creek to the Baker Creek Trailhead, head west to Johnson Lake and the old Johnson Tungsten Mine. Read all about this interesting site under Map 20. From Johnson Lake, walk up the trail to Johnson Pass, the divide between Snake and Baker Creeks. Then you simply walk down the trail to Baker Lake, the Dieshman Cabin, and on to the Baker Creek Trailhead. By taking this alternate trail, it would give you a chance to see the old mine site, climb Pyramid, Johnson and Baker Peaks, and give you a couple of fine campsite as well. It would also add two or three kms to the 37 previously stated, making the hike about 40 kms long.

For those who prefer to ridge-walk rather than follow a trail, here's still another alternate route along this long hike. From the area of Lincoln Spring and the St. Lawrence Mine, head north to the summit of Mt. Washington and walk the ridge north. You will pass near a very good grove of bristlecone pines on the upper or western end of the East Ridge of Washington. You will then walk over the summits of Quartzite and Johnson Peaks, before arriving at Johnson Pass. This part of the trip can be done in half a day easily, and you'll have nice views all the way. It's easy walking on this ridge, and much faster than staying on the trail from Lincoln Spring or the St. Lawrence Mine, to Johnson Lake. If you take this ridge route, there's no water until Johnson Lake.

Elevations Johns Wash Trailhead, 2545 meters; highest point actually on the trail, about 3200; pass between North Fork of Big Wash and Snake Creek, 2728; Snake Creek Divide, 3018; Johnson Pass, 3432; and the Baker Creek Trailhead, 2438 meters.

Best Time and Time Needed As with climbing any of the high summits in the South Snake Range, the season for this hike will be from about mid-June until about mid-October. However, early or late in the season, you may find wet trails or a little snow in the higher places. If you go early in the season, some snowdrifts will eliminate possible water problems. Most people could walk this trail in two days, with a camp at either Big Wash Spring or along Snake Creek. But doing it in two days wouldn't really allow you time to see many of the old mines or climb any of the nearby peaks(Washington, Lincoln, Pyramid or Baker). Maybe the best plan would be to do it in three days, with camps at Lincoln Spring and Johnson Lake. This would allow you to see most of the interesting sites in the range on this one trip. Doing it in four days would allow for even more sightseeing and mountain climbing along the way.

Water Lincoln Spring, Big Wash Spring, Snake Creek, springs at the head of South Fork of Baker Creek, Johnson and Baker Lakes and along Baker Creek or South Fork of Baker.

Camping Obviously you must plan to camp near water, or carry water in a large jug to more favorable campsites. At Lincoln and Big Wash Springs, please camp back a ways from the water, so as not to disturb wildlife(or have wildlife disturb you in the night).

Geology From Johns Wash Trailhead on up until you come to the bottom of Snake Creek, you'll be hiking along *limestone* ridges, mountains and canyon walls. From a point just above the Snake Creek Trailhead you'll come to lighter colored *granite*, and you'll be with this rock until about half way down South Fork of Baker Creek, or until you get to Johnson Pass. Then it's the *Prospect Mountain Quartzite*, until you reach the valley of Baker Creek, then *glacial deposits* will be seen.

Maps USGS or BLM maps Garrison(1:100,000), or Garrison and Wheeler Peak(1:62,500), or one of the geology maps MF-1343 A, B, or C(1:62,500), or Humboldt National Forest(1:125,000).

Looking west at the East Face of Pyramid Peak, from the divide between Timber Ck. and South Fork.

This cabin was built by an old prospector named Peter Dieshman(Baker Creek).

Winter Climbing in the South Snake Range

Some of the best winter climbing around can be found in the Snake Range of Eastern Nevada. The climate is one of the driest in the USA, and there are many peaks rising above timberline. This gives one a good chance to spend one or more days in the high country, without fear of being blown off the summits or ridges by an approaching storm. Yes, storms do come in, and snow piles up deep in the upper basins, but as a general rule, this country has good weather, with occasional periods of storminess. Compare this with the American northwest and western Canada, where the rule is for bad weather, with just a few periods of clear skies now and then.

There are many peaks and even more routes to choose from, but the first part of this section deals with the personal experience of the author on one of his climbs. By living fairly close to this mountain range, the author was able to watch the weather forecasts, and when good weather came, he was gone!

This particular hike was a rather long one, which began on Lexington Creek about four kms below the junction of the South Fork of Lexington and Lexington Creek itself(a km east of the Forest Service boundary). This four day hike took the author up and over the highest peaks of the South Snake Range, including Granite, Lincoln, Washington, Quartzite, Johnson, Pyramid, Baker and Wheeler. He then walked down Lehman Creek to Lehman Caves, where his car was parked.

To get started, the author hired one of the National Park Service rangers to drive him and his car up Lexington Creek, but got only as far as where the road dips down into the creek valley. Late February snows blocked the way at that point. The ranger then drove the car back to Lehman Caves, where the author picked it up at the end of the trip.

Since it was late, the author camped right where he got out of the car. Early the next morning, Day 1, he walked up the road to the west. There was just a little snow on the road at first, but after he passed through the gate at the junction of the two Lexington Creeks, he then found total snow cover. The walking was easy on hard crusted snow, until a ways past the old 1950's dam site along upper Lexington Creek. Then the snow became deeper and snowshoes were put on. This was about where the first pine trees were encountered. Then the going was much slower. The snow instantly became rather deep and powdery, because of the shade from all the trees. An early lunch was eaten at the spring at the old Lexington Mill site at 2530 meters.

He then walked south toward Pass 2871, at the head of Big Spring Wash. The snow there was even deeper and more powdery due to the north slope conditions. For this particular trip, the author purchased and used, a medium size pair of wooden snowshoes. Since he planned to get on the high ridge running north to Wheeler Peak, it was thought that for most of the trip, the snowshoes would be carried on the pack. This was indeed what happened, and the lighter and smaller snowshoes were worth the price of a new pair(about $64 for snowshoes and bindings).

However, in the deep powder, and when you really need a pair of snowshoes, the 1.5 meter-long cross-country type are the best. The author found the shorter snowshoes sank much deeper into the powder, and if there was a crust on top of the snow, he had to be very careful when lifting the 'shoe out. Otherwise the tips would catch on the crust, resulting in a fall face first in the snow. This happened four times on this trip. The cross-country snowshoes keep you upon the snow better, and the tips don't sink in like the smaller 'shoes. As in skiing, one has to be alert and pay attention at all times when using snowshoes.

Oh longer climbing trips, where one expects lots of deep snow and where snowshoes are really needed, the longer cross-country type are the best. If one were to ridge-walk long distances, with the idea of carrying snowshoes most of the way, then the shorter and lighter weight 'shoes would be best.

Upon arriving at Pass 2871, the snowshoes were removed, and crampons and expedition overboots were put on. The reason for putting on the nylon and leather-bottomed overboots, was to help keep the feet dry. But since there were some rocks exposed, crampons were also put on, to help protect the bottoms of the expedition overboots. Between the regular boots and the overboots, was placed a plastic sack. This helped keep the feet dry from the melting snows in the warm and sunny afternoons. On a long hike or climb, keeping the boots dry is very important. In really cold weather, you won't have any trouble with boots getting wet from melting snow.

Camp I was set up on the ridge and in some trees, about half way between Pass 2871 and Granite Peak. Day 1 lasted 8 hours and 3 minutes and the camp was at 3200 meters elevation. This first day was the hardest of all. The pack was as big as it ever got, the body wasn't yet used to the huge pack, there was a big altitude gain, and lots of deep powder(about a meter) in the area above the Lexington Mill site. After this first day the going was much easier.

In the afternoon of the first day(and each subsequent day), the sleeping bag, boots and expedition overboots were all laid out over the tent to dry. For the most part they were dry upon retiring for the night, but in the morning the stove was used to thaw and warm up the boots. This practice was for the author, and will be for you, standard practice every afternoon and morning, for longer winter climbs.

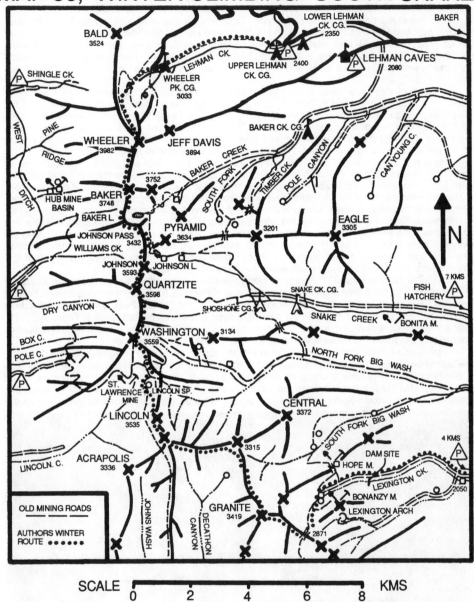

Be sure you have extra fuel for your stove, so you can dry and warm up boots each morning. An alternate procedure would be to place the boots in the sleeping bag each night. Always do your best to keep boots from getting wet in the first place.

Another reminder for those who might choose a winter climb of several days where they plan to stay on the ridges and away from any running water. You'll have to melt snow for water. This means carrying a lot more fuel than one would need on a summer hike; and more fuel than would be needed if you were planning to camp near a water source.

The author uses a small Optimus 100, kerosene stove, and it took about 1 to 1.5 hours each night to melt enough snow for supper, breakfast and the next days lunch. For a quick exit in the mornings, and to take advantage of the hard frozen snow, one must melt the snow at night. If the nights are extremely cold, then you must keep the water in one or two water bottles in the sleeping bag with you; otherwise, it's hard to pour *frozen water* out of the bottle in the mornings.

Here are some tips on how to melt snow. Take a large plastic bag, or the stuff sack for your sleeping bag, and fill it with the slushiest and wettest snow you can find. Any snow partially melted by the sun is best. Place the sack next to the stove, which melts it down a little more. As snow is melted, pour the water into a cup or bottle, and refill the kettle with more snow. Remember, the more melted the snow is when you place it in the kettle, the faster it will melt-down to water. It will also take less fuel.

The type of stove one takes is a matter of personal preference. The author uses a kerosene stove. If you're out traveling in any Third World country, like all over South America or in the Himalayas, you can find kerosene in virtually every village. If you spill kerosene in your tent, it won't light, or burn your tent down, as gasoline would. These are two reasons he prefers kerosene. But it's sometimes a little hard to find kerosene these days in this country. The very best stove to have would be one which can burn several different kinds of fuel, then you can always find something.

Day 2 was a much easier day. The author first walked the frozen and crusty ridge to the top of Granite. This was easy on the south facing part of the ridge-top. Just before the summit of Granite, and on the east face, the snow was soft and often knee-deep in places, but this didn't last long. From Granite, the windblown and rocky northwest ridge was used in heading north. The wind must howl pretty hard on this ridge at times, because almost all the snow was blown away.

Between Granite and Peak 3315, the ridge averages about 3100-3200 meters altitude and is tree covered; thus the snow is not blown off, nor is it made extra hard by strong winds. One could likely get away with putting a tent up on this ridge, even with an impending storm. The author kept his expedition overboots and crampons on, although snowshoes would have worked equally well. This part of the hike is up and down, and the snow much softer than on the higher ridges.

Just to the west of Peak 3315, the ridge finally rises above timberline, which means the winds are unobstructed. For the author this meant the snow was either rock-hard, or it was completely blown off the ridge. For about half the distance between Peak 3315 and Lincoln Peak, the author walked on bare ground; or next to bare rocks on the rock-hard snow. This was the last week of February, 1988, after a warm spell and during a drier than normal winter. Walking along the summit ridge toward Lincoln, one has some fine views of the North and Northwest Faces of the peak.

From Lincoln Peak, one must drop down into the forest zone before reaching Mt. Washington. The author once again had to use snowshoes for about 3 kms to gain access to the upper south face of Washington. In this area, it would be fairly easy to get to the St. Lawrence Mine, but there is a rather deep little canyon running down the mountain just east of the old cabins and mine. Also, the author never saw Lincoln Spring. It has such a small discharge, it's likely buried for the winter by the

A winter scene at the old Lexington Mill site in Lexington Canyon.

first snow of each season.

The author made Camp II at the end of the second day, just north of Lincoln Spring and just east of the St. Lawrence Mine. The second day involved 8 hours of walking, and camp was made at 3265 meters elevation.

Another thing you might think about before starting out on a long climb such as this one, is some kind of a first aid kit. With some people these things can get out of hand, but if you need something, you'd best be prepared. Normally the author takes only a small box of bandaids; some will want more than that. Besides some kind of first aid kit, you should consider taking a small bottle of aspirin. At the end of a long day with a huge pack, and at higher altitudes than you're accustomed to, aspirin helps you relax and sleep better. This is true for any high mountain camp.

On a long hike, where you're washing pots and pans with your hands, you may find the skin around your finger nails becomes cracked and sore. The reason for this is that high mountain air is a lot drier than you realize. This is not just a problem for Himalayan expeditions. A little hand location helps prevent the cracking in the first place, and bandaids help them heal.

During this four day climb, the author walked from about 7:30 AM until 3:30 PM each day, then camp was set up and everything had a chance to dry in the afternoon sun. Some may want to spread things out when eating lunch around mid-day. However, for this trip the author chose to get out and climb early, then set up camp early, and dry everything at that time. This allowed him to take advantage of the hard frozen snow in the mornings. It took the author about 1.5 hours each morning to heat water, cook breakfast, eat, thaw and warm up boots, pack up the camp, and start walking.

Going up the south face of Washington was easy. The snow was very hard, partly due to the winds, but mostly because it faces directly south. The south facing slopes remember, are sun-drenched, and the snow partially melted in the afternoons; then the snow re-freezes at night and is much harder in the morning hours. The upper part of Washington, that part above the bristlecone forest, was again blown clean of snow for the most part, and the author walked on rocks part of the time.

From the summit of Washington to the north ridge of Wheeler Peak, there are no more trees on the ridge. Snowshoes or skis are normally not needed along this part of the climb, but that would depend on the wind conditions just after each storm. Normally you'll find very strong south winds ahead of an approaching cold front; and strong northerly winds blowing as the storm moves on to the east and out of the area. It's definitely not a good idea to place a tent on this ridge, unless you're sure of continued good weather.

Just on the north side of Washington, and on it's upper East Ridge, is a fine grove of bristlecone pines. Taking fotos of this stand of trees is even better in winter than in summer. And it's only a 100 meters out of the way. Just north of this grove of bristlecones, the areas of limestone rock ends, and the quartzite(and some granite) rocks begin. The next peak north is Quartzite Peak, named so

At the summit of Granite Peak, looking south.

because it's the most southerly of all the quartzite rock summits in the South Snake Range.

Getting up Quartzite was easy and fast, perhaps as easy in winter as it was in summer. From there you'll have a simple walk to the summit of Johnson Peak, at 3593 meters. Johnson is made of granite and is the same kind of rock as one sees at Johnson Lake below. Between Johnson Peak and Johnson Pass, the going can be a little slow because of the little pinnacles and roughness of the ridge line; but the author found traveling this part in winter, with snow filling in some of the gaps, was easier than in summer.

Johnson Pass, 3432 meters, is a broad and flat region, devoid of snow much of the time, apparently due to strong winds. From there one can get down to Johnson Lake rather easily, and view the cabins and some of the remains of the old Johnson Tungsten Mine. On the author's winter visit, there was about 1.5 meters of snow at the cabins just east of the lake. The author had hoped to get to water there, but the lake and spring were frozen over. The cable-way up to the mine was still visible, but the old motor and other equipment left there after the avalanche of the early 1930's, was buried. Read more about the Johnson Mine under Map 20, The Johnson Lake Hike.

Climbing Pyramid Peak is very easy from Johnson Pass, whether it be winter or summer. The author simply walked up the southwest ridge right to the summit in about 30 minutes or less. At the time, the winds had blown most snow off the ridge, which made this winter climb as easy as in summer.

From Johnson Pass, you have a choice of two ways to get to the summit of Baker Peak. One can stay on the ridge-top, which skirts to the south, then west, of Baker Lake; or you can drop down to Baker Lake, then walk up the south face of Baker Peak. It might be easier to take this latter route, because the south slope of Baker is sun drenched and should be easy walking much of the time. This would also allow you to camp in the shelter of trees, and give you fine views of the Baker Lake Cirque in winter.

The alternative is to ridge-walk all the way from Johnson Pass to Baker Peak. But this is surely the hardest part of the entire South Snake Range Summit Ridge to negotiate. But this is the route the author took. The difficulty lies in the many small peaks or pinnacles along this "cockscomb" ridge. The best thing to do is to stay down 25 to 50 meters on the south or the west face, rather than right on the ridge crest. By doing this, you can avoid the up and down nature of the ridge-top. The author found the going slow in this part; partly because of the larger meter-sized boulders, and partly because the snow in between the boulders was softer than expected. It was a battle between hard rocks and soft snow.

The author made Camp III high on the south ridge of Baker Peak at an altitude of 3640 meters. Walk-time for Day 3 was 7 hours and 40 minutes. This camp was right on the ridge, because the weather looked good for the next 12 hours. Up to this camp, it had been three days of perfect weather. But by the next morning, Day 4, clouds came in, ruining any hope for more really good fotos for the rest of the trip.

The upper East Ridge of Mt. Washington and the bristlecone pines.

Once on the south ridge of Baker Peak, the going was again easy on rock-hard snow. It will be easy to get to both the east and west summits of Baker, even in winter. From Baker to the summit of Wheeler Peak was another easy walk, but it does steepen on the south ridge. And the higher you go, the harder the snow. The snow was so hard in places, no footprints were left behind. From along this ridge between Baker and Wheeler, you'll have some good foto opportunities of the north face of Baker.

From the summit of Wheeler, one could easily ridge-walk east to the top of Jeff Davis, then go on down the East Ridge to the visitor center at Lehman Caves. But the normal route down is along Lehman Creek. This may be the best and surely the most used way up and down the mountain.

The author had planned to take a full five days for this mini-expedition, and explore the Wheeler Cirque Basin and reach the summit of Bald Mountain as well, but bad weather changed all plans. He instead went straight down to Stella Lake, put on the snowshoes, and walked down canyon. The snowshoes were taken off about half way down Lehman Creek, then it was walking in wet snow to the end of the plowed road at Upper Lehman Creek Campground.

This same trail had been used off and on all winter by several other groups going to Wheeler Peak, so it was well used and easy to follow. This last day was on relatively good snow, at least for snowshoeing or skiing. From the Wheeler Peak Campground to the Upper Lehman Creek Campground, is a distance of 7 kms and it took 1.5 hours. The author then walked down the road to Lehman Caves, a distance of about 5 kms, making the fourth day, 7.5 hours long. The paved Wheeler Peak Scenic Drive is cleared of snow on a year-round basis, up to the big sweeping curve in the road at the lower end of the Upper Lehman Creek Campground.

It's hoped this brief description of one of the author's personal experiences will help those who have had less time in the mountains in winter. In the beginning part of this book is a further discussion on some of the equipment one must have for a successful winter climb.

Normal Route to Wheeler Peak

For those who would just prefer to climb Wheeler Peak and not get involved in some kind of mini-expedition to a dozen peaks, here's how it can be done. The normal route up Wheeler in winter is along Lehman Creek. In summer this route is seldom used, because nowadays you can drive all the way to the upper basin along the Wheeler Peak Scenic Drive. However, in winter this paved road is closed, requiring hikers to use the old route or trail to Wheeler Peak, the one used before the road was built.

From Lehman Caves and the visitor center to Great Basin National Park, drive down the road in the direction of Baker, but after one km, turn to the left, or north and onto the Wheeler Peak Scenic Drive. After 3 kms you'll pass the Lower Lehman Creek Campground on the south or left. After another km, you come to a big curve in the road, which is where you can enter the Upper Lehman Creek Campground. During the winter months, the road is cleared of snow up to this point, but only the lower campground is kept open on a year-round basis. This is the only campground in the park open

Cabin near Johnson Lake, with a meter and a half of snow on the ground.

for 12 months a year.

You can park there at a parking lot on the curve and walk west into the upper campground. After another 500 meters or so, you'll come to the actual trailhead with a sign pointing out the way. It's 7 kms to the upper basin and the Wheeler Peak Campground. This trail is often used in winter for ski touring and by climbers heading for Wheeler Peak, so it should be easy to follow at all times. The trail zig zags some, therefore is not too steep.

At several locations along this trail are small springs or short streams. This water should be excellent, especially in winter, as there are no cattle anywhere near the area. If you should hike this trail in summer, take water right from one of the springs.

At the western end of the Wheeler Peak Campground, is a big wooden trail sign showing a map of the Wheeler Peak area. From this spot, go about due west and along the summer trail heading for Stella Lake. For those winter climbing, it's probably just as easy to stay on or near the summer trail to the summit. From near Stella Lake, the trail zig zags up to the ridge-top to the west, then heads south along the main ridge running between Bald Mtn. to the north, and Wheeler to the south. This ridge will either be wind-blown and have rock-hard snow on it, or parts of it will have had the snow blown completely away by strong winds.

The hardest part of the climb may be getting from the basin floor up to the ridge-top which is just at timberline. Look for a slope that's exposed to the sun; because shaded or sheltered slopes remain soft and powdery, and are difficult to walk up. You'll likely have to use snowshoes or skis to get up to the ridge, but from there to the summit, you can climb with regular boots(crampons are not normally needed on this normal route).

If you're an advanced cross-country skier, then skies may be the best bet in the deep snow. However, the Lehman Creek Trail does have a lot of trees, with low branches and some steep parts. If you're not real good on skies, then better try cross-country snowshoes instead. They'll be a lot safer and simpler to use; and just as fast, if not faster.

If the snow conditions are right, this climb of Wheeler Peak can be made in one long day. Mike Nicklas, a park ranger, once climbed Wheeler via the Lehman Creek Trail and this route just described in 6 hours. Coming down took him about another 2 hours, for an 8 hour day. This was in late February, and after a long dry and warm spell. He used cross-country skis up until the ridge, then ridge-walked with regular climbing boots to the summit.

On another mid-March climb, the author walked up the Lehman Creek Trail to the Wheeler Peak CG. He got about half way up this trail before he had to put on snowshoes. Near Stella Lake, he turned northwest, and made a beeline to the summit of Bald Mountain. The summit was reached in 3 hrs.; 7 min. An easy climb, and the best place to get good fotos of Wheeler and Jeff Davis Peaks. After an early lunch at the summit, he headed down to Stella Lake, then more-or-less along the summertime trail into about the middle of the Wheeler Cirque Basin. Then on down the trail to the car, in a total round-trip time of 7 hrs.; 7 min. Snow conditions were about as good as could be expected and the weather clear and mild.

There are other possible routes up Wheeler Peak as well. One would be the East Ridge, which runs from behind Lehman Caves right up to the summits of Jeff Davis and Wheeler. Early in the season, and before much snow is on the ground, you might drive up the gravel road toward the Baker Creek Campground, and get on the ridge from the same place as the summer hike describes. However, the park service closes this road in winter, to prevent it from being rutted by vehicles when the road base is saturated by melting snow. You could walk up this road however, or walk right from the visitor center. One could also walk(with permission) into the park residential area just south of the visitor center, and get onto one of the branches of the East Ridge, and go up from there. If using the East Ridge route, remember to stay on the south side of the ridge-top, to take advantage of the harder wind-blown snow. With the right snow conditions, this would also be an easy, but long one day climb.

Another way to Wheeler Peak would be from the west side of the range and Spring Valley. The best route up in winter from the west would be up Shingle Creek and the ridge just to the south. You probably won't get too far up the road from the highway from about December 1 until early March, but you can always walk the last little ways. If you use this route after late March, you will likely be able to drive about as far as in summer. Read about the access route and see the map under Map 6, Wheeler Peak--West Face Route. A high clearance vehicle will help in getting close to the base of this ridge.

One could also climb Wheeler Peak from the Hub Mine Basin, but getting to the beginning of this route is even more difficult than to Shingle Creek.

Keep in mind, the coldest 90 days of the year in this part of the country is from November 23 until February 23. Usually during this period, you will find powdery snow in the upper basins. Early in the season, say late November, there won't be much on the ground, so it shouldn't slow you down too much. But later in the year, in December, January and February, you'll normally find lots of deep powder, making travel slow and difficult.

If you'll wait until March, to allow the higher sun and warmer temps to compact and settle the

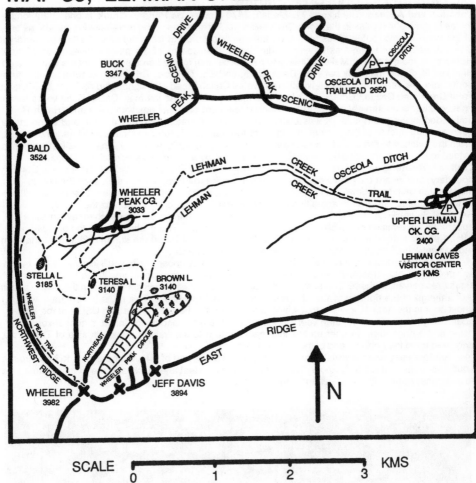

snow, it'll be much easier climbing. If you wait until April, it's possible you could do this climb of Wheeler Peak, or any other high mountain, without snowshoes or skis--depending on the year. Another reason to do a climb early in winter, or wait until March, is that there isn't as much snow at lower elevations. This makes it easier to get up the access roads and closer to the mountains in your car. Another good reason for going in March, is that you'll have much longer days than in December or January. Remember, you'll have the same amount of daylight on March 21, as you will on September 21.

Access routes to other Mountains

If you're heading up Baker Creek to Baker Lake or Baker Peak in the dead of winter, expect to walk from the beginning of the gravel road which runs up to the Baker Creek Campground and Baker Creek Trailhead. This would be a 7 or 8 kms walk from the Baker–Lehman Caves Road.

If you're going to Mt. Washington via Pole Canyon and the Wheeler Peak Mine, expect to walk the last 3 or 4 kms up to the mine in the middle of winter. In late March though, you could likely drive to the mine, before beginning the walk up the old 4WD road to the summit. If you're hoping to enter the mountains along Snake Creek, then you will always be able to make it up to the fish hatchery, but in the dead of winter, not far beyond.

If you're planning a winter climb, it's always best to stop at the park visitor center at Lehman Caves, to check on road conditions and let the rangers know of your plans. Also, it's possible to hire one of the park employees to drive you out to some remote starting point, and drive your vehicle back to the park headquarters, as did the author.

Mt. Moriah–Hendrys Creek Route

Location and Access The hike to Mt. Moriah, 3673 meters, via Hendrys Creek, is one of the longer routes to the highest peak in the North Snake Range. It's also one of the more popular, as well as one of the more scenic routes. This hike is on the southeast side of the mountain. Getting to Hendrys Creek is easier, and with less driving on dirt roads, than to any of the other trailheads on Moriah. Here's how you get there. Make your way to the Border Inn, located on the Utah-Nevada state line on Highway 50-6, the main link between Delta, Utah, and Ely, Nevada. Drive east about a km and turn north onto the very good and all-weather graveled Callao Road. It's signposted for Gandy, Partoun, Trout Creek and Callao. Go about 13 kms to a major junction. As the main Callao Road veers to the right, you continue straight ahead to the stone monument and mail box with the name "Hatch Rock" embedded in the south side. It was built by a guy named Hatch, who has a cabin and some stone quarries at the mouth of the canyon. From there the road slowly turns to the left and heads northwest. From the junction to the end of the road on Hendrys Creek is about another 7 kms. This last section is a good road, and maintained by the BLM. It can be used by any car under normal conditions.

Trail or Route Conditions The trailhead on Hendrys Ck. is located at the Forest Service boundary, and where they have put up a barricade on the road where it once crossed the creek. You may want to park back down the road about 200 meters, so as to park in the shade of some tall willows. In the beginning, the trail is actually along an old road, which once ran up to the pre-World War I Hendrys Sawmill. A third the way up the canyon, you'll see an old stone chimney on the right, apparently the remains of a cabin, which is that old sawmill site. This is about where the old road ends. After that, it's a good trail all the way into the lower basin just below the summit ridge of Moriah. In recent years the Forest Service has done some trail maintenance.

When you reach a meadow area in the lower part of this upper basin, you'll likely lose the trail in an area of an old sheepherders campsite(2700 meters). At that point, you'll see many trees with signatures carved on them. The author ended up hiking up another trail not shown on the maps, and in the drainage to the right(shown on this map with the route symbol). This route is very easy walking and it seems the natural way(the trail which is shown on the Forest Service and USGS maps actually goes straight ahead a ways, then veers to the left or northwest, and heads into a minor canyon, before rising to the ridge-top). Further up this little canyon, turn to the west at the south side of The Table, and head up to the northern end of the summit ridge.

Another easy route possibility after you reach the lower part of the upper basin, is to head up the southeast ridge of the South Peak. This would be the shortest and quickest route to the summit. It's also another route with lots of tall and straight bristlecone pines.

What remains of the Hendrys Sawmill, in Hendrys Creek Canyon.

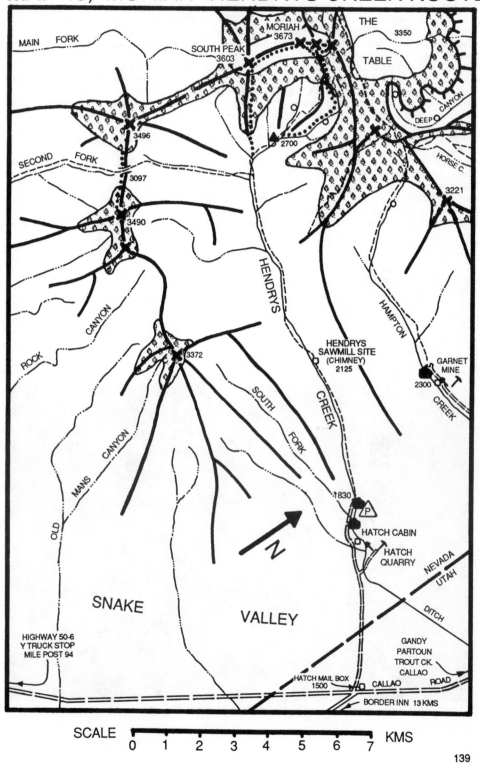

MAIN FORK

SECOND FORK

SOUTH PEAK
3603

MORIAH
3673

THE TABLE
3350

3496

3097

3490

2700

DEEP CANYON

HORSE C.

3221

HENDRYS

ROCK CANYON

3372

HAMPTON

HENDRYS
SAWMILL SITE
(CHIMNEY)
2125

GARNET
MINE
2300

CREEK

OLD MANS CANYON

SOUTH FORK

CREEK

1830

P

HATCH CABIN

HATCH
QUARRY

NEVADA
UTAH

SNAKE

VALLEY

DITCH

N

HIGHWAY 50-6
Y TRUCK STOP
MILE POST 94

GANDY
PARTOUN
TROUT CK.
CALLAO
ROAD

HATCH MAIL BOX
1500

CALLAO

BORDER INN 13 KMS

SCALE 0 1 2 3 4 5 6 7 KMS

Near the upper end of the Hendrys Creek Canyon(below the campsite), you will see a sign pointing out an old trail to Second Fork. If you go up that canyon to the pass at 3097 meters, you can then climb two high but un-named peaks, at 3496 and 3490 meters.

Elevations Trailhead, 1830 meters; The Table, 3350; South Peak, 3603; Mt. Moriah, 3673 meters.

Best Time and Time Needed From mid-June until mid-October, but expect to run into snow high on the mountain during June and October. It's about 11 or 12 kms to the trail running off to Second Fork of Silver Creek, and about another 6 or 7 kms to the summit. This is a long all day climb for strong hikers; a two day hike for others. The author made the climb via The Table, then returned via the South Peak and it's southeast ridge. It took 4 hrs. 10 min. up; 7 hrs. 50 min. round-trip.

Water Hendrys Creek has good water and is large enough to support native trout throughout the canyon. During the summer months there may be cattle in the canyon.

Camping At or near the trailhead, and anywhere up the canyon. This is perhaps the nicest canyon in the entire Snake Range for hiking and overnight camping. That's why it's recommended some people do the climb of Moriah in two days.

Geology The entire walk from the trailhead to the base of the summit ridge is along the *Prospect Mountain Quartzite Formation.* This is the same formation Hatch is getting his building stone(sometimes called flagstone) from at the mouth of the canyon The summit ridge is composed of the *Notch Peak Limestone.* As a result of the limestone rocks and soil, there is a large stand of bristlecone pines around the perimeter of the summit ridge.

Maps USGS or BLM maps Ely(1:100,000), or Ely(1:250,000), or Humboldt National Forest(1:125,000).

An old sheepherders camp in the upper end of Hendrys Creek Canyon.

Mt. Moriah, as seen from the east, and the head of Hendrys Creek.

From Moriahs north ridge, looking northeast at The Table.

Mt. Moriah—Hampton Creek Trail

Location and Access Of the six different routes to Mt. Moriah, covered in this book, the trail up Hampton Creek is probably the best all around. If a *route normal* had to be selected, this is likely it. Here's how to get to the trailhead on Hampton Creek. Drive along Highway 50-6, the main link between Delta, Utah, and Ely, Nevada. One km east of the Utah-Nevada state line(where the Border Inn is located), turn north onto the very good graveled Callao Road heading in the direction of Gandy, Partoun, Trout Creek and Callao. Drive about 19 kms to the old Robinson Ranch(in 1987, the Iverson Ranch). Just beyond this ranching oasis, turn left, or west, and proceed up a well maintained road to the garnet mine in Hampton Creek Canyon. The road ends just above the old mining area and at a small primitive campsite.

Trail or Route Conditions Just north of the camp table located on Hampton Creek, is a lone toilet and nearby, the trailhead. Walk up this very good and fairly well used trail to the west. At first the trail is on the north side of the creek and follows along side an old ditch or canal, which once diverted water to the garnet mine. Further up, the trail heads north beside the creek. At the head of the canyon, the trail turns west along the high ridge which is about the same elevation as The Table. You'll likely lose the trail as you turn west at the head of the canyon, but don't worry, just head west toward the peaks. The closer you get, the easier it will be to find the way. Further on, the trail follows along the south side of The Table, and directly toward the head of Big Canyon. At a convenient place, leave the trail, and climb southwest over two minor peaks before arriving at the highest summit of Moriah, at 3673 meters. It's an easy walk all the way, and it's hard to get lost.

Elevations Trailhead, 2300 meters; The Table, 3350; Mt. Moriah, 3673 meters.

Best Time and Time Needed The normal hiking season on Moriah is from about mid-June on through about mid or late October, but each year is different. You'll surely find some snowdrifts near the summit in June and October. It's approximately 13 kms to the summit, and a long day hike. The average hiker should be able to make it there in 4 to 5 hours, and 8 to 10 hours round-trip. The author made the summit in 3 hrs. 10 min.; and round-trip in 6 hours.

Water Hampton Creek has a year-round flow which begins at the spring in the upper canyon. There is no water on The Table.

Camping There's a good campsite with a table and toilet near the creek at the trailhead, or at other sites downstream a ways.

Geology For most of the trip you'll be walking over the same type rocks you find on Wheeler Peak, the *Prospect Mountain Quartzite*. The Table is made of this rock, but some areas right at the head of Hampton Canyon are made of limestones of the *Pioche and Corset Spring Shales*. The summit ridge of Moriah is composed of the massive *Notch Peak Limestone*.

Maps USGS or BLM maps Ely(1:100,000), or Ely(1:250,000), or Humboldt National Forest(1:125,000).

From The Table, looking southwest at the northern part of the summit ridge of Moriah.

MAP 41, MORIAH--HAMPTON CREEK TRAIL

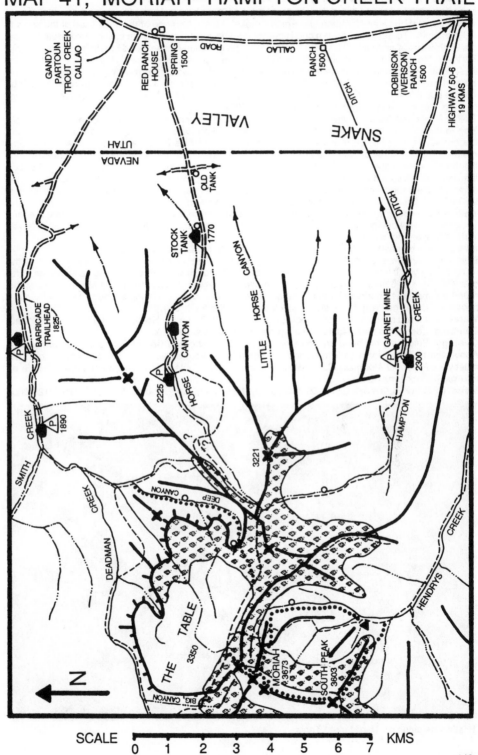

SCALE

0 1 2 3 4 5 6 7 KMS

Mt. Moriah--Horse Canyon Route

Location and Access One of the shortest routes to Moriah is via Horse Canyon, on the east side of the range, and between Hampton and Smith Creeks. This is also one of the least used of the ways to the mountain. To get there, drive along Highway 50-6, to a point about a km east of the Border Inn and the Utah-Nevada state line. Turn north onto the good graveled Callao Road heading towards Gandy, Partoun, Trout Creek and Callao. Drive about 30 kms, passing two occupied ranches, and turning west right at the red ranch house, with a good spring nearby. Go up this mostly good dirt road and into Horse Canyon. The higher you go, the worse the road is, but most cars, driven with care, should be able to make it to the end of the road. At the trailhead are several large ponderosa pines, and a sign reading, *"Horse Canyon Creek Trail: Moriah Table 5(8 kms), Big Canyon 8(13 kms)"*.

Trail or Route Conditions At the trailhead, there are two trails; one crosses the creek and makes a big loop to the south high above the stream; the second and perhaps the most used, goes up right along the creek. Further up, the two trails meet at the creek, and it's in this area you'll have to do some route-finding. The trail crosses the creek, then goes up the slope a ways to the north. Somewhere on this mostly open slope, it turns to the southwest, and heads up canyon. The author never did get on the one indicated on the maps of the area. On the way up, the author went north all the way to the ridge-top, then southwest until meeting the better trail coming up Hampton Creek, then headed west to the summit. On the way back, he went down Horse Canyon and found the trail on the north side of the creek, about where the maps have it. But then near where he lost it in the first place, he lost it again. Eventually it all worked out, but in the upper half of the canyon, you'll have to get up the best way you can, with or without a trail.

Elevations Trailhead, 2225 meters; The Table, 3350; Mt. Moriah, 3673 meters.

Best Time and Time Needed The normal hiking season is from mid-June until mid-October. With all the route-finding you'll have to do in the upper part of the canyon, it's slower than hiking up Hampton. This one will take 5 or 6 hours(maybe more) for the average person to reach the top of Moriah, making the round-trip maybe 10 hours or longer. The author made the summit in 3 hrs. 55 min.; the round-trip in 8 hours(he started half way between the stock tank and the trailhead).

Water At the red ranch house, the stock tank(1770 meters?), and in Horse Creek above the trailhead.

Camping Best at the trailhead, or half a km below; or at the stock tank.

Geology Below the trailhead are limestones from the *Pioche and Corset Spring Shale Formations.* Above the trailhead for a short distance are some intrusive *granitic* type rocks. Above that, it's mostly the *Prospect Mountain Quartzite,* which covers The Table. Moriah's summit ridge is made of the *Notch Peak Limestone.*

Maps USGS or BLM maps Ely(1:100,000), or Ely(1:250,000), or Humboldt National Forest(1:125,000).

Bristlecone pines on The(Moriah) Table.

MAP 42, MORIAH--HORSE CANYON ROUTE

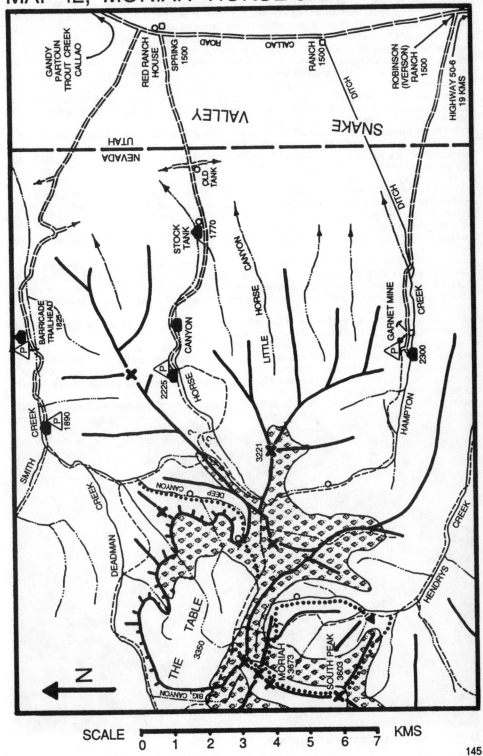

SCALE   KMS

0   1   2   3   4   5   6   7

Mt. Moriah--Smith Creek Route

Location and Access Of all the routes to Mt. Moriah, the one via Smith Creek, is the longest. This route is better for those who would like to make this climb in two days, or just do some camping in a wilderness setting. Smith Creek is located to the northeast of Moriah. To get there, first make your way to Highway 50-6 and the Border Inn at the Utah-Nevada state line. Drive a km to the east and turn north on the good graveled Callao Road heading for Gandy, Partoun, Trout Creek and Callao. Drive 30 kms; past two occupied ranches, then to a sometimes-used ranch house painted red. Go about half a km past this red ranch house, and turn west or left. Drive another 11 kms to the dirt barricade inside the mouth of Smith Canyon. This is where you start walking. Hopefully the Forest Service will remove the barricade and allow vehicles to go on to the actual end of the road, where are found shade trees, water, and a much better campsite than at the barricade. The reason for the barricade is that it's at the boundary of the proposed wilderness study area.

Trail or Route Conditions From the trailhead, walk two kms up to where the road really ends, then walk the trail up along the creek for half a km to where Deadman Creek enters from the south. There is no real Forest Service trail in this canyon, but there are trails made by fishermen and hunters, and deer, big horn sheep and cattle. The trails shown on the map are old, probably from the 1920's, and are all but useless. Might as well just make your own way along game trails. As you go up Deadman Canyon, you'll be zig zagging up along the stream. You can walk up any of the three small streams which head on The Table. The route up each canyon is about the same in difficulty, with only a little bushwhacking. The going is slower than if you are walking up a cleared trail. Once on The Table, you can then see and make your way to Mt. Moriah.

Elevations Barricaded trailhead, 1825 meters; end of road, 1890; The Table, 3350; Mt. Moriah, 3673 meters.

Best Time and Time Needed From mid-June until mid-October, but each year can be different. A round-trip climb of Moriah from this route is long and slow; probably in the neighborhood of 10 to 12 hours, for a strong hiker. A two day hike is recommended if this route is taken. The author went only to the bristlecone stand just north of the northern peaks at the head of Big Canyon and returned, all in 7 hrs. 25 min.

Water Water is in Deadman Creek and Deep Canyon, and down to as far as the upper and older trailhead(1890 meters). The lower trailhead(1825 meters) is dry.

Camping In any of the canyons enroute to Moriah, and at the lower trailhead.

Geology The big canyon walls at the mouth of Smith Creek Canyon are composed of limestones of the *Pioche and Corset Spring Shales*. At the end of the road, and on up over The Table and to the base of the peaks, you'll find the *Prospect Mountain Quartzite Formation*. The peaks themselves are made of the *Notch Peak Limestone*.

Maps USGS or BLM maps Ely(1:100,000), or Ely(1:250,000), or Humboldt National Forest(1:125,000).

October at the upper trailhead on Smith Creek.

MAP 43, MORIAH--SMITH CREEK ROUTE

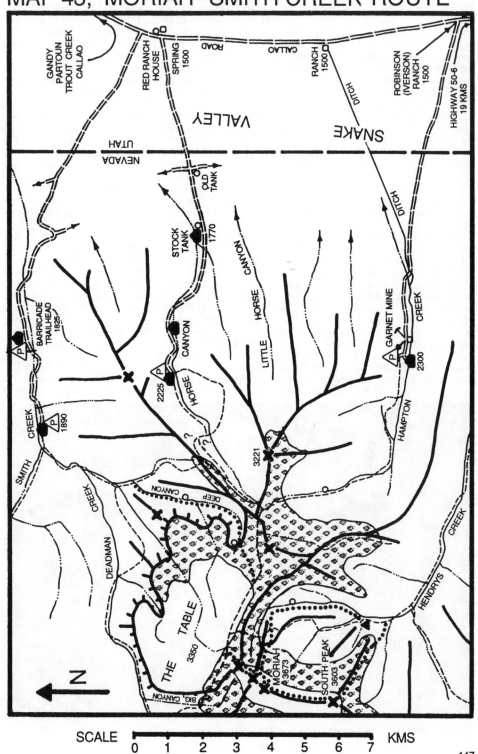

SCALE

0 1 2 3 4 5 6 7 KMS

Mt. Moriah–Four Mile Spring Route

Location and Access Depending on your mode of transportation, this hike using the road(and trail) to the east of Four Mile Spring, and to the top of Mt. Moriah, could be the shortest and easiest way; or it could be one of the longest routes(but still very easy) to the mountain. To reach the trailheads, drive along Highway 50-6 to the area just west of Sacramento Pass. Between mile posts 80 and 81, turn north onto the very good and well maintained Eight Mile Ranch Road, which runs along the east side of the northern end of Spring Valley. After 11 kms, you'll pass the road and ditch coming down from the Negro Creek Ranch. Drive north another 7 kms, and you'll come to a cattle guard and fence. Turn right or east on a rough road, and drive 4 or 5 kms to a little pass just to the north of Four Mile Spring. Those with cars or low clearance vehicles, had better stop at that point. Just above the Car-park is a very steep section of rough road going up to a kind of plateau at around 2800 meters. It's this steep part that will stop many vehicles. But if you can make it up and on top, then the road improves and it's an easy drive to the Moriah Cabin and the 4WD Trailhead near the mouth of Big Canyon. From the cattle guard at 2750 meters, it's 4 or 5 kms to the Moriah Cabin; another km to Deadman Spring; and another 2.5 or 3 kms to the 4WD Trailhead. The road to the Car-park could possibly be used in wet weather, but beyond that point it's a dry weather track only, especially on top where it's made of dirt. If you're there after a stormy period in summer, better use the Car-park no matter what your vehicle.

Trail or Route Conditions While there are many little side roads taking off from this main road running to the 4WD Trailhead, just stay on the most used track. One shouldn't have any trouble finding the way, whether driving or walking(as did the author). At the 4WD Trailhead is a sign stating, _Big Canyon Trail: Moriah Table 2(3 kms), Hendrys Creek Trail 3(5 kms), and Hampton Creek Trail 5(8 kms)._ From that point, you walk a rather good trail along a contour line to the bottom and toward the head of Big Canyon. This canyon, from it's head down to about where it empties into Deadman Canyon, was once filled with a glacier, therefore it has a "U" shape to it. At the bottom of Big Canyon, you then begin to climb back up the other side zig zag fashion. As you start the climb up, you'll begin to see scattered bristlecone pines in the forest. Once you reach the top of The Table, the bristlecones become stunted and twisted. The trees on top of The Table and just north of the northern peaks are the most fotogenic on Moriah. From the bristlecone stand, head due south for the north peak. Go over the first two lower summits any one of several ways, then ridge-walk southwest to the highest peak at 3673 meters.

Elevations Car-park, 2075 meters; top of plateau, 2750; Moriah Cabin, 2990; Deadman Spring, 2865; 4WD Trailhead, 3000; The Table, 3350; and Mt. Moriah, 3673 meters.

Best Time and Time Needed For those driving to the 4WD Trailhead, from July first until mid or late September; but from the Car-park, it can be climbed from mid-June until mid or late October. The walking distance from the Car-park to the 4WD Trailhead is about 15 kms and another 5 kms to the

October scene. Moriah as seen from near the Moriah Cabin.

MAP 44, MORIAH--FOUR MILE SP. ROUTE

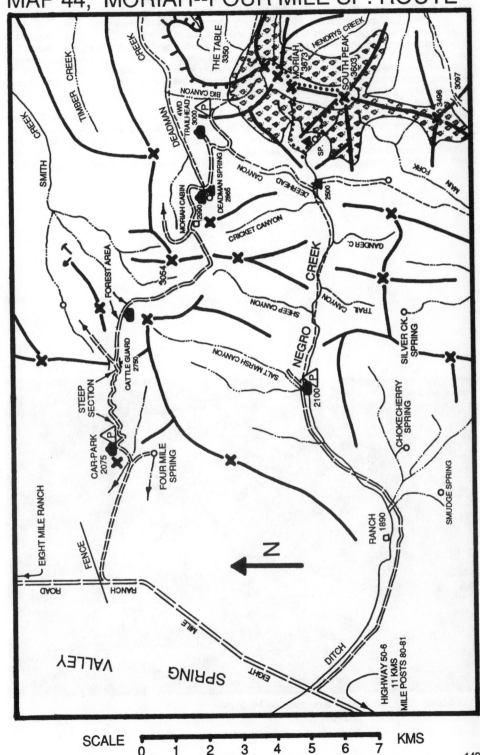

SCALE |————————————————| KMS
0   1   2   3   4   5   6   7

summit. This means a 40 km walk, round-trip. Sounds impossible to some, but the walking is very easy all the way. The author walked to the summit and back to the Car-park at 2075 meters, in 8 hrs. 35 min. round-trip. From the 4WD Trailhead, it's only about 1.5 hours to the summit.

Water If you're camping at the Car-park, be sure and have water in your car. If driving up, you can get water from the very good Deadman Spring. There's no water anywhere else along the road or trail. Four Mile Spring is to the south of the Car-park a ways and at the end of a rough road. You'll have to look for one of several of these springs. Best to bring water in your car to the Car-park.

Camping At either trailhead, or best at the Deadman Spring. The Moriah Cabin is open and free to use, but please keep it as clean as when you found it. It will sleep about 4 or 5 people on the floor. There are two small tables and two brooms inside.

Geology There are too many formations to mention, but the rocks at the Car-park and on The Table are composed of the *Prospect Mountain Quartzite*. In between those two areas, the rock is mostly limestone. The summit ridge of Moriah is made of the *Notch Peak Limestone*, giving rise to many bristlecone pines surrounding the highest peaks.

Maps USGS or BLM maps Ely(1:100,000), or Ely(1:250,000), or Humboldt National Forest(1:125,000).

The Moriah Cabin, located to the northwest of Mt. Moriah.

Deadman Spring, with just the top of Moriah showing in the background.

BIG CANYON TRAIL
● MORIAH TABLE   2
● HENDRYS CR. TR. 3
● HAMPTON CR. TR. 5

The 4WD Trailhead, just to the north of the summit of Moriah.

Mt. Moriah--Negro Creek Route

Location and Access This route to Mt. Moriah is up Negro Creek. Negro Creek drains the west slopes of Moriah and flows west into Spring Valley. Years ago there was a wagon road up this canyon, but it's been washed out in many places. There hasn't been a motor vehicle past the trailhead for years, which makes it a fine wilderness hike once again. To get there, drive to the area west of Sacramento Pass on Highway 50-6, and to between mile posts 80 and 81. Turn north onto the good and well maintained Eight Mile Ranch Road running north along the east side of Spring Valley. After about 11 kms, turn east toward the mouth of Negro Creek. After 5 or 6 kms, you'll pass the Rogers or Negro Creek Ranch at the mouth of the canyon. In another 5 or 6 kms you're at the trailhead. Any car can make it all the way.

Trail or Route Conditions From the trailhead you begin to walk up the old road, but the stream occupies the former road bed. Stay to the left and walk a cow trail for a ways. In the first 3 kms, there will be several places like this, where you have to walk one of many cow trails around places where the creek has totally washed out the road. This means there will be no more motor vehicles in the canyon. Even with the washouts and minor detours, you can move along quickly and easily. Further up, the canyon widens some and there are less willows and trees. When the old road finally peters out and heads south across the creek, you head east up stream. There are many different routes up to the summit ridge, but the one the author has taken twice, is the one up past the spring at the western base of the peaks. From the spring veer left and get up on a forested slope and a ridge coming down from the South Peak(3603 meters). Walk up this steep, but easy slope to the South Peak, then north to the main summit.

Elevations Trailhead, 2100 meters; head of the canyon, 2500; Mt. Moriah, 3673 meters.

Best Time and Time Needed As usual, from about mid-June until mid-October, but expect some snow on the peaks both early and late in the season. From the trailhead to the summit it's only 12 or 13 kms, but in places it's a little slow. Therefore, it will take the average person all day for the round-trip. The author's last trip took him to the top of the South Peak in 3 hrs. 5 min.; the round-trip, in 5 hrs. 35 min.

Water Negro Creek is a good stream, with trout. It begins at the spring at the base of the summit ridge, and flows into Spring Valley. Expect to find cattle in the lower canyon throughout the summer.

Camping There's no shade at the trailhead, but you can still camp there. Or drive back down the road a ways, and look for trees.

Geology Along much of the way, you'll see *Prospect Mountain Quartzite,* especially on the north side of the creek. Further up, you'll see limestone rocks from various strata, notably the *Guilmette Limestone.* At the west base of the summit ridge, you'll see the *Eureka Quartzite;* and the summit ridge itself is made of *Notch Peak Limestone.*

Maps USGS or BLM maps Ely(1:100,000), or Ely(1:250,000), or Humboldt National Forest(1:125,000).

The north slopes of Moriah, seen from the head of Big Canyon.

MAP 45, MORIAH--NEGRO CREEK ROUTE

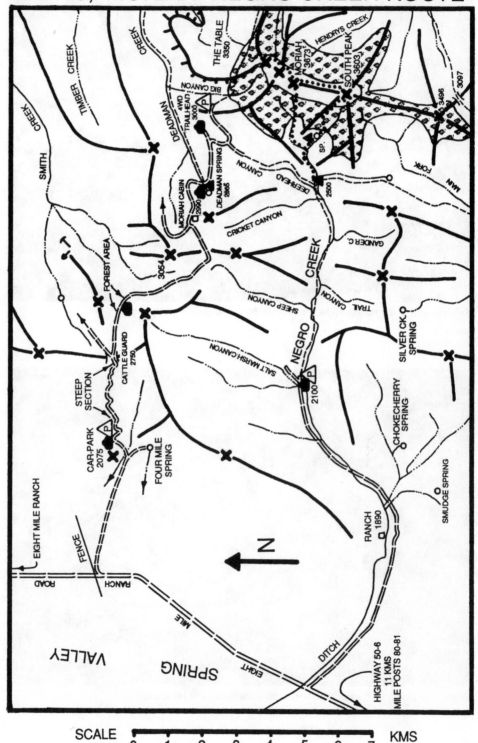

SCALE

0 1 2 3 4 5 6 7   KMS

Telefoto view of the northwest face of Moriah, from near Deadman Spring.

Bristlecone pines, on the northern end of the summit ridge of Mt. Moriah.

A winter view from the summit of Moriah.   Looking northeast at the north peaks and The Table

A late October scene along Hendrys Creek.

Winter Climbing--North Snake Range and Mt. Moriah

Hendrys Creek Route

This winter route to Mt. Moriah is the same as the one described on Map 40, Hendrys Creek. The author did this climb in mid-March 1988, after a cold spell, and toward the end of a relatively dry winter season. If you want to climb Mt. Moriah in mid-winter, this is likely the best all-around route to take.

To get to the trailhead, drive along Highway 50-6, the main link between Delta, Utah, and Ely, Nevada. About one km east of the Border Inn, which is right on the Utah-Nevada state line, turn north onto the Callao Road which runs towards Gandy, Partoun, Trout Creek and Callao. This Callao Road is a county maintained road and should be considered an all-weather, mostly gravel highway. Drive about 13 kms north of Highway 50-6 and you'll come to a major junction. If you turn left, you'll end up at the Y Truck Stop. If you veer to the right, you'll end up at the old Robinson Ranch and points north. However, proceed straight ahead and to the stone monument-like mail box with *Hatch Rock* engraved on it. From there, proceed north, then northwest toward the mouth of Hendrys Creek Canyon.

This last 7 kms of road is well used and maintained, because the Hatch guy still gets up there to mine the building stone at the mouth of the canyon. Just inside the canyon you'll see the Hatch Cabin and some of his equipment off to the right near the stream and willows. From the Hatch place to the trailhead is about half a km. This last part of the road is rougher, but any car can make it up.

The 7 kms of road from the Hatch mail box to the trailhead may be muddy in places if the weather is really wet, but stormy times are rare, so you'll likely not have any trouble. The trailhead is just at the Forest Service boundary and at a relatively low 1830 meters altitude. The low elevation of this trailhead is the major reason why this route to Moriah might be the best all around way to get to the mountain during winter.

You can camp at the trailhead, and the water in Hendrys Creek should be excellent at that time, because there won't be any cattle up stream during the winter months. There's a trail beginning at the left, which skirts around a washout of the old road. After 100 meters, you'll cross the stream to the east side, then walk the old sawmill road for 3 or 4 kms, then it gradually peters out. In recent years the Forest Service has gone into this canyon and has done some trail maintenance, at least up to about the campsite at 2700 meters. It's easy to follow the road or the trail all the way up the canyon.

On the author's trip in mid-March, he didn't find any snow on the trail until about the old Hendrys Sawmill site. Not far above the old ruins, snowshoes were put on, but at times there were bare spots on the trail. Approaching the campsite at 2700 meters, the meter-deep snow was compact and rather hard, but snowshoes were required all the way. The trail up to the campsite is a gradual climb and should be easy cruising for cross-country skiers, whether going up or down. Hendrys Creek was only

The North Face of Moriah during a winter climb.

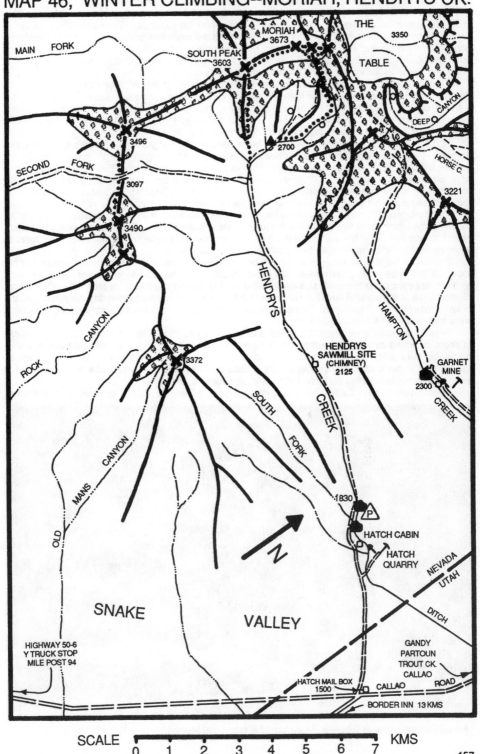

MAIN FORK

MORIAH
3673

THE
TABLE

3350

SOUTH PEAK
3603

3496

DEEP CANYON

HORSE C.

SECOND FORK

3097

2700

3221

3490

HENDRYS

HAMPTON

ROCK CANYON

HENDRYS
SAWMILL SITE
(CHIMNEY)
2125

GARNET
MINE
2300

CREEK

3372

CREEK

SOUTH FORK

OLD MANS CANYON

1830

P

N

HATCH CABIN

HATCH
QUARRY

NEVADA

UTAH

SNAKE

VALLEY

DITCH

HIGHWAY 50-6
Y TRUCK STOP
MILE POST 94

GANDY
PARTOUN
TROUT CK.
CALLAO

HATCH MAIL BOX
1500

CALLAO

ROAD

BORDER INN 13 KMS

SCALE

0   1   2   3   4   5   6   7   KMS

partially covered with snow, and it appeared that during the 1987-88 winter, one could get water directly from the stream in many locations, even in places above the campsite.

The author walked from the trailhead to the campsite at 2700 meters in just under 4 hours. This was in an afternoon, and he used snowshoes for about half the distance. Water was taken out of the stream, so melting snow wasn't necessary. Please read the route description under *Winter Climbing-- South Snake Range and Wheeler Peak*, for more discussion on some of the problems one encounters when winter climbing in this region. Some of that discussion centers on which is best, snowshoes or skies; melting snow for water, drying bedding and boots, etc,.

From the campsite in upper Hendrys Creek, you will have a choice of three routes to the summit. One is to head due north and to the right slightly and stay in the creek bottom where the route symbol is shown on the map. This route is easy, but in winter, the snow will be deep and powdery in places. Use skies or snowshoes on this one. At the head of the canyon you can either head straight for The Table, or veer to the left or west, and climb an eastern ridge of Moriah.

Another route from the campsite, would be to head north, but get on the ridge between the two streams. The author found this free of snow on the lower part, but then up high, it was soft powder, and snowshoes had to be used for a ways. Part of the old Hendrys Creek Trail runs up part of this ridge, but there's no use trying to follow it in winter. If you stay on this ridge-top, you will gradually curve around to the west and be on an eastern ridge of Moriah. Once above timberline, the snow is hard and compact, and skies or snowshoes won't be needed.

The third possible route up from the campsite, might be to veer to the northwest, and head up another ridge which terminates in about the middle of the eastern face of the summit ridge of Moriah. Expect to find this ridge fairly steep with deep and soft snow. At the top of this one, you'll have to continue west to the summit ridge, then north to the main summit.

The author walked up the ridge due north of the campsite, and came down the canyon east of this ridge. Of the three route possibilities from the campsite area, the canyon to the east, with the route symbols, appears to be the easiest, therefore the recommended approach. It took the author 2 hrs., 15 min. to reach the summit from the campsite at 2700 meters. Later that same day, he packed up the tent and returned to the trailhead. The entire second day; the climb to the top, and the long walk back to the trailhead, took 8 hours and 10 min.

When snow conditions are at their best, such as what you should find in March, it's likely you can do about the same as what the author did. That is, take half a day to reach the campsite at the base of the peaks, then reach the summit the morning of the second day. The afternoon of Day 2 will be enough time to get back to the trailhead. In the dead of winter, with a lot more powdery snow, and at lower elevations, better plan on three full days for this route to Moriah.

If you arrive on The Table after a long dry spell, you'll likely be able to walk on top of the wind-

A telefoto lense view of Wheeler Peak, from the summit of Moriah.

MAP 47, WINTER CLIMBING--MORIAH, FOUR MILE SP.

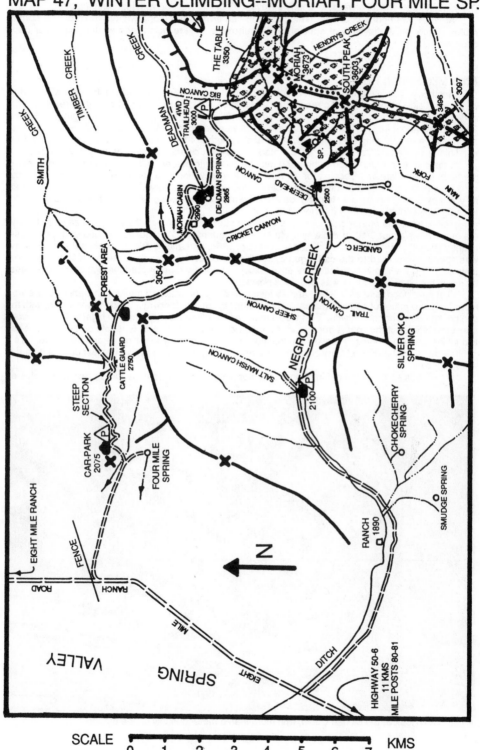

SCALE | 0 1 2 3 4 5 6 7 | KMS

blown snow, but if there's been storms not long before you're arrival, you'll need skies or snowshoes. The summit ridge should always, or nearly always, be easy to walk on with just climbing boots.

At times, crampons could be useful, but you can always get along without them on the normal routes. Only on some kind of special or difficult route on the north face would you ever need crampons.

Four Mile Spring Route

Another good way to the summit of Moriah during winter, is the one up from the Four Mile Spring, on the west side of the range. To reach the Car-park, drive along Highway 50-6, to the area just to the northwest of Sacramento Pass. Between mile posts 80 and 81, turn north onto the Eight Mile Ranch Road. Drive about 18 kms on this good graveled all-weather road, until you come to a cattle guard and fence, then turn east onto a rough road. After about another 4 kms, veer to the left or north, and drive to a little pass marked Car-park, at 2075 meters. Only high clearance cars can may it to that point. If you're there after a recent storm, this road may be muddy in places, but should be passable most of the time, even in winter. Because of it's relatively low elevation and sunny western exposure, most vehicles can likely make it to the Car-park almost the year-round. Have a supply of water in your car, as you may or may not be able to get good water from Four Mile Spring. At the Car-park, is a good spot to camp, but it could get windy if a storm blows in.

This is what the author did. Getting a very late start, he walked up the steep zig zagging road to the east. After about 9/10 of the way up to the cattle guard at 2750 meters, he had to put on cross-country snowshoes. This was the first day of spring, 1988, and after a drier than normal winter. Snow was spotty on the road to the cattle guard, but once on top, the flatter terrain was totally snow covered. The walking was mostly very easy, except where the road passed through some pine trees, then with the shade, the snow was deep and powdery.

Just after noon, and after 2 hrs. and 25 min. of walking, he reached the Moriah Cabin. There was more than one meter of snow at the cabin, but it didn't block the doorway. Inside it was warm, with the sun beating down on the outside. This would make an excellent place to spend a night or two. The walls aren't insulated, but the roof is good, and it's dry inside. It will sleep 4 or 5 people on the floor. It has two tables and two brooms. Please keep the place clean for those who will come and use it later. It's a publicly owned cabin(Forest Service), and you have their permission to use it. Just care of it as if it were your own.

Lunch was eaten at the cabin, then the author walked to very near Deadman Spring for fotos of

A mid-March look at the Moriah Cabin, with more than a meter of snow on the ground.

Moriah, then returned to his car over the same route. The total round-trip time was 5 hrs. and 13 min., with mostly very good or ideal snow conditions.

Under similar snow conditions, in late March(with long days), with an early morning start, and with a late arrival back at the Car-park, it's possible for a very strong hiker with skies, to climb Moriah in one day from the Car-park. But it would take in the neighborhood of 12 hours, round-trip! Most people however, should plan on doing a winter ascent along this route in about three days: Perhaps an easy half day to the Moriah Cabin; then a full day from the cabin to the summit and back; and an easy third day to return to the Car-park. Another alternative would be to take a tent and camp somewhere near the base of the peak, making the ascent and return to the car in a long second day. However, most people would enjoy it more, if they did the trip in three days, staying two nights in the Moriah Cabin.

This is perhaps the best route of any in this book for cross-country skiing. Once you reach the area above the cattle guard at 2750 meters, then it's mostly open and wind-swept, and flat to rolling hill country, with almost no trees. If you stay on the road, then you can go right through the one stand of trees very easily, without fear of crashing. This is also an excellent place to have and use the longer cross-country snowshoes.

From the Moriah Cabin, you can walk along the road to the 4WD Trailhead, or just make a beeline cross-country and save a lot of walking. When you arrive at the summertime 4WD Trailhead, just head up Big Canyon to the south. The trail from there on will likely be obscured by deep snow. Toward the upper end of the canyon, zig zag your way up to the east or left, and to the top of The Table. At that point you'll be in a scattered stand of bristlecone pines, which gives one some fine foto opportunities of both the trees and the summit region. From the bristlecones, make your way south and up to the north peaks, then on to the summit. You'll need snowshoes or skies up to The Table, but once onto the summit ridge, you can do it without. You'll not even need crampons, unless you hope to do a more difficult north face route or something. If it's a clear day, you'll have some fine views of Wheeler Peak to the south.

The western slope of Mt. Moriah in the month of March.

Part IV--Lehman Caves

Discovery

The story behind Lehman Caves begins with a man named Absalom S. Lehman, more commonly known as Ab. He was born in Ohio, but as a young man he migrated west with the army of gold seekers heading for the California Gold Rush. He was one of those who didn't strike it rich.

Ab's next stop was Australia, where he eventually found a wife, and had two children. Things went well for a while, then his wife and one daughter died. Some time after that he returned to California in 1861, and from there ended up in the silver boom in eastern Nevada. After a number of stops in various mining camps, he reached White Pine County in 1867. As far as prospecting and mining were concerned, Ab never did hit pay dirt.

Finally in 1869, and after many failures in the prospecting business, Ab finally decided he could make more gold or silver by suppling food to the miners, rather than trying to dig it out of the ground. So he settled on a small ranch about 3 kms east and downhill from where the present day cave facilities are situated. He diverted water from Lehman Creek and a nearby spring, to grow a garden and an orchard of apple, peach and apricot trees. Because the ground was rocky and covered with cobblestones, he used these to build a house, corral and fences. Eventually he had nearly one whole section(one square mile, or 640 acres--250 hectares) as part of his ranch and farm.

The year 1885 is when Ab is said to have discovered the entrance to the cave. There are many tales as to the circumstances surrounding the discovery. It could have been that he knew of the cave before that time, but simply didn't take the time to explore further. It was an 1885 newspaper account which first brought the caves to the attention of the world.

Actually, Ab Lehman was just the last of the long line of discoverers. In 1938 and 1964, archaeological digs were made at or near the cave entrance. Found were from 12 to 26 human skeletons and the bones of many other animals. It couldn't be determined if the cave was used for ceremonial burials or if the bodies were simply dropped into the first chamber. Also, at or near the mouth, were found fire scars and pieces of pottery. So the Indians knew of the cave long before white men came to the valley.

Development

After Ab's discovery, he made announcements in local newspapers, and ended up guiding 800 people through the cave the first year. This began a new era for Lehman, for from then on, all his energy was spent in advertising and promoting his cave.

In the beginning, ladders were installed at several locations in the cave, especially at and near the original entrance. Work was done on narrow passages, and later, the ladders were replaced by stone or cement stairways. He promoted the cave in newspapers, both local and national, and even had an exhibition at one state fair in Reno.

Sometime later, Ab began to make facilities at the cave. He built a new ranch house and planted another orchard. This he called the *Cave Ranch*. In 1889, he put his lower ranch up for sale, and finally sold it for $3000 in September, 1891. It went to C. W. Rowland. It was about this same time, Lehman became ill and landed in a hospital in Salt Lake City. He died there on October 11, 1891, at the age of 64.

The next year, an executor for Lehmans estate, sold the Cave Ranch to Rowland for $700. The Cave Ranch consisted of 7 acres(2.8 hectares), but the cave entrance was still on public land, and has remained so ever since.

In the years immediately after Lehmans death, not much is known or written about the cave. There surely must have been visitors, but no more improvements were made. Obviously, C. W. Rowland didn't share the same enthusiasm as Ab about the development of the cave.

In 1909, much of the Snake Range was made a part of the newly designated Nevada National Forest. At a later date it was expanded, and at that time, 1912, Lehmans Cave was included in the forest boundaries. Still later, the name of the forest was changed to Humboldt National Forest. Even with the change of ownership of the Cave Ranch and the cave itself, there was still no development of the cave. It wasn't until the 1920's, that things began to change.

In the year 1921, a Tonopah mining broker by the name of C. C. Boak, became interested in the cave. He along with Nevada Senator Tasker Odie began a campaign to have something done about the situation. A year later, on January 24, 1922, Lehman Caves was officially included in Americas list of national monuments. On August 6, 1922, there was a dedication ceremony at the caves, in which 500 people attended.

In the beginning, the Forest Service was the supervising agency for the caves, but because of lack of experience, the agency turned the project over to Clarence T. Rhodes. Rhodes was then

GEOLOGY CROSS SECTION-LEHMAN CAVES

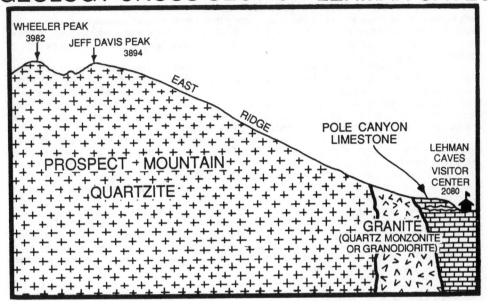

LEHMAN CAVES WALKING TOUR

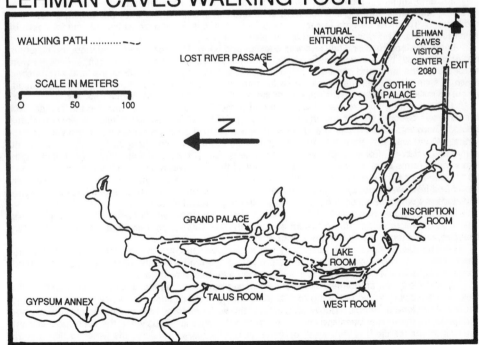

owner of the old Cave Ranch, so he was the natural candidate for supervisor of the new national monument. He was to guide people into the caves and collect fees(which he was allowed to keep).

The Forest Service immediately began to sink money into the caves and to improve the facilities, both inside and out. New stairways were made, some floors were leveled, and walking paths made. Outside, tents were put up in the orchard, a dining hall built, and the access road improved. As time went by, cabins were built for overnight accommodations, and eventually a dance hall and swimming pool were included.

Later on, Rhodes decided he wanted out. Perhaps the business wasn't all that good. For what ever reason, he ended up selling his private holdings to the state in 1932 for $15,000. The next year, it was deeded over to the Federal Government. About this same time, there was a reorganization in Washington under the Roosevelt Administration. On August 10, 1933, the supervising of the park was changed from the Forest Service to the National Park Service. At that time Lehmans Caves included one full section--a square mile, or 640 acres(about 250 hectares).

With the passing of time, more improvements were made. In 1939, an entrance tunnel was built, replacing the cricking wooden stairway at the natural entrance to the original cave. Throughout the years only candles, coal oil lanterns and carbide lamps were used to illuminate the darkened passages, but in 1941, electric lights were installed. This totally changed the caves. The effect was, it put things in proper perspective. Instead of darkened recesses, one had a full view of the various chambers. This made the cave seem much smaller than before.

Further improvements were made. Some handrails were installed, and in 1958, the walkway was paved throughout the cave. In 1961, the Talus Room was opened to visitors for the first time, lengthening the tour by 300 meters(in the early 1980's, this room was closed, because of the danger of falling rocks). In 1962, a new visitor center was built, which today houses GBNP headquarters, a small natural history bookstore, a restaurant and gift shop. In 1969, a new exit tunnel was drilled, making the entire walk almost horizontal.

Natural History of the Cave

Lehman Caves, like so many other famous grottos in North America and the world, have been created out of limestone rock. The geologic formation involved is the *Pole Canyon Limestone,* which originated something like 560 million years ago in what we call today the Cambrian Period. Other limestone caverns are Mammoth Cave in Kentucky and Carlsbad Caverns in New Mexico.

In Cambrian times, the region of eastern Nevada was a low trough forming a shallow inland sea. At times, sediments entering this sea were sand and silt; at other times limey oozes simply settled to the bottom. The Pole Canyon Limestone was formed by this limey ooze which was made mostly of small sea shells. This deposition went on for millions of years.

Later, the land rose and fell, and was buckled and bent. This continued throughout the history of not only Nevada, but the world as a whole. When the area was in a state of uplift, sediments were eroded from the land, and carried to some distance sea for deposition. When the land was pushed down to form a sea, then new rocks such as limestone, dolomite, and shales were the end result. About 65 million years ago, it was uplifted for the last time, ending all new marine deposits.

It's been during this last period, from the end of the Cretaceous Period and into the Tertiary, that the land has become as it is today(see the *Geology of the Snake Range* in another section of this book). There was much buckling and bending, which caused great pressures inside the various rock strata. Along with the great pressure, heat was generated, which changed the original rock into something different. For example, when sandstone is compressed and subjected to heat, it changes into various forms of quartzite. This is the history of the Prospect Mountain Quartzite, which makes up the summit regions of Wheeler Peak. When shales(which are formed in shallow seas--usually inland and fresh water beds) are subjected to heat and pressures, they are changed into slates. When limestone is treated the same way, it turns into various grades of marble.

This is what has happened with the Pole Canyon Limestone, which has five different members. The one member which is represented in Lehman Caves, is one that has been slightly changed, and is today a very low grade marble.

Lehman Caves have come about very late in geologic time, just in the past 4 or 5 million years. The bending, buckling and uplift had, for the most part, ended when the cave began to be formed. That's explains why although the statra is tilted, the cave runs almost horizontal.

Limestone caves are formed by water percolating down through the cracks and crevasses in the rock, and dissolving away part of the rock to form underground cavities. Evidently, pure water cannot dissolve limestone or marble. But when rain falls, the water absorbs carbon dioxide from the air, and later picks up more from decaying vegetal matter on the ground. Thus when the water gets into the bedrock, it is essentially a very weak carbonic acid. This is what allows the water to dissolve the limestone or marble, thus creating the caves.

The next step in the building of caves such as Lehmans, is the stage of deposition. After percolating water made the empty cavities underground, the climate of the region became drier, and the water table dropped. So instead of the cavities being filled with water, they became filled with air. This coupled with some openings to the cave, allowed for a certain amount of evaporation. While there continued to be some water in the caves, as there is today, there was a drying out effect.

While there is some limestone still being dissolved in the water, the smaller amount of water is exposed to the air, thus some of the water evaporates. This leaves the solids, which it has just dissolved on the way down, on the ceiling or floor of the cave. These end up as icicles-like features on both top and bottom. Those emanating from the ceiling are called *stalactites*; those from the floor are called *stalagmites*. There are many other depositional features in the cave, each with it's own descriptive name.

Much of the information in this chapter comes from the small booklet entitled,"*The Lehman Caves Story*". It's put out by the Lehman Caves Natural History Association, and is on sale at the park headquarters at Lehman Caves. You might buy this before or after your tour of the caves. Another publication is titled, *"Lehman Caves"*, and is also on sale at the visitor center.

When you get there you can take the cave tour which lasts 1.5 hours. The inside temperature of the caves is a constant 11 degrees C.(52 F.), so take a jacket to keep warm. Also, the humidity is nearly 100% all the time. You'll pay $3(1988) to go on a guided tour, which is conducted several times daily. More tours are conducted in the busier summer season. If you're heading there on a busy weekend, such as Memorial Day, Fourth of July, 24th of July(a Utah--Mormon Holiday), or Labor Day, you are advised to telefone in advance and make a reservation. On Thanksgiving, Christmas and New Years, the cave and visitor center are closed; otherwise, they are open seven days a week.

At the visitor center is a small museum, a bookstore, and a restaurant and gift shop(which operates from April through October). A short movie is presented, which you can view before or after the cave tour. Nearby is one of the original cabins at the cave, which now has a small exhibit. Behind the visitor center is a short, self guided, nature trail running through the pinyon-juniper forest. Pickup a pamphlet at the front desk, which describes the vegetation along this paved path. Just to the northeast of the visitor center is a small picnic site, with tables, a toilet, and drinking water. Lehman Caves, as well as all of Nevada, uses Pacific Standard Time.

A look at the mines at Hogum, with Wheeler Peak in the background. From near Goody Station.

The Story of Bristlecone Pines

One of the major attractions of the Snake Range, Great Basin National Park and especially Wheeler Peak, is a grove of bristlecone pines on the northern slopes of the Wheeler Peak Massif. In 1964, one of these twisted and gnarled and half dead bristlecones was found to be 4900 years old. This find, more than any other scenic attraction, has put Wheeler Peak and the surrounding area on the map.

The story of bristlecones of course goes way back in time, but events in this century have led to their recent "discovery". According to one story, it all started back in the 1920's, with three expeditions to the American southwest, sponsored by the National Geographic Society. Those expeditions studied the Indian ruins of Pueblo Bonito, located in Chaco Culture National Historic Park, New Mexico.

The studies were led by a Dr. Douglass, who studied the age of the logs in the buildings of the pueblo. It was determined that at least one tree used in the construction was cut in the year 700 AD.

The method used in those studies to age-date wood has become known as *Dendrochronology.* This is the study of trees and the chronology of tree rings. Simply put, this is the counting of tree rings in one sample to determine dry or wet periods in the past history of the tree. In wet and warmer years, the tree rings are thicker or wider than in dry and/or cold years. Since weather patterns run in cycles, so do tree ring patterns. In the American west, wet and dry cycles run in about 20 year intervals. By knowing and understanding the differences in tree rings, you can cut down a living tree, and match it up with logs which were cut at some earlier time. Thus you can set dates, such as when the Anasazi Indians abandoned their homes in the Four Corners region. You can also reconstruct past weather patterns.

Starting with a known dated sample, one can use the tree ring patterns to correlate with similar patterns on much older and now dead specimens. By obtaining older and older samples, one can decide in the exact year when a tree was cut down to build an Indian cliff dwelling.

If one has an old log or a tree stump to work on, then all one needs to do is count the rings. But if one wants to test a living tree to determine it's age, but doesn't want to cut it down, another method must be used. This involves boring a small hole in the tree and taking out a sample of the tree rings. In doing this, a kind of drill or brace and bit is used. This is commonly called an *increment borer.* It's a long hollow metal bore, attached to a handle which is used to turn the bore. After the bore is drilled into the tree, it is then removed, along with a pencil-thin sample of the inner part of the tree. These tree ring samples can then be counted allowing the tree to live on.

After Dr. Douglass, perhaps the next most important personality in the quest for old trees and dendrochronology used in age dating various things, was Edmund Schulman. He and his fellow professors at the Laboratory of Tree Ring Research, at the University of Arizona, began to study trees while looking for evidence of past climatic changes. Since their studies involved past climates, they were interested in the oldest trees they could find. The work really started in earnest in 1953, but things began to happen the year before.

At the end of the summer field season of 1952; Schulman was testing some old Douglas firs near Sun Valley, Idaho, when they came across a limber pine with one side completely dead. They took a bore sample, but didn't reach the heart of the tree. Even with the incomplete sample, they knew they had an old one. The next summer the researchers returned, cut the tree down and carted off one section to California for further study. It later proved to be 1650 years old.

During this early period of searching for old trees, numerous specimens were found. A 860-year old ponderosa pine in Bryce Canyon, and a 975-year old pinyon pine in central Utah were discovered, along with a 600-year old Douglas fir in Mesa Verde National Park, Colorado.

With all the growing interest in old trees, Schulman and others were told by Inyo National Forest rangers of an old bristlecone located in the White Mountains in extreme eastern California near the Nevada line. A local ranger, A. E. Noren, had found and named the largest tree in the area. It measured 11.25 meters in overall circumference, and had been called the Patriarch. This tree was found to be about 1500 years old.

One thing led to another, but before they could seriously test some of the really old trees, they would have to figure out a better way to take core samples than to drill a straight hole. In the end, they found that by taking a series of borings, then by using overlap matching similar to the methods used in the pueblo roof beams, they could accurately count the number of tree rings in even the most twisted and gnarled of bristlecones.

In 1956, Schulman and Ferguson were certain they had found trees nearly 4000 years old. But they had trouble in the matching of rings. More samples were needed, so in the summer field season of 1957, Schulman along with M. E. Cooley, went back again to the top of the White Mountains and to the driest parts of the big grove there. Finally they found the place they later called Methuselah Walk.

THE GREAT BASIN (and other nearby Physiographic Provinces)

Half-dead bristlecone pines at the bottom of the Wheeler Peak Rock Glacier.

There they found the right combination of factors to preserve trees the longest. It was at the highest altitude for survival, there were outcroppings of dolomite rock(similar to limestone), and it was at one of the drier parts of the grove. At that point, it was estimated that the annual rainfall was only about 25 cms, even though it was at an altitude of about 3350 meters. The White Mountains sit in the rainshadow of the Sierras.

In this grove, they found several trees over 4000 years old, and the grand daddy of them all was one listed at a confirmed 4600 years. Even with this discovery, no one was ready to ax the redwoods, which up until that time were considered the oldest living things. To date, the oldest living and precisely dated redwood or sequoia, is set at 3307 years of age(in 1987). However, John Muir is said to have counted 4000 rings on one dead tree in a burned out area in the 1880's. But no one has found that tree stump to confirm it.

The collections and studies made by Schulman, Ferguson and Cooley, in 1956 and 1957, were reported in an article in the *National Geographic* magazine in March, 1958. Just prior to that, in January 1958, Schulman died unexpectedly. Because of that story, the bristlecones received worldwide attention, and the U.S. Forest Service, in the course of developing the Ancient Bristlecone Pine Forest recreation area, designated one stand the Edmund Schulman Memorial Grove. This grove is located in the Ancient Bristlecone Pine Forest in the White Mountains of California, just east of Bishop.

In the years after Schulmans death, C. W. Ferguson continued work in the same bristlecone forest. In the February, 1968 issue of *Science,* Ferguson reported research done on dead trees, in addition to live specimens. The tree rings in the oldest live trees, including the one at 4600 years of age, were matched with dead trees; which, even after death, show remarkable resistances to weathering. The result was a chronology of 7117 years of continuous tree ring counts(through 1968).

In the years following the research in the White Mountains, there were a number of people out looking for even older trees. One of these men was Donald R. Currey, then at the University of North Carolina, now(1988) the Chairman of the Geography Department at the University of Utah.

Curreys work took him to the Snake Range and the Wheeler Peak area. In 1963 and 1964, during studies of Recent glaciation(Little Ice Age--within the last 10,000 years) in the mountains of the southwestern United States, a number of bristlecone stands were encountered. His first objective was to try and date some of the more recent periods of glaciation. It turned out to be the find of the century. He located and studied the oldest bristlecone pine and the oldest living thing ever found on earth by man; a tree very near 4900 years of age.

Currey selected the Wheeler Peak stand which is actually just north of the summit of Wheelers east peak, generally known as Jeff Davis Peak. This oldest tree, which he called WPN-114 is, or was, before it was cut down, located on the highest part of the lateral glacier moraine on the east side of the lower end of the present rock glacier. See the hiking maps of Wheeler and Jeff Davis Peaks. The altitude of the site is at 3275 meters, and on morainal deposits, which are derived from the Prospect Mountain Quartzite Formation.

The forest at that point is made up almost exclusively of bristlecone pines, but as one walks down the slope and into areas with more favorable growing conditions, one sees many limber pine(*Pinus flexilis*), and Engelmann spruce(*Pices Engelmann*). It's these three trees you'll encounter as you walk through the Wheeler Peak Ancient Bristlecone Pine Forest.

Tree WPN-114 had a dead crown of just over 5 meters high, and a 6.4 meter circumference about half a meter above the ground. The tree was without bark, except for one strip about half a meter wide on its more protected north side. The present ground surface is more than .6 of a meter above the original ground level when the tree first began to grow. Because of the twisted nature of the tree, it was necessary to cut it down, with the permission, aid and comfort of the Forest Service. One section was removed to be studied in a lab. The author never did find the remains, but has been told it still lies there beside the stump.

In counting the rings, which must have been quite a job, they had to do some overlapping and matching to fit things together. According to Currey, *the derived radius measured 2.28 meters to the pith, which was 2.5 meters above the original base, and encompassed 4844 counted rings. Allowing for the likelihood of missing rings and for the 2.5 meter height of the innermost counted ring, it may be tentatively concluded that WPN-114 began growing about 4900 years ago.*

On how to get to this grove of trees, read under Map 11, The Bristlecone Pine Trail. But there are other groves around too. One of the best groves is high on the western end of the East Ridge of Mt. Washington. This very fine stand sits on the highest part of the East Ridge, just northeast of the summit of the mountain. These trees are easily as fotogenic as those on Wheeler, but it lacks the huge massive peak and rock glacier as a background to a foto. There's also another pretty good grove on the south face of Washington. Read about how to get to this one under any of the several maps(25 through 29) on Mt. Washington.

Perhaps the third best grove, at least for taking fotos, is the one on the summit and south face of

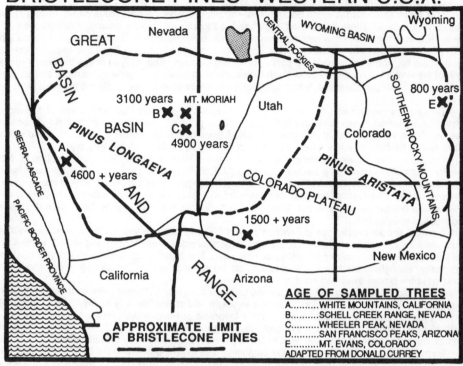

BRISTLECONE PINES--WESTERN U.S.A.

GREAT

Nevada

Wyoming

CENTRAL ROCKIES

WYOMING BASIN

BASIN

SIERRA-CASCADE

3100 years   MT. MORIAH

B ✘ ✘

BASIN   C ✘

4900 years

PINUS LONGAEVA

A ✚

4600 + years

AND

Utah

Colorado

SOUTHERN ROCKY MOUNTAINS

800 years

E ✘

PINUS ARISTATA

PACIFIC BORDER PROVINCE

COLORADO PLATEAU

1500 + years

D ✘

New Mexico

California

RANGE

Arizona

**APPROXIMATE LIMIT
OF BRISTLECONE PINES**

AGE OF SAMPLED TREES

A..........WHITE MOUNTAINS, CALIFORNIA
B..........SCHELL CREEK RANGE, NEVADA
C..........WHEELER PEAK, NEVADA
D..........SAN FRANCISCO PEAKS, ARIZONA
E..........MT. EVANS, COLORADO
ADAPTED FROM DONALD CURREY

A good place to see bristlecone pines is on the upper East Ridge of Mt. Washington.

Eagle Peak. Read about it under Maps 21 and 22. This grove, like the one on Washington, sits atop the Pole Canyon Limestone, and it's fairly easy to reach.

After these three stands in the South Snake Range, probably the best site is on Mt. Moriah in the North Snake Range. There the summit ridge has bristlecones all the way around. Perhaps the best site to view both these skraggly looking trees and to have the peak in the background, is right on top of The Table, just north of the summit ridge. There are some good ones on The Table itself, and others just over the lip, or rim, and inside the upper part of Big Canyon. This canyon drains the area directly north of the summit. Like the Wheeler Peak Grove, many of these trees grow out of rocks and soils of the Prospect Mountain Quartzite, which appears to make living even more difficult than if it were on limestone.

These sites mentioned are some of the best places to see this tree, with some of the most twisted and gnarled specimens, but bristlecone pines grow all over the North and South Snake Ranges. From the top of Mt. Washington, and on all three high ridges running south, are found many bristlecones. All three of these ridges are made of limestone, the bedrock this tree prefers.

The author hasn't seen the top of the ridge above the Minerva Mines, but given the altitude, the limestone formations making up the ridge, and the drier conditions, he guesses they are there in large numbers, as they are on Acrapolis Peak. One local rancher told the author, "*if you gave a man a chain saw and let him start cutting, and kept him supplied with gasoline, he could never in his lifetime cut down all the bristlecone pines in the Snake Range.*" Simply put, this tree is definitely not on the endangered species list!

A typical site for these trees is between about 2800 and 3350 meters; on the drier slopes with a southerly component(almost never on the cooler more shaded north faces); and almost always on rocky soils derived from either limestone or dolomite. The trees which are the oldest and best for fotography, are right at the tree line, and usually on the summits of peaks or on ridge lines, and in the worst possible places trees can survive.

The bristlecones are usually less than one meter in diameter, but some grow up to two meters or more across. They are typically 5 to 10 meters in height, but at tree line may be only 3 or 4 meters tall and very squat. Lower on the slopes and in more favorable growing areas, you'll see some trees grow up to 25 or 30 meters and look just like any other loggable tree. The big grove on the south face of Washington is the best place to see what some might call, "a commercially valuable stand".

Some people may have trouble in the beginning distinguishing between the bristlecones and the limber pines. Bristlecones usually have medium long needles, in groups of five, and are thickly clustered in the last 25 cms of the tips of branches. They look like the tail of a frightened cat. The limber pines on the other hand, have longer and lighter colored needles and are very much clustered on the very tips of their branches. The cones of bristlecones have, as you might expect, many small bristles covering the outside, and are chocolate colored when alive and on the tree.

Much discussion is heard on why bristlecones grow to be so old. Some of the ideas brought forward are. They are always at a high altitude environment, where it's cold and dry, and relatively free of insects. These conditions help more than any other factors, to preserved dead trees. A second reason, they grow more slowly in the normally arid southwest. The slower they grow, the older they can live--seems to be a rule of thumb. Also, the ground is sparsely covered, which prevents the spread of forest fires. The highly resinous nature of the compact wood provides resistances to moisture and decay. And the retention of needles for 20 or 30 years insures a somewhat stable photosynthetic capacity that can carry a tree over several years of stress(drought or extra cold weather years).

If you do much reading on the subject, you'll see two names applied to this tree. One is *Pinus aristata*, the other *Pinus longaeva.* Since most of the literature on the subject was published before 1970, you may see either of these names applied to the Great Basin bristlecones.

Finally in 1970, a guy named Bailey made an attempt to settle the issue. He drew a boundary along the Colorado River. Those bristlecones in Colorado, Arizona and New Mexico are to be called *Pinus aristata*; whereas those trees found west of the Colorado, in Utah, Nevada and California, are classified as *Pinus longaeva.* Whether or not these names stick will remain to be seen, but there has been subsequent research done, and it was found that the terpenoid chemistry and crossability of the two trees provide support for two separate species.

The map shows the approximate boundary of the bristlecones which are almost all confined to the Southern Rocky Mountains, the Colorado Plateau, and the Great Basin Provinces. Almost all mountains in the Great Basin of California, Nevada and Utah above about 2800 meters will have some bristlecones on them; more on those with limestone summits. Refer to the various hiking maps to see the extent of the bristlecones in the Snake Range. In doing so, you'll notice that most of them are found on Mt. Washington and points south.

Close-up look at a bristlecone pine limb. Note the needles are in clusters of five.

Bristlecone pines on the East Ridge of Mt. Washington.

History of Mining in the Snake Range

Throughout the history of the whitemans occupation of the Snake Range, mining has been perhaps the most dominant, yet the most sporadic, occupation in the area. The earliest claims were filed in 1869, and since that time, millions of dollars worth of gold, silver, lead, zinc, copper, tungsten, garnets, phosphate(bat guano), and building stone have been blasted and dug out, and hauled from of these hills.

As time went on, and as new mining areas were discovered, mining districts were formed. In the area covered by this book, nine such districts have been set up. They include: Mount Moriah Area, Sacramento, Black Horse, Osceola, Tungsten, Snake, Mount Washington, Lexington, and the Shoshone Districts. The history of each and the minerals mined is covered below. Much of this information comes from the *Nevada Bureau of Mines and Geology Bulletin 85, 1976, and the PH.D. dissertation of Robert S. Waite.*

1. Mount Moriah Area

This region is probably the least known, the least mineralized, the least successful, and the latest to be exploited, of all the districts discussed. Several mines and prospects are located on the slopes of Mount Moriah in the North Snake Range, most of them on the east side in the watersheds of Smith Creek, Horse Canyon, Hampton Creek and Hendrys Creek.

The Galena, Monitor Gulch, or Kaufman Mine in Horse Canyon was operated in 1948, when 33 tons of lead-zinc ore containing a little silver and copper were produced.

The Silver Peak Mine, is located somewhere north of Peak 3054(see Map 44, Mt. Moriah--Four Mile Spring Route) and at the head of Smith Creek. Recorded production totaled about 17,000 kgs of lead, 8 kgs of silver, and a small amount of gold recovered from 26 tons of concentrate shipped from a small mill at the site in 1925. The lead-silver ore bodies are replacement deposits in a marbleized zone of the Pole Canyon Limestone along a fault line.

The most unusual mineral mined in the Moriah Area, has to be garnets. Almandine garnets occur in a placer deposit(in loose alluvial gravels) along the floor of Hampton Creek Canyon about 3 kms above it's mouth. Remains of a washing and concentrating plant, and an old cabin are visible there today near the end of the road. Records of production are unknown, but shipments were made in the early 1960's. The deposits are along one km of the canyon floor, and to a depth of 30 meters. The source of the garnet is a quartz lens exposed along one side of the canyon. The size of the garnets range up to about one centimeter.

In recent years, about the only mining in the district has been the quarrying of building stone,

Building stone from the Hatch Rock quarries near Hendrys Creek.

MINING DISTRICTS IN THE SNAKE RANGE

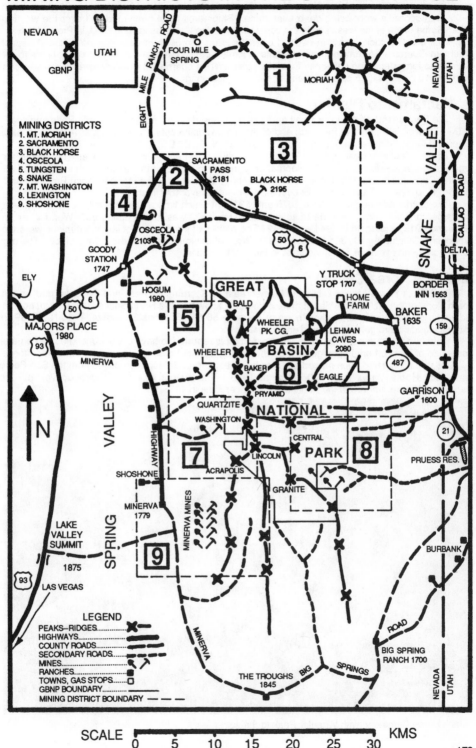

NEVADA
UTAH
GBNP

MINING DISTRICTS
1. MT. MORIAH
2. SACRAMENTO
3. BLACK HORSE
4. OSCEOLA
5. TUNGSTEN
6. SNAKE
7. MT. WASHINGTON
8. LEXINGTON
9. SHOSHONE

1

FOUR MILE SPRING

EIGHT MILE RANCH ROAD

MORIAH

NEVADA · UTAH

SNAKE VALLEY

CALLAO ROAD

3

SACRAMENTO PASS 2181

2

BLACK HORSE 2195

4

50 · 6

DELTA

OSCEOLA 2103

ELY

GOODY STATION 1747

HOGUM 1980

GREAT

BALD

Y TRUCK STOP 1707

HOME FARM

BORDER INN 1563

BAKER 1635

159

50 · 6

MAJORS PLACE 1980

93

5

WHEELER PK. CG.

LEHMAN CAVES 2080

MINERVA

WHEELER

BASIN

BAKER

487

6

EAGLE

GARRISON 1600

N

PRYAMID

QUARTZITE

NATIONAL

21

WASHINGTON

CENTRAL

VALLEY

7

LINCOLN

PARK

8

PRUESS RES.

HIGHWAY

SHOSHONE

ACRAPOLIS

GRANITE

MINERVA 1779

MINERVA MINES

LAKE VALLEY SUMMIT 1875

SPRING

9

BURBANK

93

LAS VEGAS

LEGEND
PEAKS–RIDGES..........
HIGHWAYS.................
COUNTY ROADS..........
SECONDARY ROADS......
MINES.......................
RANCHES...................
TOWNS, GAS STOPS.....
GBNP BOUNDARY..........
MINING DISTRICT BOUNDARY – – –

MINERVA

ROAD

BIG SPRING RANCH 1700

THE TROUGHS 1845

BIG SPRINGS

NEVADA · UTAH

SCALE   0   5   10   15   20   25   30   KMS

173

sometimes called flagstone. The Star Dust or Hatch Mine, consists of about 20 small quarries on the slopes and ridges of Hendrys Creek Canyon, and several others in the South Fork of Hendrys. There are even sites on the ridge between Smith and Deadman Creeks. The first recorded production was in 1955, with sporadic work being done ever since. Shipments have been made all over the western USA. Some of the stone was used in the construction of the library building at BYU, in Provo, Utah.

This building rock, is a thin-bedded quartzite, that comes from near the top of the Prospect Mountain Quartzite Formation. The quartzite is jointed in two directions nearly at right angles to the bedding to form slabs and columns of various sizes. When quarried, it usually comes out in sections from 3 to 10 cms thick, 25 cms wide, and about a meter in length.

2. Sacramento District

The Sacramento District is a small area just west and downhill from Sacramento Pass and south of US Highway 50-6, right at the north end of the big sweeping curve. It includes several small gold, silver and tungsten mines in Sections 17 and 18, T. 15 N., R. 68 E.

The earliest discoveries were of gold and silver bearing veins, which were the basis for organization of the district in 1869. Soon after, mines or prospects such as the Armstrong, La Plata, Aurora, Constitution and the Sacramento were slightly developed. The Independence Prospect and the Oro Fino Vein on Sacramento Hill both assayed out at favorable figures.

The district was neglected from 1875 until 1915, at which time a tungsten mill was erected near Sacramento Pass. Scheelite(one of several tungsten ores) was mined during both World Wars; in 1915 and 1916, and again in 1941 and 1942. The names of the three most important mines were the Woodman, Guilded Age 1, and Guilded Age 2. No further work has been done there since. The ore came from quartz veins in limestone beds in the Pioche Shale.

3. Black Horse District

The Black Horse Mining District is located east of Sacramento Pass and Osceola, and on the south slope of the Mt. Moriah Massif more commonly known as the North Snake Range. Most of the old workings are found about 3 kms north of Highway 50-6 in Sections 23 and 24, T. 15 N., R. 69 E. Minerals mined were gold, silver, lead and tungsten.

Gold, the first mineral to be mined in the district, is reported to have been found speckled on the underside of an overhanging ledge by a cowboy riding a black horse taking refuge from a rain storm. By 1905, the district had been named and was being explored. Gold was produced from the San Pedro and Black Horse Mines from 1906 through 1913. The district was then unproductive until the discovery of lead-silver ore at the Pauline or Bellander Mine in 1933.

Black Horse Cemetery, with Wheeler Peak to the south.

OSCEOLA AND HOGUM GHOST TOWNS AND THE WEST AND OSCEOLA DITCHES

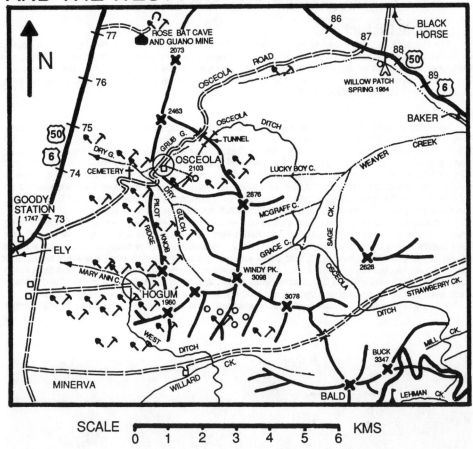

Gold ore was first milled in an arrastra in 1909 and in an amalgamating mill in 1910. Tungsten ore was concentrated in a 25 ton plant at the Gold King Mine in 1943. A tungsten ore named scheelite was produced from the Gold King(Black Horse) Mine intermittently from 1943 to 1953.

The most important mines in the district have been the Black Horse(near the former site of the old ghost town of Black Horse--gold silver, tungsten), Bellander(lead-silver) and Tilford(gold and silver). The ore bodies at all three sites are veins along faults and replacement deposits in limestone.

Black Horse Town
The real boom hit this mining district in 1906. That's when miners moved into the area in large numbers and erected a tent city. Within a year, the population was estimated to be 400. There were three stores, three saloons, two boarding houses, a blacksmith shop, barber shop, school, post office and a house of ill repute. The boom lasted 7 or 8 years, then when the richest ores had been mined out, the town was abandoned. All you'll see there today are the old mines scattered about, an empty townsite, and a miners cemetery. At the cemetery is one old miners grave and that of another person dating from the mining era. In addition, there are two new graves, placed there in 1987 and 1988. From this cemetery, one has a fine view of Wheeler Peak to the south.

Get there today, by driving north from Highway 50-6, between mile posts 87 and 88. This is just west of the Willow Patch Spring and Campsite. Head due north on a very good gravel road for about 3 kms. At that point is a road junction. To your left and straight in front of you is the former town site. Nothing is visible from the road. To reach the cemetery, turn to the right or east, and drive another 200 meters or so, and on the right (south) side of the road is the small cemetery.

4. Osceola District

The Osceola District, possibly once called the Centennial District, is the only site in the county which has been predominantly a placer gold mining district. It includes the Hogum, Weaver Creek, and Summit areas, as well as the principal lode mines, which are in the Dry Gulch Area around Osceola. The district covers both sides of the ridge crest and the western slope of the Snake Range from Osceola summit south to Willard Creek.

Osceola

Lode gold(that found in solid bedrock) was discovered in August of 1872 by Joseph Watson and Frank Hicks, in the Exchange Claim located on the northeast slope of Pilot Knob Ridge above Dry Gulch. Two months later the Osceola Mining District was organized. Other discoveries of gold bearing quartz veins followed quickly in five principal groups of mines. They were: Gold Exchange, Mary Ann Canyon, Summit, Whitney and Mulligan. The most extensive underground workings were in the Star, Crescent, Time Check, Cumberland and Exchange Mines of the Gold Exchange group on Pilot Knob. The first ores were milled in arrastras. By 1878 about 100 lode claims had been staked, and a five-stamp mill had been constructed in Dry Gulch a km below the town center.

In about 1877, a tent city of from 400 to 600 miners, had sprang up over night. Osceola grew steadily for the next five years, until the population was estimated to be about 1500 people. By the early 1880's, there were three stores, a post office, restaurant, butcher shop, a blacksmith shop, a jail, an assay office(still standing?), and three saloons. About this same time, a weekly newspaper was founded, the *Osceola Nugget*, a four page publication. At one time there were 20 buildings lining main street, which was in Grub Gulch(sometimes called Wet Gulch). Most of the miners lived in tents, which were placed on small platforms dug out on the side of the hills overlooking the town site.

Not only were there the usual Anglo-Saxon element to the new mining town, but also a fair number

Osceola Cemetery.

of Chinese. They had come to America to help build the transcontinental railroad, but when those jobs ran out, they went into other fields of employment. They arrived at mining camps, such as Osceola, and were hired as cooks, laborers, laundrymen and eventually helped to build the Osceola and West Ditches.

Placer gold mining was hampered from the start by lack of water. Small springs in Wet Canyon yielded about four liters in 15 minutes. Consequently two ditches were constructed beginning in 1886.

In 1886, a man by the name of Benjamin Hampton organized the Osceola Placer Mining Company. He secured over 400 hectares of land in Dry Gulch and Mary Ann Canyon, then bought several ranches in Spring Valley and their water rights, and proceeded to built the West Ditch. It began way to the south, at the mouth of Williams Canyon. From there water was diverted north past Hub Mine Basin, and later included the water from Pine, Ridge, and Shingle Creeks. Further north it intercepted Willard Creek, then contoured around the face of the mountain and into Mary Ann Canyon, where it ended. It was built during 1886 and 1887, at the cost of $85,000.

About this same time the Osceola Ditch was built. Hampton and his mining company went to the east side of the range and bought more ranches and water rights. The end result was an even longer ditch than the first. The Osceola Ditch was 29 kms long and originated on the middle part of Lehman Creek. In all, the water from Lehman, Mill, Sawmill, Strawberry, Sage, Burnt, and Weaver Creeks all flowed together and eventually to Osceola.

It was completed in 1889 and the total cost of both ditches was in the neighborhood of $200,000 to $250,000. All together about 300 men helped in the construction. Several kms of flumes had to be built over loose rock or sandy places, and over ravines. Lumber for the flumes was brought in from Hendrys Creek Sawmill on Mt. Moriah, and from the sawmill on the upper part of South Fork of Big Wash. Also, a 200 meter tunnel was blasted out to get the water from the east to the west side of the divide. To increase the water supply of Lehman Creek, a small dam was built to enlarge Stella Lake, just west of present day Wheeler Peak Campground.

With a good water supply, hydraulic mining, ground sluicing, and sluice box methods were employed until 1900, when a combination of light snowfall, leaky flumes, water theft from the ditches, and other factors caused placer mining to be discontinued.

Today you can still see the remains of the Osceola and West Ditches. Look at the hiking maps of the west side routes to Baker and Wheeler Peaks to see the location of the West Ditch. The Osceola

The old concentraing mill at Osceola.

Ditch can be seen about half way up the Wheeler Peak Scenic Drive. There's a sign and a parking lot, and a short trail to the ditch(see Map 39, Lehman Creek Trail). There are many locations you can see either ditch, but in many cases, roads now cover up the old waterways.

Since 1902, there has been a small but steady production of both lode and placer gold nearly every year to the present. The best gold production years were from 1939-1941, when $200,000 was brought in. For all production of all minerals in the Osceola District, the best year was in 1940, when the combined value of gold and silver was $257,000. A total of 31 lode mines and 44 placers have been reported and operated from 1902 until the present.

Tungsten was discovered in 1916 and a two-stamp mill was built at the Pea Ridge Mine from which both gold and tungsten concentrates were recovered. In 1942, tungsten ore was discovered and mined at the Black Mule and Dirty Shirt gold mines. Tungsten concentrate from the Three Sisters placer mine and the Shipper underground mine was produced in 1954 and 1955. Most of the tungsten ores from the Osceola, Sacramento and Black Horse Districts were milled at Goody Mill or Station on Highway 50-6, between mile posts 72 and 73.

The rock in this district has been faulted and bent, so there's a jumble of formations. The oldest rocks exposed are the Precambrian McCoy Creek Group, mostly quartzite. Above that are the Prospect Mountain Quartzite, Pioche Shale and the Pole Canyon Limestone.

Most of the lode gold has been deposited in quartz veins which are a result of the faulting, then the cracks were filled in and replaced with the quartz, thus the concentration. The placer gold has been found in the bottom of Dry Gulch and Grub(Wet) Gulch near the townsite of Osceola, and in Mary Ann Canyon near Hogum. Concentrations tend to be highest just below the lode deposits, and to as deep as 60 meters. The placer gold is generally very fine, but one nugget found weighed in at about 11 kgs. This well may have been the largest nugget ever found in Nevada. The largest deposit of tungsten was found in scheelite bearing quartz veins of the Prospect Mountain Quartzite and in the Dirty Shirt Mine of Mary Ann Canyon.

If you visit Osceola today, you'll find the same placer mining activity going on just west, or down canyon, from the old town site. There are a couple of operators there today, working with trommel screens and other equipment. On top of the ridge just south of Dry Gulch, is the old town cemetery, and just up canyon from the main workings is an old red colored concentrator, which can be seen easily from the road. At the old town site itself, there is one building still standing. This is the assay office, which is made of stone. This old structure stands next to a trailer home, where one of the present

Osceola Arch to the left, the Rose Bat Cave in the center, and the tailings from the guano mine tunnel near the bottom of the foto.

owners of the area lives. The owners have asked the author to inform interested visitors they are welcome, but they would appreciate it if they are contacted first.

The easiest way to reach Osceola is to make your way to Goody Station, on Highway 50-6, between mile posts 72 and 73. From there turn northeast and drive 5 or 6 kms up a well used gravel and rocky road. Near the mining areas, look for the cemetery next to the road on the left(north)side. If the weather is good, you can also come in from the east side, and from mile post 87 on Highway 50-6. This section of road is normally good, but may not be passable in bad weather.

The Rose Bat Cave and Guano Mine

The most unusual mineral mined in the Osceola District was phosphate, more commonly known as guano. This was actually bat guano from the Rose Bat Cave. There's some interesting history behind this cave. Early in this century, sometime around 1913, someone realized there were economic possibilities for the guano. In those days guano was used for making fertilizer and gunpowder.

Not much could be done at first, because the cave was mostly vertical and the guano was difficult to reach and get out. But in 1926, a horizontal tunnel was blasted out about 25 meters below the caves natural entrance. This 40 meter-long tunnel led to the lower part of the cave and the roosting chamber. A short set of tracks were laid inside the tunnel, and ore cars were used to haul the guano out. This made mining easy and it lasted off and on for several years. It's been many years now since this operation closed down.

Throughout the year there are four varieties of bats which inhabit the cave. They include the Big Brown, the Little Brown, and the Big-eared Bat. They apparently live in the cave on a year-round basis, but are few in numbers, traveling in groups of 50 or so. The fourth variety is the Mexican Freetail Bat. This is sometimes known as the Guano Bat, and is the one which has contributed most of the guano to the cave.

The Mexican Freetail is a migratory bat, which spends the winters in Mexico, then flies north in the warm season. The Rose Bat Cave is one of the most northerly roosting places for this species. These bats reach the cave usually sometime in April and head south again in about September.

Because the cave is so large and because of the unusual mining activity which took place there, the Rose Bat Cave and Guano Mine was declared a national historic site on December 22, 1970. The cave is on BLM(public land) just north of Osceola and can be visited by anyone.

Just inside the natural entrance of the Rose Bat Cave.

To get there, drive along Highway 50-6, between Sacramento Pass and Goody Station. At a point just north of mile post 77, look directly east and you'll see the cave at the base of the huge cliffs. At the same location, turn off the highway and onto a rough road heading east. It's about 2 kms to the cave and mine, but the second km is rather steep. Any higher clearance car can make it there, if driven with care. There are no gates or private land to cross to reach this historic site.

At the cave-mine site, you'll first come to the tunnel below the natural entrance. You may smell the guano as you approach the tunnel, as there's a draft coming out. You can enter the tunnel with a good light, where you will see evidence that tracks had once been laid, to facilitate hauling out the guano. This lower chamber has a very high ceiling, and it takes a strong light to see that far.

Between the tunnel and the natural entrance, you'll see more evidence of the old guano mining operation. As you walk up the slope on a steep trail, you'll also see the large limestone Osceola Arch, just in front of you to the north of the cave. The last 10 meters or so in front of the natural entrance is steep, but anyone should be able to handle it. Just inside the entrance, is a large room, which immediately drops down into the upper chamber. The majority of the bats apparently roost in the lower chamber, which has been opened up with the tunnel.

If you're in the area during the summer months, and want to see the bats exit, be there at about sundown, and you may see something interesting.

5. Tungsten District

The Tungsten District, also known as the Hub District, is nearly coextensive with T. 13 N, R. 68 E.(36 sections) on the west slope of the Snake Range. It includes Wheeler and Baker Peaks along the summit ridge, and the Hub Mine Basin at the base of the west ridge or face of Baker Peak. The huebnerite-scheelite bearing veins of the Hub Mine area are the only deposits in the district known to have been productive.

Huebnerite(another type of tungsten ore) was first identified in the Hub vein in 1889, and the district was organized in 1890. During this first year of operation, 10 tons of concentrate was shipped, but recoveries were too low to be profitable.

In 1910, a 50-ton gravity-concentration mill was constructed in Hub Basin, supplied with water by a 2 km long ditch from Williams Creek. The mill operated for a short time in 1911 but closed owing to low prices for tungsten. The mine and mill were reopened in 1915 due to the war and the need for tungsten in armament.

From 1917 to 1951, the district was inactive, except for dismantling the mill. In 1952 and 1953, some huebnerite-scheelite concentrate obtained from dump ore was recovered and shipped out for processing.

Mining cabin in the Hub Mine Basin.

The principal formation underlying the Hub Mine Basin is a granite, or quartz monzonite intrusion. The next formation up is reported to be the Stella Lake Quartzite, listed by some investigators as the lower part of the Prospect Mountain Quartzite. The minerals are found in five prominent quartz veins cutting across the granite, but not into the quartzite.

6. Snake District

The Snake District, sometimes known as the Bonita, includes the drainage areas of Snake and Baker Creeks on the east slope of the Snake Range. This district was first set up in 1869, then reorganized in 1873. By 1913 it was renamed the Bonita District, after Camp Bonita and the Bonita Mine on Snake Creek.

The earliest discoveries were specimens of silver ore in 1869, but little if any work was done in the area. Scheelite bearing(tungsten) veins along Snake Creek were discovered in 1913 and a shipment of concentrates was made the same year from the Tilford(Bonita) Mine. The ore was treated in a two-ton experimental mill at the camp.

There was tungsten ore mined higher up the canyon at Johnson Lake and Mine after 1913, and especially during World War I. It was concentrated at a small mill about 1.5 kms below Johnson Lake. Read all about this mine and mill in the hiking section under Map 20, Johnson Lake Hike--Snake Creek Trail.

Lead ore was shipped from the Poljack Mine in Young Canyon in 1929. Young Canyon is to the east and northeast of Eagle Peak. Seven tons of ore yielded three tons of lead, about 70 kgs of copper and some silver, all valued at $450.

Later on and in the 1940's, the floor of Snake Creek Canyon below the Bonita Mine was explored for placer scheelite. A dredge was set up and work was done on a section about 400 meters long and a 100 meters wide. Little ore was recovered, but the old dredge used is still sitting there on the south side of the road along Snake Creek. The Bonita Mine located just above the canyon floor, is situated in veins of quartz within the Pioche Shale Formation. If you drive to the north of the old dredge and into a little side canyon coming down the southeast slope of Eagle Peak, you can see the ruins of an old cabin and loading area. If you spend time in the area, you might find more.

7. Mount Washington District

The Mount Washington District, formerly known as the Lincoln District and more recently as the St. Lawrence or Mount Wheeler District, covers the west slope of the Snake Range from Williams Canyon nearly to Shoshone. It includes Mt. Washington and Lincoln Peak on it's eastern boundary.

The first discovery was the Washington copper-lead-antimony deposit in 1869. The Lincoln

In Snake Creek Canyon is this old dredge, near the Bonita Mine.

District was then first organized, and at the time included the Snake and Lexington areas. There were many claims staked out, but little if any production took place in those early years. Some work was done in the late 1880's, including erecting some of the cabins still standing at the St. Lawrence Mine. The first recorded production was in 1911, with a shipment of 22 tons of lead-silver ore from the St. Lawrence Mine. Read all about the St. Lawrence Mine in the hiking section under Map 29, The St. Lawrence Mine Hike.

Exploration for tungsten ore was begun in about 1952 at the Mount Wheeler Mine, located in Pole Canyon, just west of Mt. Washington. About 1000 tons were produced through 1955. At about that time, it was theorized that if a tunnel or adit were drilled from the mouth of the Wheeler Peak Mine in Pole Canyon, due east under the mountain, they would intersect the main vein which is so prominently exposed at the St. Lawrence Mine on top of Washington. So in 1956 and 1957, two kms of tunnels were cut. They never did make contact with the rich lead-silver fissure, but instead discovered a very rich heretofore unknown beryllium deposit.

Exploration was continued through 1962, and some ore was stockpiled. But the price of beryllium was too low to sell at the time, and this underground mine couldn't compete with the open pit mine at Spore Mountain, located northwest of Delta, Utah. In recent years however, the price of beryllium has gone up, while at the same time the costs of production at Spore Mtn. has increased and their ore quality has diminished. The present owners of the Wheeler Peak Mine say it's only a matter of time before this beryllium mine reopens. Beryllium by the way, is the space age metal which is lighter than aluminum and stronger than steel.

The geology in the Mt. Washington area goes like this: at the bottom is the Prospect Mountain Quartzite, while up from there it's the Pioche Shale, Pole Canyon Limestone, Lincoln Peak Formation, Johns Wash Limestone, and the Corset Spring Shale. All the beds dip to the south as a result of being uplifted by the intrusion of Tertiary granite to the north.

At the bottom of the Pioche Shale, is a member called the Wheeler Limestone. This is where the beryllium deposits are found in the Wheeler Peak Mine. On top of the mountain, the Pole Canyon Limestone is exposed, and it's in this formation that the rich St. Lawrence Mine is found. The ore bodies themselves are replacement deposits within narrow veins of quartz or calcite along fault lines.

8. Lexington District

The Lexington District includes the watersheds of Big Wash, Lexington Creek and Black Canyon(south of Lexington Arch), on the east slope of the southern Snake Range. There has only been one productive mine in the district in recent years, and that's the Bonanzy or Lexington Tungsten Mine near the head of Lexington Creek, just over the ridge from Lexington Arch.

One of the mine tunnels at the St. Lawrence Mine.

The first reported mining activity in this area was in 1883, but nothing came of these early explorations for gold. Right at the end of the road in Arch Canyon, you'll see the remains of an old gold mine, which still has claim notices. But no work has been done in it in years.

In 1916, some promising claims were prospected for tungsten in the upper Lexington Canyon. The earliest report of production from the district was in 1918, when the Bonanzy Mine yielded scheelite tungsten ore worth $20,000. A 50-ton concentrating plant was constructed in 1941, and during the next two years, concentrate worth $80,000 was taken out. Little or no work has been done there since.

The Bonanzy Mine is located on top of a saddle just to the east of the Lexington Mill site in upper Lexington Creek Canyon. See Map 34, Granite Peak, for a close look at the area. On the saddle, are a number of prospects and adits, including two shafts; one vertical and one inclined at 50 degrees. The scheelite ore is concentrated in calcite veins in the Lincoln Peak Limestone, which is exposed at the surface. Underlying the blue limestone is a granite type intrusion of porphyritic quartz monzonite.

9. Shoshone District

The Shoshone District on the west slope of the range, is better known in recent years as the Minerva District. It includes T. 11 N., R. 68 E., and extends from the site of the old Shoshone post office in the northwest corner to Silver Chief Canyon in the south.

Silver chloride was identified in the Indian Vein on Mineral Hill one day in 1869 when an Indian led some miners to the outcrop of what is now the eastern part of the Scheelite Chief Vein. Ten claims were staked that day and the Shoshone District was founded. In the next several years many claims were filed, but little work was done except on the Indian Queen Mine, where a 25 meter shaft was sunk in 1874. It was apparently deserted after 1876, as there are no records of activity until 1911. That's when 22 tons of lead-silver ore was produced and shipped.

Scheelite in quartz veins was discovered in 1915 and mined by the Minerva Tungsten Corp. from 1916 to 1918. This of course was during the First World War when tungsten was needed in the arms industry. At that time the area was called the Minerva District. At Minerva, a tent city sprung up over night, but then permanent buildings replaced the tents. Approximately 200 men were employed there during the war. About that time a post office was opened at the old Swallow Ranch(in the area called Shoshone) about 3 kms north of Minerva.

The ore was milled in a 150-ton concentrating plant at Minerva, but it was dismantled in 1923. One account says part of this mill was destroyed by fire. A small production of tungsten was reported in 1932, and 41 tons of low-grade gold-silver ore was shipped in 1934.

Tungsten mining was revived in 1936, when Tungsten Metals Corp. explored the mines. In 1938, the corporation built a 75-ton plant, enlarging it to 150-ton capacity in 1940. This was located at the

At the head of Lexington Creek is the old Lexington Mill site.

south end of the paved road running along the east side of Spring Valley, and at what is now called on maps of the region, Minerva. The author calls this road the Minerva Highway. All the mining took place to the east and southeast of Minerva.

The mines were again reopened with the advent of World War II in about 1939. This was a boom era which ended for the most part in 1945. There was sporadic mining until the Korean War, when another blimp in notice on the production chart. Little work has been done there since the mid-1950's.

In the area of the tungsten mines, which are all on the west side of the big ridge running south from Lincoln and Acrapolis Peaks, there is found the massive Pole Canyon Limestone. The 300 meter thick section at that point has been informally divided into three members: Upper Black Limestone, Upper White Limestone, and the Lower Black Limestone Members.

Within these various members are the ore bodies. The scheelite is found in calcite and quartz replacement fractures which coincide with old faults. Within a 4 km section(north to south), there are seven veins running east-west, which contain most of the ore bodies. The major mines are, from north to south: the Hill Top, Tungsten Queen, Everett Mines, Oriole, The Chief, and the Silver Bell. Other mines mentioned in the literature are the Tony, Zigzag, Canary Yellow, and Lone Buck.

See the hiking Maps 32 and 33, for a better look at where the Minerva Mines are located.

What remains of the old Minerva Mill site. Wheeler Peak in far background.

An antique well drilling outfit, near The Chief Mine, southeast of Minerva.

A look down on The Chief Mine, located southeast of Minerva.

Geology of the Snake Range

The newly formed Great Basin National Park and the Snake Range of eastern Nevada, are part of what geologists and geographers call the *Great Basin*. The Great Basin makes up about half of what is known as the *Basin and Range Province* of the western USA.

The Basin and Range Province includes all of Nevada, parts of eastern California, southeast Oregon, southern Idaho, western Utah, the southern half of Arizona, southern parts of New Mexico, and the extreme western tip of Texas. This entire region consists of about 200 mountain ranges and an equal number of valleys or basins.

The Great Basin part takes in all of Nevada, the western third of Utah, small parts of eastern California, the southeastern corner of Oregon, and a very small section of southern Idaho. The Great Basin consists of dozens of mountain ranges running north-south which are separated by valleys, most of which are closed and have no drainage.

The Great Basin is subdivided into five physiographic parts: (1)The *Central Area*, of elevated basins and ranges; (2)The *Bonneville Basin*, east of the central area, and making up all of western Utah; (3)The *Lahontan Basin*, west of the central area in western Nevada; (4)The *Lava and Lake Area*, in the northwest corner, is mostly in Oregon; (5)and the *Southern Area*, which includes Death Valley and southern Nevada. The Snake Range and Great Basin National Park sit on the boundary of the Central Area and the Bonneville Basin.

The geologic history is pretty well summed up in the structural cross section. It shows the evolution of the Great Basin in very simplified terms.

Of Precambrian times, not much is known of the Great Basin, because the oldest rocks are not exposed, and therefore can't be studied. In late Precambrian, prior to 600 million years ago, there was a geosyncline or basin in the Southern Area, where at least 10,000 meters of sediments accumulated. This geosyncline is not shown on the cross section because its extent is not known. The Precambrian rocks are buried in most other parts of the Great Basin, therefore can't be analyzed.

In Paleozoic time(from about 600 million up to 225 million years ago) a second geosyncline occupied much of what is now the Great Basin and in it another 10,000 meters or more of sediments accumulated(stage 1). This is when Snake Range formations such as the Prospect Mountain Quartzite and the Pole Canyon Limestone were formed. In the Central Area, which includes the Snake Range, and other areas to the east, there are formations of carbonate rocks(limestone and dolomite) and shale; toward the west there are formations derived in part from volcanic eruptions. Some folding and faulting took place at various times during the Paleozoic, but the resulting structures are not shown on the evolutionary cross section.

In Early Mesozoic time(stage 2, and from 225 million up to 180 million years ago) a third geosyncline developed and another 10,000 meters of sediments accumulated. These sediments are largely derived from volcanics and erosion of other land forms. This third geosyncline was to the west of the Snake Range region.

In the middle and late Mesozoic time(stage 3 and from 180 million up to about 65 or 70 million years ago) a batholith formed at the site of the Sierra Nevada(not shown) of California, and the Mesozoic and Paleozoic formations in the Great Basin were folded, thrust faulted, and uplifted to form the mountains from which sediments were carried eastward into the Cretaceous geosyncline that had occupied the site of the Rocky Mountains and Great Plains.

Later(stage 4), the igneous or volcanic activity that had begun much earlier in the Sierra Nevada spread eastward, and stocks and laccoliths were intruded into the deformed Mesozoic and Paleozoic rocks. This may have been the time where some of the granite or quartz monzonite rocks at the head of Baker and Snake Creeks were intruded into the rock which now make up the Snake Range.

In about the middle Cenozoic time(from about 40 million up to 25 millions years ago), the Great Basin began to be block faulted, and this faulting has continued to the present time(stage 5). Volcanism(not shown), which was sporadic during the early Cenozoic, became extensive during the stage of block faulting. Along the north side of the Great Basin, lavas and other eruptives completely buried the faulted and folded older rocks.

As block-faulting progressed, sediments derived from the up-faulted blocks were deposited in the basins. In some, the fill is enormously thick. Death Valley for example, is estimated to contain 2500 meters of fill. Death Valley therefore has been down-faulted 3 kms below sea level, but has been kept nearly filled with sediments derived by erosion of the neighboring uplifted blocks.

Dominant Rock Formations in the Snake Range

With all the block and thrust faulting which has taken place in the Snake Range, it's impossible to

EVOLUTION OF LANDFORMS--GREAT BASIN

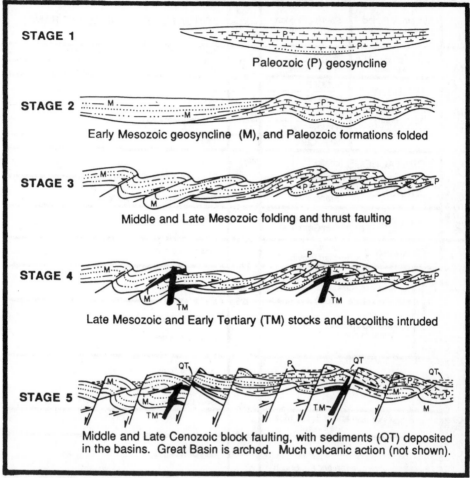

STAGE 1

Paleozoic (P) geosyncline

STAGE 2

Early Mesozoic geosyncline (M), and Paleozoic formations folded

STAGE 3

Middle and Late Mesozoic folding and thrust faulting

STAGE 4

Late Mesozoic and Early Tertiary (TM) stocks and laccoliths intruded

STAGE 5

Middle and Late Cenozoic block faulting, with sediments (QT) deposited in the basins. Great Basin is arched. Much volcanic action (not shown).

FROM CHARLES B. HUNT, PHYSIOGRAPHY OF THE UNITED STATES

draw an accurate geology cross section. Therefore, the geology time table along with a stratigraphic section are shown. The stratigraphic section is very simplified.

Here are just a few of the more important formations you might encounter when hiking or climbing in the Snake Range and in the Great Basin National Park.

Prospect Mountain Quartzite This quartzite formation, like all others, was originally sandstone, and probably laid down in an environment like todays Sahara Desert. It dates from the beginning of Cambrian times, or about 600 million years ago. Later it was covered up and squeezed and pressurized to create quartzite. This quartzite is pinkish gray to light olive gray on fresh fractures, and it weathers to a rusty brown or tan. This is the most dominant formation in the Snake Range, both north and south. All of Bald, Wheeler, Baker and Quartzite Peaks are made of this formation, along with parts of Pyramid and Eagle Peaks. On Mt. Moriah, you'll see this formation on The Table, sometimes called Moriah Table, and all over the eastern half of that mountain range. It's about 1500 meters thick.

GEOLOGY TIME TABLE--SNAKE RANGE

Era	System or Period (rocks) (time)	Series or Epoch (rocks) (time)	Age (millions of years)	FORMATIONS IN THE SNAKE RANGE
CENOZOIC (Age of mammals)	QUATERNARY (Age of man)	RECENT	.01	Sand dunes Younger alluvium
				Talus and colluvium —— Rock glacier —— Landslides ——
		PLEISTOCENE	2.0 to 3.0	Pluvial lake deposits Glacier moraine
	TERTIARY (third, from the 18th-century classification)	PLIOCENE	7	Alluvium
		MIOCENE	25	Conglomerates
		OLIGOCENE	40	
		EOCENE	60	— Needles Range Formation —
		PALEOCENE	65	— Older Conglomerate —
MESOZOIC (Age of reptiles)	CRETACEOUS (chalk)		135	— Rhyolite porphyry dikes and sills =
	JURASSIC (Jura Mountains, France)		180	Quartz Monzonite Granodiorite
	TRIASSIC (from three-fold division in Germany)		225	
PALEOZOIC (Invertebrate forms abundant and varied; first appearance of fishes, amphibians, and land plants)	PERMIAN (Perm, a Russian Province)		270	Arcturus Formation
	CARBONIFEROUS International name	PENNSYLVANIAN American name (from abundance of coal)	325	— Ely Limestone —
		MISSISSIPPIAN American name	350	Chainman Shale
				Joana Limestone
				— Pilot Shale —
	DOVONIAN (Devonshire, England)		400	Guilmette Formation
				Simonson Dolomite
				Sevy Dolomite
	SILURIAN (an anient British tribe, the Silurs)		440	— Laketown and Fish Haven Dolomites —
	ORDOVICIAN (an ancient British tribe, Ordovices)		500	Eureka Quartzite
				Lehman Formation and Kanosh Shale
				Juab, Wahwah, and Fillmore Limestones
				— House Limestone ■
	CAMBRIAN (Cambrian, the Roman name for Wales)		600	Notch Peak Limestone
				Corset Spring Shale
				Johns Wash Limestone
				Lincoln Peak Formation
				Pioche Shale
				Prospect Mountain Quartzite
	PRECAMBRIAN (Primitive life forms)		3500 or more	Osceola Argillite(Misch and Hazzard-1962)
				Shingle Creek Quartzite

Pole Canyon Limestone This formation was laid down in an ocean or sea environment in middle Cambrian time, about 560 million years ago. In the Snake Range, it is alternating light and dark massive limestone, up to about 600 meters thick. Parts of this formation have been marbleized, as seen in Lehman Caves and at the summit of Eagle Peak. This formation is synonymous with Mt. Washington, and it's prominent southwest and east ridges are made of it. It's also the formation which makes up the south half of the summit of Eagle Peak. In the North Snake Range, it's the formation which makes up the massive gray walls of lower Smith Creek Canyon. It's seen in Horse Canyon and Hampton Creek as well.

Lincoln Peak Limestone This limestone formation was formed in late Cambrian times, about 525 million years ago, and at the bottom of a sea or ocean. This is the limestone you'll see on the lower western, northern and eastern slopes of Lincoln Peak, and on the east slopes of Central and Granite Peaks. In the southern Snake Range, it's about 1400 meters thick and is the first formation above the Pole Canyon Limestone. Whitebread, who studied this formation, says it is, "thin-bedded, medium-dark-gray limestone and shaly limestone".

Notch Peak Limestone Notch Peak Limestone was also laid down in an ocean environment in late Cambrian times, about 510 million years ago. It gets it's name from the very prominent Notch Peak in western Utah, not far east of Wheeler Peak. In the Southern Snake Range, it's 500 to 600 meters thick. This formation is seen on the southeastern part of Lincoln Peak, the eastern part of Granite Peak, and forms the northern part of the big ridge running between the Minerva Mines and Acrapolis Peak. In the North Snake Range, this is the gray limestone making up the summit ridge and all the high peaks of Mt. Moriah.

House Limestone Many geologists place this formation in the Pogonip Group. This group of rocks is about 1100 meters thick, but the House Limestone part is maybe 200 meters thick. This limestone was laid down in the bottom of a Cambrian and Ordovician sea or ocean, about 500 million years ago. It's prominently exposed at the summit of Lincoln Peak, and along the Highland Ridge to the south.

Laketown and Fish Haven Dolomites These two dolomites are usually classified together, and makeup a formation about 200 meters thick. They date from around 440 million years ago, and like limestone, were also formed in the bottom of a sea or ocean. The difference between limestone and dolomite, is that dolomite has a much higher percentage of magnesian. You'll see this formation only if you climb Granite Peak. It forms all of the top part of the peak and is very dark gray. The peak was apparently misnamed because of it's color, for there is no granite anywhere near the peak.

Intrusive Rocks These rocks were once molten magma deep within the earth, but sometime during Jurassic times(middle Mesozoic--between 180 and 135 million years ago), it was pushed upward through fractures in the earths crust. Had they made it to the surface, they would have formed volcanos and lava flows. But they didn't quite crack the surface, so they could only cool slowly underground. This slow cooling allowed various minerals to crystallize and separate to form a speckled or salt and pepper like rock commonly called granite. Geologists classify the different types of granite according to appearance and mineral content. In the South Snake Range, and from place to place, they are called granodiorite, quartz monzonite, and porphyritic quartz monzonite. Few people can tell the difference, so they're usually lumped together and called "granite" or "granitic type rock". Often times, there will be mines or mineralized areas, at or near the contact zone of granite and various other formations.

You'll see these rocks from the Hub Mine Basin(west of Baker Pk.), and over the summit ridge to the east, including Johnson Peak. Also, parts of Pyramid Peak and all the upper Snake Creek Basin are made of these granite rocks. There's also some granite exposed between Sacramento Pass and Bald Mtn., and to the south in Lexington Creek Canyon.

A winter scene in the Wheeler Peak Cirque Basin. Northeast Face in background.

Winter camp, on the upper south slopes of Baker Peak.

Further Reading

An Ecological Study of Bristlecone Pine in Utah and Eastern Nevada, Hiebert and Hamrick, *Great Basin Naturalist,* July 1984.
Ancient Bristlecone Pine Forest, Russ and Ann Johnson, Sierra Media, Inc., Bishop, Calif..
An Ancient Bristlecone Pine Stand, Eastern Nevada, Donald R. Currey, *Ecology,* Vol. 46, No. 4.
Bristlecone Pine, Oldest Known Living Thing, Edmund Schulman, March, 1958, *National Geographic Magazine.*
Bristlecone Pine: Science and Esthetics, C. W. Ferguson, *Science,* Feb. 23, 1968.
Geology and Mineral Resources of White Pine County, Nevada, Bulletin 85, 1976, *Nevada Bureau of Mines and Geology.*
Geologic Map of the Wheeler Peak and Garrison Quadrangles, Nevada and Utah, USGS Map I-578, Donald H. Whitebread.
Geologic Map of the Wheeler Peak and Highland Ridge Further Planning Areas, White Pine County, Nevada, USGS Miscellaneous Field Studies Map MF-1343-A.
Geophysical Map of the Wheeler Peak and Highland Ridge Further Planning Areas, White Pine County, Nevada, USGS Miscellaneous Field Studies Map MF-1343-C.
Mineral Resource Potential Map of the Wheeler Peak and Highland Ridge Further Planning Areas, White Pine County Nevada, USGS Miscellaneous Field Studies Map MF-1343-B.
The Proposed Great Basin National Park, Robert Starr Waite, Ph.D. dissertation, UCLA, 1974(Geography).
Playing God in Yellowstone, Alston Chase, 1987, Harcourt Brace Jovanovich, Publishers
White Pine Lang Syne, "A True History of White Pine County, Nevada", Effie O. Read, 1965, Big Mountain Press, Denver.

Other Guide Books by the Author

Climbers and Hikers Guide to the Worlds Mountains(2nd Ed.), Kelsey, 800 pages, 377 maps, 380 fotos, waterproof cover, US $19.95 (mail orders US $21.50).
Utah Mountaineering Guide, and the Best Canyon Hikes(2nd Ed.), Kelsey, 192 pages, 105 fotos, waterproof cover, US $7.95 (mail orders US $8.95).
Canyon Hiking Guide to the Colorado Plateau(2nd-Revised Printing), Kelsey, 256 pages, 117 hikes and maps, 130 fotos, waterproof cover, US $9.95 (mail orders US $10.95).
Hiking Utah's San Rafael Swell, Kelsey, 144 pages, 30 mapped hikes, plus lots of history, 104 fotos, waterproof cover, US $7.95 (mail orders US $8.95).
Hiking and Exploring Utah's Henry Mountains and Robbers Roost, Kelsey, 224 pages, 38 hikes or climbs, 163 fotos, including The Life and Legend of Butch Cassidy, waterproof cover, US $8.95 (mail orders US $9.95).
Hiking and Exploring the Paria River, Kelsey, 208 pages, 30 different hikes from Bryce Canyon to Lee's Ferry, including The Story of John D. Lee and Mountain Meadows Massacre, 155 fotos, waterproof cover, US $8.95 (mail orders US $9.95).
China on Your Own, and the Hiking Guide to China's Nine Sacred Mountains(3rd, and Revised Ed.), Jennings and Kelsey, 240 pages, 110 maps, 16 hikes or climbs, waterproof cover, US $9.95 (Please order this book from Milestone Publications, P.O. Box 35548, Station E, Vancouver, B.C., Canada, V6M 4G8).

Distributors for Kelsey Publishing
Please write to one of these companies when ordering any of Mike Kelsey's books.

Primary Distributor
Wasatch Publishers, Inc., 4647 Idlewild Road, Salt Lake City, Utah, 84124, Tele. 801-278-3174

Alpenbooks, P.O. Box 27344, Seattle, Washington, 98125, Tele. 206-672-9316
Banana Republic, 175 Bluxome Street, San Francisco, California, 94107, Tele. 800-527-5200
Bookpeople, 2929 Fifth Street, Berkeley, California, 94710, Tele. 800-227-1516

Canyon Country Publications, P.O. Box 963, Moab, Utah, 84532, Tele. 801-259-6700
Gordon's Books, 2323 Delgany, Denver, Colorado, 80216, Tele. 303-296-1830
Many Feathers–Southwestern Books, 5738 North Central, Phoenix, Arizona, 85012, Tele. 602-266-1043
Mountain 'n Air Books, 3704 1/2 Foothill Blvd., La Crescenta, California, 91214, Tele. 818-957-5338
Quality Books(Library Distributor), 918 Sherwood Drive, Lake Bluff, Illinois, 60044, Tele. 312-295-2010
Recreational Equipment, Inc.(R.E.I.), P.O. Box 88126, Seattle, Washington, 98188, 800-426-4840 (Or check at any of their local stores).

In the **UK** and **Europe**, and the rest of the world contact:

CORDEE, 3a De Montfort Street, Leicester, England, UK, LE1 7HD, Tele. 0533 543579

From Johnson Peak, looking at Wheeler, Baker, Jeff Davis, and Pyramid Peaks.